# BREAK UP OR BREAK THROUGH

# BREAK UP OR
# BREAK THROUGH

A Spiritual Guide to Richer Relationships

## Dina Bachelor Evan, Ph.D., MFCC

alyson books
los angeles | new york

MANUFACTURED IN THE UNITED STATES OF AMERICA.

THIS TRADE PAPERBACK ORIGINAL IS PUBLISHED BY ALYSON PUBLICATIONS,
P.O. BOX 4371, LOS ANGELES, CA 90078-4371.
DISTRIBUTION IN THE UNITED KINGDOM BY
TURNAROUND PUBLISHER SERVICES LTD.,
UNIT 3, OLYMPIA TRADING ESTATE, COBURG ROAD, WOOD GREEN,
LONDON N22 6TZ ENGLAND.

FIRST EDITION: JUNE 2001

02 03 04 05 **a** 10 9 8 7 6 5 4 3 2

ISBN: 1-55583-639-9

LIBRARY OF CONGRESS CATALOGING-IN-PUBLICATION DATA
EVAN, DINA BACHELOR.
    BREAK UP OR BREAK THROUGH : A SPIRITUAL GUIDE TO RICHER RELATIONSHIPS /
DINA BACHELOR EVAN.—1ST ED.
    ISBN 1-55583-639-9
    1. GAY COUPLES—RELIGIOUS LIFE. 2. INTERPERSONAL RELATIONS—RELIGIOUS
ASPECTS. I. TITLE.
BL625.9.G39 E93 2001
158.2—DC21                                        2001018812

**CREDITS**
COVER DESIGN BY PHILIP PIROLO.
COVER PHOTOGRAPHS BY PHOTODISC AND CORBIS.

This book is dedicated to my beloved children, Lauren, J.D., and Mia; my grandchildren, Brittany, Brianne, Taryn, and Paige; and my sisters in Spirit in the Circle of One—Mia, Suzanna, Jackie, Donna, Marilu, Lydia, Anne, Jeanne, Lauren, Jean, Lynn, Carolyn, Naunie, Heather, Yoli, Irene, Catherine, Terry, and Julie—who have all had the integrity and courage to stay fully present as we find our way to Oneness and Spirit.

# Contents

# Introduction

*I am honeycombed and*
*faceted with iridescent*
*shimmering spirit.*
*In the center of my being*
*You are.*

*Though winds may spiral in chaos*
*and bring illusions of separation and pain,*
*they will move through me*
*and beyond me*
*For in the center of my being*
*You are.*

I never came out. I came home.

Before I knew I was a lesbian, I lived in a straight world as a visitor, never knowing why I didn't fit in, and trying everything I knew to feel at home. Four children and a whole life later, I discovered I was a lesbian in straight lady's clothing. Finally, in the midst of an acquiescing sigh, I understood. I felt so much relief, I could hardly contain myself. The kind of relief you feel when you find the perfect outfit, one that makes you feel 10 pounds lighter and irresistibly attractive. I bubbled. I blissed. I relished. I rejoiced. I relaxed. Now I was a spirit in lesbian clothing. Little did I know what this revelation would require.

Certain things in life act as spiritual wake-up calls. The car that nearly misses you as you step off the curb. The person whose eyes meet yours across the room in the silent recognition that you are, without ever having met, inextricably entwined. The flight you missed that crashes. And...discovering you are a lesbian. If you are conscious, being gay or lesbian is the fire that moves your soul instantly into the college of courage.

When you're straight no one knows at first glance whether you have integrity or personal pride, but, generally speaking, whatever way you act with your partner, unless you're abusive, is sexually acceptable. It does not require an act of courage to outwardly demonstrate your love. But once you realize you're lesbian or gay, every question about your level of emotional courage is instantly in your face. It hovers in the air between you and your beloved as you step out the front door of your home and must decide, "Do I keep holding her hand, or let it go?" It goes with you to work and creeps into your awareness when an associate asks about getting together for dinner and says she wants you to meet her husband and can't wait to meet yours. It hangs on the telephone line when your family wants to know who you're dating, if it's serious, and "when can we meet *him*?" It defines how far up the ladder you may go in the entertainment industry, in the insurance industry, in the health care industry, and into the category known as the typical American family.

The depth of my new discovery first rippled through me when my youngest daughter asked, "How can you be a lesbian? You're not *with* anyone." And I answered, "How can you be straight? Neither are you." At that point both she and I understood the issue was not about choice. She was the only one with a choice, and, unlike my oldest daughter— thank God—she chose to love me anyway.

My oldest daughter, on the other hand, being a Jehovah's Witness, called to tell me she wanted me to be at the birth of her firstborn child. She had chosen to separate herself from the rest of the family, and I hadn't seen her for several years, so I was elated to hear her voice. I remember that call as if it happened yesterday, even though it was more than 18 years ago. "I want you to be at the birth," she said, "but of course you won't be able to spend time with this child after it's born. You know…because of your lifestyle"

My heart dropped to the floor, and after I found the strength to speak again, I said, "I'm sorry, honey. I can't bond with this child and then have it leave my life like you did. I love you, but I can't be there." She and I didn't see each other again until many years later when I met her two children, was asked again if I still was with a woman, and then was once again literally and metaphorically shown to the door.

Being gay or lesbian is a spiritual assignment that has to do with integrity, authenticity, compassion, and love. Being a woman who loves women is the fire in my spiritual process this time around. It's the purifier of my soul. If I am to be authentic, that part of who I am must be honored. If I shrink back from it, I have dishonored my own choices in this incarnation to stand up and be who I am. I cannot extricate my love for women from who I am spiritually any more than I can extricate my love for Spirit from who I am. They are magically interwoven to create the tapestry of my soul. Each time I stand up for either, I am made more whole, more powerful, and more real. Each time I stand up, I proclaim that being a lesbian is not about who I love, it's about *how* I love. Deeply. Powerfully. From my soul. That's why it's heartbreaking to me to watch us fall into the same old relationship traps that have done us and the straight world in for as long as I can remember.

This book is about relationships and *spirituality*. Spirituality encompasses, embraces every aspect of life. It does not, however, refer to dogma, doctrine, or any specific organized religious belief. Spirituality is an internal sense of connection and harmony. It's a congruency between my values and my actions. It's an awareness that I am inextricably connected at the core to every living thing and that all of it is God, whatever you perceive God to be. It's because of our spirituality that we speak and act ethically. Spirituality is the core of every successful relationship. Whether your spirituality comes in the form of a love of nature, a principled and respectful process with others, or an awe for every living thing, at the core of the most profound love in the universe, there is Spirit. It's the stunning awareness that what I do to you, I do to me— and what I do for you, I do for me. It's the grace of knowing only love matters.

Throughout time, every group of people has been measured by the strength of their relationships to Spirit, to themselves, and to one another. Our statistics for long-term committed relationships leave a great deal of room for improvement. In the straight world nearly 60% of marriages end in divorce. In the lesbian and gay world nearly 80% of all relationships never reach the long-term commitment phase, and those that do often succumb to the either the pressure of society and its morals or the lack of respect in our own communities for commitments. According to The National Coalition of Anti-Violence Programs, 25% to 33% percent of all same-sex relationships are abusive, a rate equal to that of the heterosexual community (*Out* magazine, February 1998).

If we stop and look at these bleak realities, how could the end result be any different, given the foundation on which most relationships, including ours, are based? Today we are selling relationships, gay and straight alike, in much the same way we sell used cars. We simply tell the customer what he or she wants to hear and let them deal with the truth later. You can learn quickly in lesbian bars how to persuade a woman into giving you exactly what you want, or you'll quickly get the idea of how to capture the heart of Mr. Right in men's bars. If you don't pick this mentality up in bars, you might also buy into these "code and rules" because they filter into our awareness by osmosis, advertising, and word of mouth.

I grew up in an empty room. I'd be kidding myself if I didn't admit that's one reason why relationships are a priority in my life. I have also discovered they are the finest route to enlightenment—the best personal growth activity on the planet. I've spent the majority of my life focused on relationships—learning about them and teaching about them. I have a 98% success rate with couples who come to me for counseling wanting to fix their relationships. Couples who come to have a safe place to break up also often find themselves scratching their heads and changing their minds as they begin breaking through instead of breaking up. Most of us want to be the best we can be for ourselves and our partners. And what most of us need are the tools with which to do relationships better. We have very few "out" role models. The majority of couples in long-term relationships are not the ones we see depicted in the news, in personal ads in our magazines, or even at podiums as our political leaders.

We also need to unplug from the tricks and gimmicks of most self-help books, which teach you to be inauthentic, mostly sexy, and less than who you are. A multitude of books offer slick techniques for getting your man or woman, but most of us still don't know how on earth we will keep him or her once having "captured and bagged" this most prized possession. Many books tell us the most important thing in our lives is our connection to others. The problem is, we don't know how to connect deeply enough to be able to keep our beloved once we find that precious person. Because of this inability to connect deeply, most of us still feel single even when we are in long-term relationships. You now know how to push, pull, and promote yourself into being that elusive object of someone's affection, but how do you keep the game afoot, keep the relationship alive, keep the love growing—especially if the person you've been promoting so intently isn't really who you are inside, but who you're pretending to be?

The problem with many concepts is obviously that **they start off with a lie** and you must become the lie if you use them. What happens once you have "gotten" your man or your woman? Do you continue to try to be someone you are not throughout the rest of your relationship in order to "keep" your partner? Who is your partner supposed to connect with if the person you're being is not really you at all? We live in a society addicted to sameness. We don't feel we have "made it" until we do it exactly as the heterosexual community has done it. In our community, women don't feel they have made it until they have repeated the mistakes men have made. Hence, we now have a flourishing number of gay sex clubs for women, and we are now less invested in monogamy. Most men will be the first to tell you they have not mastered the art of true intimacy, yet women often long to emulate them. What if you, in truth, are a scared little girl or a self-conscious guy who has not yet mastered the art of self-esteem? This may be the case for many of us, as evidenced by the fact that most of us are sleeping together by the second date. Mind you, this is long before we even really meet the *real person* to whom we have given our bodies. Is it any wonder we find ourselves getting ready to pack up after three months of pseudo-honeymooning when the *real* person shows up and we're aghast? We are stunned at who he or she really is, and at ourselves.

The problem with many concepts being sold by the millions today is that they start off with a lie and you must become the lie if you use them. Could that be why most of us feel so phony, as if we don't know who we are? We, as gays and lesbians, have generally been given the message that we don't fit into society's idea of legitimate relationships. Then, when we finally find a relationship, we don't feel as if we fit there either unless we're being someone our own community tells us we should be. We must be hot. Smooth. On. The perfect body. The perfect body. The perfect body. The feminist activist. The AIDS activist. The media watchdog. Top. Bottom. Butch. Femme. The perfect body. The perfect body.

We focus on sex, not love. They are not the same thing. The Aug. 19, 1997 issue of *The Advocate* features an article on "The Best and Brightest Under-30 Set." And just why are these starlets the best and brightest? I assume, given the list, that it's because they are first sexy, then young, then smart, then gay, then lesbian. Not a single mention until you get to page 59 that these are also conscious, courageous, incredibly dedicated spirits. Sexy and young take first and second place on the cover and in our lives. That's what sells. That's what we are still selling, even when it's not real.

## What's the Problem?

Something is inherently wrong with the way we do relationships. In fact, something is inherently wrong with the way we do life. It's limited, superficial. There's a huge error in our thinking. We've always thought if we could just get a partner who loved us, life would be fulfilling and complete. Most of us have already found out that's not true. Big surprise! When has anyone ever been able to give you acceptance, affection, or love that you, while feeling unworthy, were able or willing to receive? When someone said you were beautiful, if you did not yourself believe it to be true, were you willing to believe it from someone else? If your partner told you how much you were loved, but you secretly felt unlovable, were you able to accept how much your partner really cared? Chances are your answer is a resounding *no*. So, then, what good is there in finding partners if once we have them we cannot let their love in or create successful relationships? **The bottom line is that we have not yet realized that the work to be done in relationships is work we must do on ourselves.** It's time to analyze our own personal, individual ability to be a loving, supportive, and present partner. Without this capacity, we cannot truly create what we say we want: long-term, committed relationships that work. This is our spiritual work individually and as a community. It's also the secret to creating successful relationships. In fact, working on yourself is the secret to a fulfilled and happy life. We need to see our mate, relationships, and family as the foundation of our power and our peace. Relationships are the fire in our soul's growth, both individually and collectively.

No partner can give you security, safety, or love unless you're willing to give that to yourself first. I know you hate hearing that because your heart longs for someone else to do it for you. But as long as you hold on to that illusion, you will remain empty-handed, feeling alone inside. You will never get to a point where you feel safe, or loved, by manipulating or changing your partner to get these needs met. I once worked with a young gay client who grew up feeling unattractive, overweight, and unlovable. He became the funny man on campus in his youth in order to make friends and cover up his pain. In his 30s, he lost 60 pounds, worked out at the gym regularly, looked fantastic, and still came into my office weekly, filled with the grief of not being good enough to get a partner. There was always someone in the bar who looked better, sexier, and who went home with a lover every night. He hated that lifestyle, but could not conceive of any other standard by which to measure himself. "In the men's community," he told me, "if you're not young and sexy, you're not anything. It's all about how you look." Most of it still is, and now that standard has also crept into the women's community, because we keep using the same tired role models.

That shocking awareness was not new to me. While serving as chair of a major AIDS organization, during one board meeting I began by asking everyone to tell his or her coming-out story. Twelve people went around the room telling their personal stories. A family member—an uncle or grandfather—had introduced every one of the men to sex as a child before they were even teenagers. After the meeting I asked these men if they were monogamous in their long-term relationships. Not one man was able to tell me he had been able to keep his commitment to this ideal—the ideal he had wanted and committed to early on in his relationship. When I asked them why, they all said, "It's all about sex, not intimacy."

My heart felt so sad and overwhelmed. How could I even begin to tell them what they were missing? We must see that emulating what has been done in the past by the straight community, or our own community, lacks vision and provides no real role model. Heterosexual divorce rates are increasing to more than 60%. The rates for straight women having affairs are also on the rise. In our community these numbers are not available. But ask yourself. How many gay and lesbian couples do you know who have long-term, fully committed monogamous relationships? How many carry on deep, meaningful conversations that result in positive resolution and problem solving? To do that, we must become safe with ourselves and our ability to do it differently, better. We don't feel safe with each other. Or more to the point, we don't yet feel safe with ourselves. How do we get there?

*You* must be the one who changes. **You must be more focused on what it is inside you that prevents you from feeling love** than on how to get your partner to be more loving. The greatest, the only, place of power for making change is in us. Even if society were to embrace our lifestyles fully, my guess is that we could not maintain long-term committed relationships because we have not worked on ourselves.

*It's not necessary to be forever seeking love.*
*It's only necessary to discover your barriers to receiving it.*

## A New Attitude

Love and the opportunities to create loving relationships are everywhere. You could walk out your door this morning and get a partner if that was all you wanted. It's not all you want. What you want is to be loved. Deeply and profoundly accepted and loved. You may miss your chance, or have already missed many chances, because most of us don't even recognize this possibility when it arrives. We have no reference point for it. We haven't yet even learned how to love ourselves.

Being gay is the fire in our process. Once you have discovered you are gay or lesbian, you have taken your first step on an exciting road of self-discovery that demands you love yourself if you are to be authentically happy. The world isn't necessarily applauding your discovery and loving you to pieces just because you are gay. Chances are, your parents are not applauding your discovery. Chances are, you may not be ready to applaud either. It takes a while of acclimating and adjusting to this new reality. Then there's the business of finding someone you'd like to date. Once we have managed to find a mate, we are still at the beginning, the work has only just begun. This is when we each must be willing to change drastically, and this change must start with our initial idea of *why* we want a relationship in the first place.

Having a partner is not the answer to your problems. Having a partner is the bonus, a gift, the frosting on the cake. But the cake—the real challenge and assignment in life—is to be the best human being you can be. This means getting rid of those selfish egotistical behaviors and learning how to love with an open, unconditional heart. This is still your responsibility and your first priority. Your partner is simply a precious mirror, a priceless gift the universe gives you, who will reflect back to you how well you're doing. **And the truth is that if you stay focused on your own growth, your integrity, your willingness to stay present, and your ability and capacity to love, your relationships in every area of your life will be successful.**

## Is This All There Is?

In the past, we have been primarily focused on how to get a mate, which we have been taught to do by any means and at any cost. We must now take an in-depth look at our faulty thinking and be willing to change the core ideas we have about ourselves and our relationships to our mates and everyone else in our lives. Let's look at this dilemma. When you pretend to be someone you are not, and in turn seek out someone who is not being him or her self, what is the result? Two disappointed people who somewhere down the line feel tricked, betrayed, and more desperate than before. We end up in relationships with a glazed look on our faces, asking the question in that old Peggy Lee song, "Is That All There Is?" Then, at some point we "numb out" inside and decide that any relationship is better than none at all, so we settle for less than we really want and deserve. We do this while living with the frustration and fear of having to keep up the charade.

## It's Time to Rock the Boat!

Our society is addicted to the status quo. Don't rock the boat. Don't expect change. Puh-leeze! Men have to change. So do women. Everyone on the planet must change if we are to survive. Besides, when you are in a conscious relationship, you are both constantly changing. Frankly, we had all better change, because there are very few of us who can say that our lives or our relationships are spiritually and emotionally fulfilling. Change is what keeps you and your relationship alive and exciting. Change is what offers new purpose, new potential, new vision, and new paths.

In some ways, we are lucky. We have skipped the *Men Are From Mars* syndrome. We get both without having to worry about it. How many of you would really like to create a planet where you both get to develop and enjoy all of your Mars and Venus parts instead of perpetuating the differences between gender roles? We all have both of these planetary aspects within our personalities. What's more, if we are to be whole human beings, we cannot shuffle off onto our partners those aspects society has attributed to one gender role or the other. Two halves do not create a whole when it comes to relationships. Two halves create disappointing, broken relationships.

Whenever you make someone else responsible for something you refuse to acknowledge in yourself, he or she will soon feel objectified and resentful. Let's say you refuse to face some issue inside yourself that prevents you from feeling safe and instead you insist on your mate making you safe by being constantly at your side. It won't be long before your partner grows tired of always having to be your protector and doing your work for you about this issue. Another example might be that you're forever asking your partner to assure you that you are beautiful because you don't believe it. These are both issues that require you to do your own healing.

We have assigned roles to male, female, butch, and femme, and demanded each gender stay within its narrowly defined ranks, expressing only narrowly defined attributes. The result is that women have incredible amounts of denied rage. Tied up in our rage is extraordinary power, but it too is denied. So, we are still asking for permission to be equal. Men have been forced to deny their suffering and their incredible capacity for sensitivity. Neither gender has been encouraged to be all it can be: free from roles. And both are angry as hell at each other because they feel pressure to be someone they are not. At the same time, Spirit is pushing all of us to be who we really are. Do you hear the conflict? Does stepping away from this gender identification mean we cannot encourage each partner in the relationship to contribute what he or she does best? Not at all. Without gender issues, we might be able to offer to the relationship, and each other, the very best of what we have no matter what.

When we honor and deeply connect with each other, what is at the core of our being is what we find irresistible. It is simultaneously neither gender and both. It is Spirit. Yet, that irresistible something is often lost in our transition into mate relationships.

Gender issues are just another detour away from intimacy, and even though it can be great fun at times to play male/female role games, our gender has little or nothing to do with the truth of our being, the truth of Spirit, or our ability to connect profoundly. No matter who you are, what gender you are, what gender role you identify with, what color you are, what height, shape, or nationality you are, you are unique, and your gifts are critical to your relationship. When individual gifts are given freely out of a desire to share and not a need to survive or follow an assigned gender role, both individuals are blessed and fully participating in the success of their relationship.

In our society a greater percentage of breakups are now being instigated by women. Women have found that being limited to a certain set of responsibilities, even in gay relationships, does not take into account many of their abilities and talents. If pushed into limited gender roles—in any kind of relationship—we soon feel unappreciated and unchallenged both mentally and spiritually. Shared responsibilities and fluid roles in a relationship allow both partners and their children to benefit from the individual gifts and gender differences of both parents. Parents who feel satisfied with the quality of their lives are far more present and emotionally available to their children.

## The Truth of Who We Are

Out of some incredible power in this universe everything that exists was created. In every spiritual or religious teaching, there are common threads or basic tenets. One consistent, universal truth is that this energy was "all there was" in the beginning, and that everything else was created from It. That includes you and me. We are part of this energy. This Divine energy is our core. It's the truth of who we are.

When I say to you in this book to "see the Spirit in each other" or "connect to the Spirit in each other," I am talking about getting to this realization of our own Divinity. It's not hard. In the same way, we see or recognize the nurturing "mom" part in a woman, the protective "dad" part in a man, or the professional or artist parts of each other. This time you will learn to see the Spirit—the part of each of us that is a perfect reflection of Spirit. Our separation from this truth has created so much pain and aloneness. Our separation from Spirit, ourselves, and each other has caused all the pain and selfishness in our lives and in the world. If we knew we were inherently sacred and that each person in our lives was also sacred, it would be much harder to hurt ourself or each other, abandon ourself or each other, or lie to ourself and each other. In this book I am talking about acknowledging that Spirit within and operating from that core spiritual self. Once we accept it, our relationships will become successful and filled with intimacy, better sex, and rich opportunities for growth. Sexuality and spirituality are not at odds or in conflict with each other; in fact, they empower each other. We will talk more about that in chapter five.

## Healing Yourself = Successful Relationships

To succeed in relationships, you must work on yourself, and your partner must work on himself or herself. Do you have to wait until you have done all the work and are already healed before you get started in a relationship? Of course not—not a single one of us is there yet. We are all works in progress. But you must be committed to the process of healing *yourself* and stop unconsciously placing the responsibility for your wholeness or your happiness on your partner. If you want to be in a loving, alive, vital relationship, it's up to you to be loving, alive, and vital. It is not up to your partner to create that for you. Actually, I should say you *get to* create that for yourself. When you are the one in charge, you *get to* create exactly what you want, and that is a much safer position for you to be in, because no one can know you better than you can know yourself.

For years I have been teaching in my workshops and seminars that **relationships are a sacred trust.** They are part of a Divine experiment and offer us the finest opportunity in the universe for healing ourselves and experiencing the fullness of loving and being loved.

The purpose of every relationship process and every relationship is **to find and know *you*. In the entire world, relationships are the finest tool we have to help us do that.** They are, in fact, the *only* tool that allows us to do that. You can evolve by sitting on a mountaintop somewhere concentrating on Spirit. But you have no idea how far along the path your own soul has evolved until you get off that mountain, enter into a relationship, and hear your first judgment or fear arise and create in you a desire to distance.

All our spiritual teachings have afforded us the perfect prototype for how relationships should be valued and how they can work successfully. If you're aware of those teachings and models and you are living them in your relationship, you have a high possibility for success. If you're not aware of these tools, it's time to increase your awareness and put them to use, because without them your relationships will continue to be unsatisfying and unstable. This is one of the key problems in 90% of relationships today: a lack of awareness about how relationships can work from a spiritual base and the joy that comes from doing so.

The "how to's" for successful relationships are not complex.

**Stay Present**
**Be Honest**
**Act Out of Love, Not Fear**

Until you are able to **Stay Present, Be Honest,** and **Act Out of Love, Not Fear,** you are *playing at* relationships, you are not creating real ones. Failure rates will continue to grow, and more of us will remain or continue to feel alone. No one can build a lasting relationship on a foundation of lies. As you will read in chapter seven, most of us lie to our partners, our families, and ourselves daily without even batting an eyelash. We tell our lies in the name of keeping peace or the false idea that it's our job to avoid hurting each other, and mostly, we lie out of fear. Fear that we will be abandoned. Fear that we will be found unworthy. Fear that we will once again be left alone. Fear of the fallout. Be truthful with yourself for a minute.

What do you and I want most in a relationship? Don't you dream of being able to be with someone, stripped down, emotionally nude, vulnerable and open, finally being exactly who you are, only to have your partner tell you how much he or she adores you? No pretense. No role playing. No gender shuffle. Nothing between you and your beloved, family member, or friend but the truth and love. There is no need for anything else. Wouldn't you finally feel as if you've arrived, as if you've finally made it? I'm going to show you how, through your own healing process, to find a path to yourself, then a path to your beloved, and finally a path to Spirit. I want that for you. If you've tried other techniques and still haven't found what you're seeking, then you must want it. Wanting is painful. So let's begin our journey to finding.

*The only lasting connection to another is Spirit to Spirit.*

# Stay Present

# CHAPTER ONE
## Who Are You?

*I have gone from spark to reality*
*from infant to adult*
*from shallow to deeper*
*from knowledgeable to wiser*
*from a person to a presence*
*from student to teacher*
*to student.*

*Still, I know*
*I have only begun*
*and am not yet*
*being fully*
*who I am.*

**You believe who you already are is not enough.** Society's messages and judgment has not helped that perception a great deal. Still, we can't continue to blame society for our own failures. Not being enough is your biggest fear and the motivating force behind all your efforts of trying to be someone you are not. As long as you hold on to this false belief, you won't be real. And as long as you are not real, you can't be present with yourself or your relationships. This lack of presence becomes a vicious cycle and ultimately a lifestyle.

You're a priceless reflection of Spirit, and there's nothing you need to hide or lie about. But you continue to hide, pretend, and act "as if," and as long as you do that, you will not find yourself or your beloved. The real you is behind all that camouflage, behind sexy sound bites and false selves. When you are both being real, you and your partner could sit across from each other for the next million years and there would

3

still not be enough time to know all the wondrous qualities there are to know about each other.

## Take a Look at Who You Really Are

Remember the last time you looked upon a newborn infant in awe? Here was this tiny, helpless creature, filled with wonder and openness, and unable to do a single thing for him or herself except cry to be fed or changed. Did you not feel overwhelming love for this little person who had not yet amassed accomplishments, credits, "somebodyness," or wealth? Did your heart not open to this innocent creature who was neither sexy, nor slim, nor dressed to the nines? Did you not feel this being was already worthy of being loved completely without needing to do a single thing? The miracle of this child's being is quite enough. That is how Spirit feels about you. And that is how you can learn to feel about yourself and those you love; total unconditional love for the precious being inside, not the outer accoutrements.

But instead of going inward to find the truth in ourselves and then outward to offer that truth to each other, we hide behind facades, roles, rules, codes, and separations that prevent us from knowing our true selves or sharing that Self with our beloved. These are all games and techniques. There is no game or technique under heaven that works. There is only the truth and love. You can't have *real relationships* unless you are willing to be real.

You don't have to pretend to be perfect to find a mate. Underneath all those lies that your mind or ego tells you, you are already perfect and there is nothing to pretend about. You're perfect if you are in the process of becoming a more spiritually enlightened human being, because that is all that is required. You even get to choose when and how you will do that. That is your *only job,* and it's ongoing. There is no such thing as perfection, because there is no end to this process. Just as there is no such thing as spiritual perfection, there is no state of perfection in reference to your physical body either. There is not just one kind of ultimate human that the rest of us must strive to become. One look. One personality. Not true. The closest we can come to perfection is when we are being all we can be

4

with all our individual uniqueness. Even then, since we can always become more of who we are, how could there ever be a final state at which we could arrive that could be considered perfect? Look around you. Are those people whom you love, respect, and envy, and who are in meaningful relationships perfect? I don't think so. They are every size and kind and body shape and hue, but none of them is perfect. **If they are in a successful relationship, what they are is real.**

*Authenticity means not being willing to compromise who you are in order to be what someone else wants you to be.*

If you want successful relationships, you must be real. But before you can start being real, you need to ask yourself what is stopping you. The teachings in this book are based upon spiritual truths, all of which can bring you a profound sense of realness. If you use this information, you will create ecstatic, meaningful relationships that last because you are having fun learning about yourself and growing with each other. This is the purpose of relationships, to learn about yourself and your capacity to stay present, be compassionate, and see the Spirit in yourself and in each other. Spirit designed relationships and gave us all the tools necessary to get the most from them. Together let's look at this perfect prototype.

## The Truth About Relationships

In the beginning Spirit was all there was. In order to know Itself better, Spirit—the Divine, the Source, the Universe, the Divine Mind or whatever you perceive that energy to be—created from Itself an *other* with which it could relate. It created you and me. Thus, the sole purpose for the original relationship was for Spirit to know Itself better. **And the sole purpose for our relationships is that we might know ourselves better. The moment you begin to long for a relationship, enter into one, or embrace the one you are in, you must understand the real purpose—that your unconscious need is solely to know yourself better.** To discover the real you. This is why Spirit created a relationship with us. This is why we create relationships with each other. **This discovery** requires being real, honest, and emotionally courageous enough to examine the truth of our being.

## Relationships Are About You

As I said, I can sit on a mountain and get enlightened, but until I come down from the mountain and enter a relationship, I have no way of knowing who I am or how well my soul has evolved. I have no sense of my willingness to be vulnerable. No sense of my capacity for compassion. No sense of ability to be truthful. No sense of my willingness to honor the Spirit in another. Contrary to what many self-help books will tell you, **relationships are not about what you can get from your mate or partner. They are about you and who you are willing to be and what you are willing to give as a mate or partner.**

Getting a mate is not nearly as important as knowing what to do with one after you have found him or her. And if you get a mate based upon what you think he or she wants you to be, you have started your relationship off with a lie. Soon you will start desperately looking for Mr. or Miss Right again, and you will know in the deepest recesses of your heart that something is off. Something will still be missing. Not only are you missing the point of relationships in the first place, but you are also missing. And where have you been? Sadly, we have been hiding behind illusions.

Out of fear, you have been hiding in your own self-created hell. You have been hiding behind the judgments of your parents, the judgments of society, the trauma of your abuse, or your need to be in control. You have been hiding behind your fear of intimacy, your false values and ideas about sexuality and your body. You have been hiding behind your need to be right, your self-judgments about your lovability and worth. You have been hiding behind your lack of emotional courage and the lie that you can somehow be destroyed if you are real. You have been hiding behind a selfishness that says, "If I give you what you want, perhaps I can get what I want from you." All of these are lies that your mind or ego has created. Aren't you exhausted from hiding? Doesn't your heart long to stop hiding and discover who you are? Why have you been hiding? The bottom line is that you're afraid that Spirit has lied to you and that you are really worth nothing. Unlovable.

Spirit has no concept of judgment or punishment. You are punishing yourself with your *own* judgments. Ask yourself this simple question: Why would Spirit create you, give you the task of evolving your soul through your own challenges and life processes, and then punish you for doing exactly what It has designed you to do? There is no such thing as failure. You get to drag out this painful process of pretending to be someone you are not as long as you wish, or you can remember in an instant, or in many lifetimes, what you already know to be true.

*There is no doubt in the Creator's mind about you, because there is none about Itself.*

When Spirit, the Universe, the Source, Presence—whatever you wish to call that Divine energy—created you, It did so from Itself. You are already Divine, and underneath the false ideas you have about yourself, you're pure, radiant spirit. Pure, radiant gay spirit, and the world is waiting for you to step into your rightful place in it. In this instant, right now, *you are manifesting as Spirit, diminished only by your own fear.* You are the Divine, experiencing Itself with all your judgments and limits. This is not what Spirit wants from you or for you. This is not what your beloved wants from you or for you. This is not what you, in the deepest recesses of your heart, want from or for yourself! But this is what you continue to do to yourself.

It's time to start being real and honoring yourself and your relationships as a sacred process. Don't be afraid. You have nothing to fear; in this journey to yourself you will find that you are all the things you'd hoped. You will also find that who you are is more than enough not only to find your beloved, but also to keep him or her fascinated as long as you both live. Aren't the most important people in your life right now the ones who are real? The extent to which you're capable of being real and willing to use spiritual principles in your relationships directly reflects your ability to create and maintain successful relationships. If you've used these simple principles a *little*, no doubt you have been a *little* successful in relationships. If you use these principles as the basis and foundation in your process, your relationships can not help but be successful.

**Stay Present**
**Be Honest**
**Act Out of Love, Not Fear**

## Stay Present

There has never been an instant since the moment we were conceived that Spirit has not been profoundly present with us. It's impossible for that source to have left us because we are a part of All That Is. That would be tantamount to my body disconnecting itself from my hand. There may have been many times when we were not able to experience that presence or felt lost and abandoned by it because of our own judgments. But in the darkest moment when you let go and once again were able to feel the love that had always been waiting for you, did you not realize it had never left you? Self-judgment is so powerful that it has the capacity to cut us off from our self, each other, and the energy in the universe. This is why we must resolve this issue of internalized shame. In truth, it's impossible for us to be left, for if Spirit were to leave us, it would have to leave Itself. If you just become still, feel yourself quietly let go of all those things you think you need to be and do, you will find the truth of your being.

*When we are not there for ourselves, it is impossible to know Spirit is there for us.*

Spirit just is...ever present, ever loving, and ever wanting you to know more of who and what It is by knowing more of who and what you are. Exactly the same principle is true in relationships. It's critical for you to understand that the more present you are to yourself, the more present you can become to your partner. The less present you are to yourself, the less present you will be to your partner. The more you know and trust yourself, the deeper you can move with ease and safety into the essence of your partner and the deepest intimacy you both are able to create.

When you understand this principle, you begin to also understand that what you do to your partner you also do to yourself. What you do for your partner, you also do for yourself. This sacred principle teaches us that the more we embrace the love and Spirit in each of us, the more love and Spirit we have in our lives. The more we allow for separation, the more separation exists. It's all one. Our task, then, is to remove the barriers in each of us that prevent us from loving and being loved fully. This state of becoming one with your partner results from becoming one with yourself and one with Spirit. We will talk more of this principle in the following chapters.

## How Much of You Is Present?

When I speak of staying present, I am not talking about just hanging out or spending time together. I am not talking about those of you who respond, "Well, I'm here, aren't I?" when your partner asks if you love him or her. I am talking about being present to life, to yourself, and to each other with impeccable integrity and a commitment to your own soul's ongoing growth and increasing aliveness. I am talking about being present to yourself in a way that ensures your personal and spiritual growth.

*A world event takes place when we stop trying to change others and begin to change ourselves.*

How to be truly present with another or with yourself is an art, a Zen dance and process that requires a willingness to view life and your priorities a bit differently. Do you know how to balance being present to your own needs, those of your partner, and those of a new relationship at the same time? Do you know how to be present to your beloved even when he or she is not with you? Is every part of you present to your beloved when you are making love? Do you know how to protect the love you share and intensify the depth of it, just by being more real? Is there anything in your life more important than the spiritual work you do with your partner? At some point you must become willing to ask yourself, *Why am I really here and what do I most want out of this life?* We will find those answers together.

## Be Honest

Our words and the intent behind them are incredibly important in relationships. The Torah, the Bible, all far Eastern and metaphysical teachings tell us that the words we use and how we use them are a direct reflection or expression of our inner essence. Words create our reality. The process of creating reality goes from idea-thought-image-word-concept and then to reality. Then we react. Think about that. Is there a single thing you can think of that was not first conceived in mind and then spoken? Reality is not created randomly. We create our own reality by what we think and say. The old adage "What you concentrate on, you become" is true. By making conscious decisions about our speech and increasing our ability to be honest, we take control of what we manifest in our lives and the levels of love we reach in our relationships.

Words can be used to enhance and enliven a relationship, or they can be used to create deception and fraud. Words can be used to deepen a process of connection or detract from it. Words can invite another to sit in the stillness and protection of our heart or push away a beloved one out of our own fear and denial. Words can take us deeper into our healing process and help deepen the healing of our partner or can distance and remove us from the process. We have a responsibility to use words consciously and in alignment with our true intent. We each have a spiritual obligation to speak and live the truth to the extent that we know it. When we do not do so, we send a clear message to ourselves that who we are and what we believe is not worthy of respect.

Do you know how to ask for what you need in a nonthreatening way? Do you know how to assist your partner in deeper healing? Do you find yourself confused about issues and responsibilities? Do you get lost in the words that cover your real issues? Do you believe that asking for what you need is being too "needy"? Are you afraid to hear the truth? Does telling your truth mean leaving or being left?

*Individually, our duty lies in living up to whatever amount of truth we know in any given moment.*

When we are still and aware of our connection to Spirit, we have all the answers. When your ego takes over and you move into your head, everything you say and everything you do is distorted by the past. When your ego is removed and you move back into your heart, there is nothing you do not know, and all of its truth. Together we will explore why telling our truth has become so difficult and what we can do to move back into alignment with ourselves and Spirit. From that aligned place, our choices and words are inspired, guided, and we are assured of having fulfilling and enduring relationships.

## Act Out of Love, Not Fear

What a wonderful experience that would be. In 15 years of counseling as a minister and a psychotherapist, **I have never seen a single instance when a choice made out of love for oneself or another did not result in healing.** And yet we are so afraid to choose that which is loving. Society tells us we must instead play games, give ourselves up, be phony, lie, and cheat to be fulfilled. And still we are not fulfilled. All we have accomplished is to step away from being the truly spiritual human beings we came here to be, and we have lessened our own sense of personal empowerment. Denying our own needs never fulfills us.

Opting to make choices out of love for ourselves and those we love is a quantum leap in trust. This is the key. If we make choices about the planet out of love, about our children out of love, and about one another out of love and not fear, we may survive and flourish rather than become extinct.

*Anything other than love is fear.*

We must move back into harmony with ourselves and the Spirit within us if we are to survive. There is no other way. Together we will examine why this process feels so unfamiliar and how we can make this critical and incredibly joyful life change.

Let's begin by finding out what your personal fears are and why they motivate you to play games or be someone you're not, especially when you're already so much more. Let's find out what motivates you, and how to improve these skills to create the relationships you desire. Take the following test and see how you fare.

## Spiritual Relationship Personal Inventory

Answer Each Question Always, Sometimes, or Never

1. Do you ever physically leave the premises in the midst of an argument?

2. Do you ever emotionally leave or space out during an argument?

3. Do you ever pretend to be someone you are not, to satisfy your partner or date?

4. Do you agree with your partner to avoid an argument rather than state what is true for you?

5. Do you feel "less than" your partner?

6. Do you worry that your partner will find someone else and leave?

7. Do you wonder how you feel or what you think?

8. Do you get confused about who's wrong/right?

9. Do you feel your partner fails to *get* who you are?

10. Do you feel there are parts of you that are unlovable?

11. Do you feel your partner lacks appreciation for your talents and abilities?

12. Do you feel confused about what you believe spiritually?

13. Do you feel betrayed if your partner feels differently or has a different opinion than you?

14. Do you expect things from your partner that you're not willing to give in return?

15. Do you anticipate crisis in your relationship?

16. Do you withhold information from your partner?

17. Do you use blame or shame to get what you want?

18. Are you critical?

19. Do you stockpile issues or problems and dump them on your partner all at once during arguments?

20. Do you think you have the answers for how your partner ought to be or act?

21. Do you feel betrayed if your partner needs time alone or with friends?

22. Do you feel afraid when intense feelings surface?

23. Do you fear engulfment or abandonment?

24. Do you worry about being embarrassed by your partner or his or her way of being?

25. Do you avoid talking about issues that may cause your partner to feel pain?

26. Do you use name-calling, labels, criticism, or threats when you're angry?

27. Does your partner use name-calling, labels, criticism, or threats when he or she is angry?

28. Is verbal, sexual, or emotional abuse a part of your relationship dynamic?

29. Is substance or food abuse a part of the dynamic in your relationship?

30. Is it difficult for you to acknowledge your love for your partner to friends/relatives?

31. Do you believe it's your job to make your partner happy and satisfied sexually?

32. Do you talk to others about your relationship before or in lieu of speaking with your mate?

33. Do you make disparaging remarks about your mate or his or her character flaws to others?

34. Do you divulge private intimacies/sharing to others?

35. Do you use omission to create room for doubt in order to get control?

36. Do you withhold safety with words and actions?

37. Do you answer questions with a question?

38. Do you respond to deep feeling by changing the subject?

39. Do you respond to anger with anger?

40. Do you feel anger is an unhealthy emotion?

41. Do you feel your feelings are facts?

42. Do you feel it's demeaning to apologize?

43. Do you feel you lose power, ground, face if you discover or admit you're wrong?

44. Does being wrong equate to being bad?

45. Does allowing for change equate to a lack of perfection?

46. Do you solicit information even when your partner has said he/she is not ready to talk?

47. Is it hard to take time out while feelings cool down or get clarified?

48. Do you have a friend/s who know more about what you're feeling than your partner?

49. Do you make "innocent" remarks that often hurt your partner?

50. Do you often speak of "all the others" who agree with your point of view?

51. Do you have a pattern of leaving relationships about every three months or three years?

52. Does the presence of fear mean something is wrong or you should leave?

53. Do you have feelings that appear to be too big for you to handle?

54. Do you have feelings/thoughts that you would not feel safe to share with your partner?

55. Does giving praise or encouragement to your partner make you feel sad or diminished?

56. Are you cynical about your mate or your relationship?

57. Do you believe your mate lies or has lied to you?

58. Would you believe a friend or family member instead of believing your mate?

59. Is one of the people you feel least safe with your mate?

60. Do you feel your mate needs something from you that is not being spoken?

61. Do you feel you can't let go and be vulnerable with a mate?

62. Are you able to openly cry with a mate?

63. Does it feel unsafe to get angry in front of a mate?

64. Do you and your mate lack a shared vision for the future?

65. Do you and your mate lack a shared spiritual path and process?

66. Do you and your mate fail to get involved in ongoing efforts at spiritual growth?

67. Do you and your mate have dissimilar ethics, principles, and levels of commitment?

68. Do you and your mate avoid time to just be together without friends or projects?

69. Do you feel awkward when there is silence or quiet in your relationship?

70. Do you feel like your mate is not a best friend?

71. Do you and your mate ignore opportunities for shared projects or ongoing experiences of giving back to the world or community in some way?

72. Do you and your mate spend more than 10 hours a week watching television or movies?

73. Do you and your mate ignore ways to improve your relationship, communication, or spirituality?

74. Are you missing processes or opportunities for personal, individual growth?

75. Do you lack a personal relationship with Spirit?

76. Do you have hang-ups about your sexuality?

77. Do you lack the freedom and abandon to experience joy sexually?

78. Are you hesitant to discuss your sexual satisfaction or sexual issues with your mate?

79. Do you allow yourself to experience sexual intimacy without the need for orgasm?

80. Do you become insecure when sexual activity slows down or your mate is not feeling sexual?

81. Is your mate unconcerned about your sexual satisfaction and pleasure?

82. Are you inhibited about making love in many different positions and circumstances?

83. Do you feel uncomfortable masturbating?

84. Do you withhold information about things that would give you sexual pleasure?

85. Does your mate feel he or she has failed you if you do not reach orgasm?

86. Does your mate feel you have failed him or her if he or she does not reach orgasm?

87. Do you lack knowledge about what turns you on sexually?

88. Are there parts of you that turn off when you're being sexual?

89. Does your sexual appetite feel unmatched with that of your mate?

90. Do you feel you must satisfy your mate in order for him or her to feel OK about themselves?

91. Do you forget to think of ways to provide sexual treats for your partner?

92. Are you intimidated when your partner admires someone else with an attractive body?

93. Do you mistrust your partner's level of commitment to monogamy?

94. Do you use nonmonogamy as a way of avoiding deeper intimacy?

95. Do you feel you and your mate seldom "make love"?

96. Do you and your mate have sex more often than you make love?

97. Do you connect sexually with people before you have connected spiritually and emotionally with them?

98. Do you believe some things should be kept secret between you and your partner?

99. Do you speak of your sexual relationship to others in a disparaging way?

100. Do you believe one person must always take the lead sexually?

Now, go back over the questions and tally the number of times you answered "always," "sometimes," or "never."

ALWAYS_____    SOMETIMES_____    NEVER_____

**If the majority of your answers are in the "never" category**, obviously you have done some real work on yourself. Congratulations! Now you can clean up those leftover issues and focus on how to deepen your relationship safely. You have the principles in place and you are using the tools in your relationship. Good for you. Just focus on the issues that are still unresolved and allow yourself to use the information in this book to deal with the unfinished part of your work. You're well on your way to creating conscious relationships.

**If you have a nearly equal number of answers in the "never" and "sometimes" categories**, you have also done some work. Now you can focus on those areas that you have highlighted that still need healing. Take a look at the areas that need improvement and see if they have a theme or some similarity. If they do, you still have some beliefs about yourself that are not in your best interest. Try to see what the underlying beliefs are and then concentrate your focus on the particular tools you need.

**If the majority of your answers are in the "always" and "sometimes" categories**, you're in for some wonderful discoveries about yourself. Putting the tools in this book to work for you will provide you with some freedom and self-esteem that you have been seeking. No doubt you are still operating under some misconceptions, and this is your opportunity to get off that self-defeating wheel and have the kind of relationships you deserve.

**If the majority of your answers are in the "always" category**, you're definitely reading the right book. And I'm delighted for you, because you're about to begin the journey you have waited for, the one that takes you to yourself. There is great joy in the process of letting go of those false beliefs and barriers to receiving love. You have all that joy to look forward to, starting right now, so let's begin. Let's start by examining where those barriers come from and how we can begin to remove them.

## Stay Present. Be Honest. Act Out of Love, Not Fear.

In the pages that follow, we are going to examine your ability to stay present, be honest, and act out of love, not fear. I will give you some tools for improving your ability to do this and ensure your success in relationships. We will do that by breaking down these principles and exploring exactly what they mean and how you might act or feel if you live them. We will begin with the issue of staying present, because if you're not truly present to life, yourself, and each other, none of this work can be accomplished and you're missing out on love. So, first let's see if we can find out what has prevented you from being fully present—or what you're afraid of.

## Why Can't I Be Real?

Your answer to this question lies in a place deep inside you. Many authors, some of whom call this the "shadow side," have discussed this place. I call it our red wagon. It's a place where we hold our fear and denial. After taking the quiz, you may wonder where these false ideas and fears about ourselves come from and how we can begin letting them go. Actually, this red wagon is nothing to be afraid of, because it's simply the part of your psyche that holds the issues that need healing until you're ready to bring them to light. It's a dark place without light and understanding—that's all, nothing more. It's that place inside us to which we have not yet brought love; where we hide our fears, doubts, anger and limitations, all those feelings we judge and don't want anyone else to see. It harbors fear that motivates us to lie, pretend we aren't afraid, and act as if we don't care or are someone we are not. It's our *little red wagon* full of life experiences and denial. Understanding your denial is important, because unless you recognize that many of your decisions come from these old stored pains and fear, you can't reclaim your power over them. If you understand them, you can make conscious decisions not to act out of that fear. The following are some examples of issues we all deal with. Have you ever had experiences such as these?

* You experience an instant when you are getting into your car to go to a job you hate when you realize the guy you are leaving on that doorstep thinks you're cold, uncaring, and demanding. You realize you have been that way, even in your love relationships, since your uncle Harold spanked you "for being a sissy" when you were 9 years old. Ever since, you have tried to kill any part of yourself that resembled "a sissy" in any way. Of course, in doing so, you have no doubt limited the intuitive, soft, caring, less linear parts of yourself that are dying to be expressed and be accepted by everyone around you. You'd really like to turn around, go back inside, hold your mate and tell him you love him, but you're afraid that would make you too vulnerable, put you in a position of being hurt, so instead you just go to work.

Now ask yourself, what are the ways in which you prevent yourself, out of fear, from showing love?

* You notice the false, angry part of yourself that you have been using to distance the people in your life, and you realize how isolated it has made you. Ever since you were about age 10 and overheard dad say he wished you'd been a boy, you decided you'd never let anyone get close enough to see that you're not enough, not lovable. The problem is that everything in your life, including those who love you deeply, would seem to indicate you're more than enough. In fact, you're probably an overachiever, a caretaker who tries harder than anyone to prove your worth. Unless, of course, you're still trying to prove that dad was right by consciously or unconsciously sabotaging relationships to prove you don't deserve love at all. Either way, the part inside you who still needs to prove something to dad is making you miserable, wants love,

and is sick of feeling so alone in the midst of so much love.

What old childhood judgment is still controlling your life and relationships?

* You remember some old feelings of how discounted you were as a child, and you feel outraged. Since childhood, you brag a lot, tell people often how wonderful you are, and feel crushed and outraged when your beloved does not notice every new accomplishment and every new effort you make to be special and outstanding. The truth is, you still believe what you were told as a child, and you're still trying desperately to get someone outside yourself to tell you it's a lie. Still, you don't believe them when they do tell you how great you are, so no matter how often or intently they try to convince you, it's never enough.

How are you still trying to get people to prove you are lovable, worthwhile, and desirable?

* You are staring off into space at lunch and slip into some altered state, remembering how deeply you felt loved by your first girlfriend. You realize you want that feeling back. Instead, you push the anger back down and make a decision not to talk of your desire to feel more loved by your mate. Inside, you're afraid she won't see you as lovable, desirable, and worthy. Better not to risk it, you tell yourself. Unconsciously, you still look into every new face for that special woman who you want to walk into your life and recognize your specialness. You leave yourself vulnerable to making a hurtful choice for infidelity because you won't risk going deeper emotionally with someone who really loves you.

In what ways do you hold yourself back and deny your needs out of fear of rejection?

* You're driving over the crest of Coldwater Canyon when you suddenly realize you're exhausted and have been depriving yourself. You become so filled with a sense of your aloneness that tears stream down

your cheeks. You begin to remember all the times your parents seemed to be saying your worth as a child was dependent upon how "good" you were and how many accomplishments or honors you achieved in school. Are you wondering now why you're not filled up? Are you still enmeshed in *doing* in order to become who you already are? Are you missing the opportunities for deep connection that could fill you?

Why do you think it's still so hard for you to believe you're enough, even if you never did another single thing?

* You recall how much you loved your partner but broke up with him because you had both gotten into a cycle of control and anger that neither of you was able to stop. You suddenly realize how much you had been projecting blame onto him, which was really old pain and lack of trust caused by a previous lover. Was criticism and shaming a way your parents kept you in line? Are you doing it now to your partners and yourself?

What terrible thing have you done that makes you not worthy of receiving love? No matter what your perception, what if you were already forgiven?

* You get the flu and feel fearful, angry, or sad for no apparent reason and then remember how angry your mother would get at you as a child when you became ill. Ever since, you have not let anyone care for you. In fact, at the first sign of deepening intimacy in any relationship, you create a reason to leave, distance, usually blaming the other person for not caring enough, and away you go from the very thing you say you want the most.

Is it really possible that all those failed relationships were always the other person's fault?

* You have read all the magazines and watched all the TV ads, and believe you must look thin, suave, stylish, and debonair in order to find a mate. Since that is not who you are, you have decided no one will come into your life to love you. You're tired of the endless diets, the fear

of being who you are, the phony person who comes out and acts as if he or she is someone else, and you're about ready to give up. Underneath all that acting is a really great person who has never had your approval or a chance to be fully who he or she is. Instead of feeling fulfilled, you are still empty and sad. What you really want most is someone who will love you exactly as you are. But since you won't even let yourself be that person, no one as yet has found you.

Do you even know who you are, or what you're really capable of?

Starting to get the picture? I imagine you have your own personal painful scenario, right? Now one thing is for sure, I do *not* want you to think that your red wagon issues are insurmountable. Every single one is simply an old issue that needs to be healed on your journey to yourself, and none of them is fatal. I just want you to know about them, be able to identify the feelings that come from inside, demystify them, and stop letting them roll into the *now* to control you and your relationships. We all have a personal red wagon full of life experiences that seems to creep forward and direct our behavior in our present relationships and circumstances. You are going to encounter them in this journey to your self, the authentic you, and in your discovery of your Self, the spiritual you.

Many people think they can just *get spiritual* and that will make all of their emotional troubles and pain disappear. Unfortunately, neither spirituality nor emotional growth work in that way. Once you're on a spiritual path, you will encounter the same fears and limitations you encounter in the rest of your life, only now they will impede your spiritual process. If you're in an emotional growth process, you will ultimately discover your spiritual self anyway. Either way, *you* must do the emotional work on *yourself*—all of which is spiritual, and all of which is part of your path. Haven't you known, or known of, well-established spiritual leaders with followers who have made very big, human mistakes and lost their way because they had not done their own emotional growth work? You can see these kinds of people all the time. They are the people collectors, those who need followers who perceive them as being special. They focus on money, amass wealth and control. They often gain acclaim by berating or discounting others and very often do not use spiritual principles of inclusion rather than exclusion. These folks have red wagons of their own, and ultimately they too will have to turn around and examine and heal the contents in order to move ahead spiritually.

*You are living today what you were taught to believe yesterday. You will live tomorrow what you choose to believe today.*

Your red wagon presents you with rich possibilities. It's abundant with information about you and those issues that still need to be healed. Until now, most of us have avoided these issues rather than use them in our process of healing. Intuitively, we know we all have unresolved issues that prevent us from creating successful relationships or direct us into making inappropriate career decisions and inappropriate choices about the people in our lives. From this place, all those illusions about who we are or *should* be originate. Those false ideas get created in response to these unresolved issues. We act as if those issues are too fearful to address. Yet, the Spirit inside us knows that if we can muster the courage to stare them down and resolve them, we will somehow get our lives back. Your spirit is right.

*Behind all resistance is fear.*
*Behind all fear is a lack of faith in yourself.*

When you get to these feelings and become fearful, your first instinct may be to protect yourself, to move away emotionally. If you're with another person, you may find yourself using anger, judgment, pretense, arrogance, or false selves to distance the other person. You usually get to your hidden feelings when someone or some circumstance has triggered a vulnerable place inside you. Our natural inclination is to close off, close down. Often we stop breathing and hold onto ourselves, bracing against the feelings. This is a place where you must have great compassion and understanding for yourself, the other person, and your red wagon as a teacher. You're filled with all your judgments about yourself, most of which have been handed down through the broken psyches of your parents, who were also filled with judgments about themselves. From their input and your circumstances in life, you have created all those false selves—because you fear being real.

> *Believing you are worthy of nothing is spiritual arrogance.*
> *You are thinking you know more than God.*

Your fears prevent you from feeling aliveness, love, and passion, and from feeling personal power, pride, and ecstasy. Your refusal to face your fear is the reason you keep asking yourself, *What am I doing here? What is my purpose? Why am I not happy?* In reality, those fears are part of your purpose, here to help you find yourself. They are illusions and lies made up by your mind to protect you—and now to help you grow. You can't recognize true love unless you have experienced isolation. You can't find power unless you have known powerlessness. You can't find out who you are until you have experienced who you're not. Without your fears, your false ideas about yourself, you would have no process for finding out who you are. Releasing them is your work both alone and in a relationship. All that emotion inside has a purpose, a divine purpose.

## Relationships Show Us Where Our Work Is

Relationships give us the opportunity to know what false beliefs we still hold about ourselves. Your purpose is to let them go and find your own divinity. **Your purpose is to understand that most of the feelings and judgments you still experience are not even about *now*. They are simply the result of lessons you experienced as a child and are here so that you can find yourself now.**

You're not your abuse. You're not your parents' or society's judgments. You're not any of your limited ideas about yourself. Yet without these ideas, how would you make your way to the truth of who you are? What would be the grist for the mill in your discovery process? Our process, and Spirit's process, is to know ourselves and our own divinity. To do that, we must identify and clear away the ways we are not being fully spiritual.

> *Every event and person in your life is a teacher attempting*
> *to teach you to be Love.*

You're not those old feelings and judgments. You're an adult with all the potential to be a master in life, fully loved and loving. Clients often ask me, "Why do I have to go through all this pain? How can this be part of Spirit's plan, that I have suffered so much?" First of all, your suffering was never something Spirit wanted for you. A person, not Spirit, inflicted that suffering. Suffering is created when you, as an adult, acting out of your pain, move into denial and refuse to heal. You then, consciously or unconsciously, inflict pain on yourself or another because you cannot tolerate the feelings you hold inside. In addition, when you were abused as a child, the suffering had no purpose. When you begin to deal with painful feeling in the healing process, the purpose is to release suffering once and for all. Want to stop the suffering? Stop perpetuating the illusion that you cannot deal with your feelings. Act out of your *path*, not your *pathology*.

In our collective unconscious we have become emotional sissies. We have missed these magical opportunities to evolve our own souls. Instead, we have run from them. Rather than taking the emotional and spiritual responsibility not to perpetuate pain, we act out of our old wounds and the fear they have created. Instead of acting out of the wholeness of who we really are, we allow the feelings and fears from our past to make our decisions for us. All of which happens to be a choice, by the way. This is a choice you can begin to make differently starting today.

## You Get to Choose

We each get to choose what we will empower in our lives. We can empower the belief that we are helpless, hopeless victims of circumstance and injury, or we can empower the beliefs that add to our wholeness and spirituality. People are making millions of dollars on the hope that you will continue to be *recovering* from some issue or another, rather than heal it. They are making millions on the belief that you are still somehow flawed. How long must you continue *recovering, trying, working at it,* before you just stop and simply be who you are? I don't mean to trivialize the healing process in any way, but let's face it, many of us have been victims of our childhood most of our lives. We are still invested in living the lie that we cannot get past what happened to us

10, 20, or 30 years ago. Some of us are still waiting for our parents or God to fix us. What if there is nothing wrong with us in the first place? What if we are not our wounding? What if we are more than what has happened to us?

In any given period in our lives, a thousand times a day *we make the choice* to retreat from life and its lessons or to embrace it. We *choose* to empower the love in our lives or diminish it. We *choose* to honor ourselves or perpetuate the lie that we are unlovable, unworthy, and in some way flawed. *We choose* to act out of our fear or out of love. *We choose* to act from a place of truth or from a lie. **In any given moment, we hold the possibility for our own empowerment.**

*Your worth is a given. Your grace and greatness is a choice.*

You can truly alter your life by altering your mind and attitude. It's a choice. That choice is yours. Simply ask yourself what you want and choose that which honors your decisions and your truth. You will always have some issue or another coming from your red wagon, because we are here to learn. Your choices about how to respond to each challenge and opportunity for growth make all the difference in the quality of your life and relationships. Every single choice you make either enhances or diminishes who you are—and adds to your aliveness or creates spiritual death.

I once had a very spiritual client who believed what her father had told her: She would never succeed in life. This belief was so ingrained that she sabotaged every relationship and job she had until she was well over 40! As she amassed failure after failure, she simply used each one as a confirmation and told herself, *See, my father was right. The proof is right here.* I finally told her, "You're right. God has put you on this planet to fail and be miserable. God is simply mean as hell."

"What? That's not true!" she responded instantly, nearly coming out of her chair.

"Well, you have one parent who believes it's impossible for you to fail and one who believes you can do nothing but fail. Which one will you choose to believe? It's your choice. It always has been. Choose right now." She did. It was a struggle, but she made the commitment to choose what she knew in her heart to be true about herself rather than what she had been told. Day after day, with one decision and action at a time, whenever she began to move back into her negative program of self-sabotage, she stopped herself, took a breath and asked, "What do I really know to be true for me?" She then made her decision based upon her own spiritual truth, and before long those decisions began to come naturally. The good news about this kind of healing is that because it's based on truth and truth is the natural state, once you begin the process you heal more quickly than you had ever imagined.

In much the same way that a plant reaches for sunlight, your heart and soul are reaching for deep healing states and real feelings of being connected, soul deep, right to the core of who you are. But you become afraid, because the minute you get too close to anyone, you start to feel all those uncomfortable feelings from your past begin to get unearthed.

Intimacy touches us deep inside, and when we are touched emotionally, it opens us up and up come all those nasty feelings we have stored in denial or pushed away. This is one of the major reasons so many of us avoid deep intimacy. When these feelings begin to surface, we think the intimacy is the problem, and we feel something must be wrong with our choice. Getting connected is not the problem. We are afraid to heal the old issues in order to get to what we say we want. Whatever those old issues are, you have already survived them or you would not be sitting here reading this book. Relax—whatever comes up is surfacing so that you can heal it, be done with it, and get on with your life.

## Our Predicaments

One of our predicaments in dealing with these feelings is that we are seldom present enough to ourselves, our surroundings, or each other to create the kind of union that results in a healing. *This is why relationships are critical to our process.* We are so busy acquiring food, material things, financial security, and prestige that emotional and spiritual security have become elusive, lost in the shuffle. We continue to believe that if we can only acquire enough things, mates, and partners, we will improve the quality of our lives. Unfortunately, that has not proven true, and we are still seeking that elusive *something* to fill us up. That something lies in the center of yourself and your relationships. It's the truth of your being.

> *If you measure your success in terms of praise or criticism,*
> *you will never know the truth.*
> *Listen to your own heart and the voice of Spirit inside you.*
> *That is the only truth you need to know.*

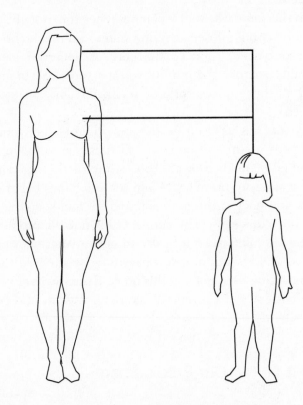

When you, as an adult, feel the feelings that you felt as a child, you can reexperience every sensation as if it is happening in the moment. In truth, these feelings are exactly *what you felt when you were small* and are *not the now feelings of you as an adult*. They are the feelings that keep you in the pain of your past. They are the pain, guilt, anger, grief, and rage in your red wagon.

Another predicament you may experience is that **your relationships are usually created out of need, fear, and denial.** They come directly from your fears; therefore, they soon become unsafe. In many misguided ways we have been connecting to each other out of our need, using each other as quick fixes so we don't have to experience our feelings. For instance, when did you last get into a relationship with an inappropriate partner or a friend, rather than feel your aloneness? Have you ever put up with outlandish behavior from a friend or family member rather than risk him or her leaving you? Whenever we do that, our relationships prove to be less than satisfying. Partners, friends, and family members become objects of filling our needs rather than recipients of our love. In the past you may have believed that if you could just find someone who loved you or thought you were special, he or she would heal your pain. That didn't work, did it? When he or she left, your sense of security left as well and you were back in the pain.

*Need is never love.*

## The Blame Game

In addition to our propensity for creating relationships out of need, we with deal two other major predicaments. The first is that we live in an era of blame—blaming our parents, our teachers, and our society or government. In fact, we have blamed everyone, with the exception of the person who has the most control: ourselves. We play the blame game with ourselves when we are afraid, when we lack trust in the truth of our being. We may be afraid of feelings, growth, truth, commitment, or learning. Underneath all the other reasons, the real cause for blaming—and predicament number 2—is that we are afraid of ourselves. We lack the faith and trust in ourselves to safely process our feelings and self-discoveries. We lack faith in ourselves to act on our own behalf, ask for what we need, create it for ourselves.

We usually play the blame game most intently just before we are about to give up and move into acceptance, about either our circumstances or the way others are acting. We play it when someone has our number and we know the game is about to get called. Then we really puff up, get louder, make threatening statements, and call the troops in. Do you know what "calling the troops in" means? That's when you tell your partner "Everyone else feels exactly as I do." about what is going on with him or her. Obviously, you have not polled everyone, and, if you had, certainly not *everyone* would agree with your point of view. But it's nevertheless a tactic we often use in the blame game, especially when we are most afraid our partner is right about what he or she is saying and we begin to feel wrong.

For some people, the game can last lifetimes. When that happens, the stakes get higher, and the game gets harder the next time around. Not only do they miss living life fully, but they also miss the extraordinary discovery of who they really are. We give up ourselves—and our dreams and visions—when we play this game.

The only people who ever win at the blame game are attorneys. They like it because it pays for their houses, vacations, and cars. The rest of us don't like it as much. When we are in it, we have this sneaking suspicion that something is not quite right. We walk away from people and situations either feeling as if we missed something important or wishing we had handled things better. We feel somehow disappointed in ourselves, as if we have cheated ourselves in some way we can't quite put our finger on. We feel ashamed, as if we have missed some special opportunity that could result in deeper, more meaningful relationships. Sometimes we feel sad and can even blame ourselves for playing the blame game.

It takes a lot of energy to play the blame game. Most of the time, we have to work hard to stay in the game. And winning isn't very fulfilling. You receive no prizes when you win this game. In fact, you have to go back to *start* again every time you win. Feel like you're doing the same relationships with different people over and over?

The blame game costs us thousands of hours, millions of dollars, and years of personal freedom. It's one of the greatest tools we've found to distance ourselves from life, from our own power, and from our divinity. We even use the blame game to distance ourselves from Spirit.

This game is a national pastime. As a community, we've been blaming society forever, and yet we've never treated our relationships with the honor they deserve. The blame game is the life-giving force behind talk shows, best-selling books, insurance companies, and courtrooms. It's the impetus behind wars, divorces, and custody battles. It's the foundational energy of prejudice, hatred, and separation.

The blame game is the response we choose when we lack emotional and spiritual courage. It's the most active game we play, until we become conscious. Then, and only then, do we realize playing this game is a deadening option that has no life-giving value. Instead, it diminishes our awareness, aliveness, and strength. It's a lie about the truth of our divinity. It's not real, and neither are you when you play it.

Once you discover that you've been playing the blame game, you have to be careful not to inadvertently go back to playing it with yourself. It's nearly embedded in our DNA. If you find, after reading this book, that you've been playing the game, simply decide to no longer play. You'll have all the tools you need to take personal responsibility. Once you've stopped playing the blame game, you can start being real and play the game of life and love, which are much more fun and rewarding.

It's important to understand that your personal decision not to play the blame game does not in any way condone or excuse the actions of those who have hurt you. Many people feel if they let go of blame, they are excusing the wrong done to them. Letting go of the game simply means you're no longer willing to let blame control your decisions and your life. Be careful, however. We are so good that we even trick ourselves into believing we don't know when we are playing the game.

We are talking about this game because it's time to get beyond it individually and as a community. We are more concerned about what society thinks of us than we are with cleaning up our own issues, our own lack of integrity, and our own self-hatred. We have not wanted to take personal responsibility for our own pain or our own path. In some ways we have acted like emotional cowards. We blame our lack of self-esteem on the nonacceptance of our parents. **Our parents at the ripe old age of 60, 70, or 80 have absolutely no responsibility for fixing us as adults.** They still have responsibility for fixing themselves, if they wish to, before they die. If they choose to do so, that's more than enough. But you and I are on our own. We get to decide what our own lives will look like. Thank heavens! I personally would never turn that responsibility over to my parents.

We also have to stop blaming society for our lack of safety and equality. We number in the millions and yet we have millions who are still in the closet. Imagine what could happen if we took one week out of the year and exchanged money only with another gay man or lesbian in support of his or her business. What if we had a national gay flu day and all of us stayed home in October on National Coming Out Day? Truth is, we have no one to blame for our lack of equality but ourselves. But we still do have internalized shame that prevents us from being proud of who we are and taking a stand against the prejudice that hurts us.

There are times when placing the responsibility for hurtful actions onto the person who took those actions is correct. This is not playing the blame game. For instance, it's important that if you were abused as a child, you do not take on the responsibility for your abuse but instead put the responsibility where it belongs, with your abuser. This process of understanding where the responsibility lies, or "what's your issue and what's mine," is also a fine dance in relationships that takes skill. You will be getting important help with this issue in chapter three when we discuss boundaries. In the meantime, remember that you use blame only when you are operating from fear and lack faith in yourself.

The last predicament is that we didn't understand the importance of dealing with the issues we hold in denial. Each is a fine tool we can use to create what we desire. Healing those issues is our secret weapon for getting what we say we want. Each issue you heal opens a space and possibility for having what you want. You cannot have what you want if you are filled up with wanting or the pain of not having. Doing this work is a gift we give ourselves. And it's even more important than that. It's your spiritual purpose.

This is the very reason the universe allows us to create life exactly as we wish it to be, so that we can learn from our process. We are creating ourselves, just as Spirit did, and we get to choose what we'll become. The universe has no attachment to your pain. It sees your pain as a part of your path that you're currently choosing so that you may learn about yourself. You may have as little or as much pain as you wish. Or you may have as little or as much love as you wish. It's up to you. The divine mind will not do that for you. That's what free will is all about. If Spirit were to make those decisions for you, It would also take away your right to your process and the discovery of your true self. Spirit works through you, as you, to create exactly what you decide to have in your life.

*We create everything we experience in life, including that which we perceive ourselves to lack.*

You get to choose whether you will have a happy life or a sad one, a full life or an empty one, a life filled with love or longing. Each of your choices is part of your path. Since the truth is that you're already Spirit, at some point in your process you will ultimately make that discovery for yourself. At some point in this life, or the next, you will get sick of berating yourself, doing without, and feeling isolated. Then you will give yourself permission to be who you really are. You can do it now or later. The universe makes no judgment on your process, and it has no desire for you to do it differently. That's why Spirit's not the one in pain—you are.

You say you wish for your circumstances in life to be different. But you're in pain because you're refusing to make the choices that will make your life better. There are times when the truth stings. And this is a time when the truth *must* sting. In fact, we must use a lightning bolt, if necessary, to jolt us out of our complacency and unwillingness to act on our own behalf. Either that or we must admit we enjoy creating the pain we are in, and we are using it to prevent ourselves from finding love and freedom. Either way, we need to get honest, live life consciously, take our power back, and stop lying about the abundance of choices we actually do have and are refusing. Every person who comes out, tells the truth, and makes decisions out of love, not fear, has chosen freedom for him or herself.

In 1982 I fasted for the Equal Rights Amendment in Springfield, Ill., for thirty-seven days, consuming only water. Only three states were left to ratify the amendment out of five holdouts. Thanks to countless hours of woman (and man) power, every other state had passed it. One by one, I watched as the insurance companies bought the legislators who had promised us their votes. The ERA never passed, but I came home with equal rights. I gave them to myself. If we want respect and honor in the world, we must be willing to learn to give that to ourselves and our relationships first.

It is of little use to be in conflict with yourself. In fact, it's excruciatingly painful. Whenever you act contrary to your own truth, you create a war inside yourself that saps your energy, diminishes your personal power, and chips away at your self-esteem. If you say you want your life to be different, *you* must make choices for yourself to make that possible. As soon as you embrace your life and every lesson you have created for yourself, you will begin to understand that *you* are the one in control and *you* have the power to change it. Change will occur naturally. The Spirit in you watches you suffer and keeps trying to tell you in every way that you have the power to change things for yourself. Every spiritual teaching known to humankind has the same message, truths, and principles. All you need to do is move to being the love that you already are. That is, in fact, your only purpose.

*Whenever you feel dissonance, stop and ask yourself, "What part of me is not aligned with Spirit?"*

There is no question for which the answer is not love. There is no wound that cannot be healed with love. There is no task that cannot be accomplished with love. And there is no relationship that will not be successful if it's lived out of love and not fear. You have the answers, and yet you still seek to be that which you are not. You still seek answers in what is less than loving—in games, techniques, and rules. Your answers are not there, I promise you.

## More About Individual Red Wagons

I discuss red wagons in this chapter because they are going to become your best friends and greatest teachers. I have two tiny Red Flyers sitting in my office to remind clients that their wagon issues are not insurmountable. Most of us feel there is something wrong with us when we suddenly feel negative emotions, or get *triggered* with intense feelings. This triggering has scared you, and you have moved away from the very thing that needs healing in order to find happiness. *Getting triggered* is the term used for what happens when someone says or does something that opens up a world of feelings that rush to the surface. Sometimes the feelings can *appear* to be unmanageable and dangerous. You can be reading a book such as this one, and something inside says, "Oops, put that down...DANGER ZONE HERE!" So you quickly put the book down and tell yourself you need something a bit lighter, perhaps an auto mechanics magazine or *Good Housekeeping*. There is nothing wrong with you when you feel these feelings. You have simply tripped upon an old, stored trauma or fearful feeling that needs to be resolved.

More often than not, instead of being curious about that voice or those emotions, you *leave* the person, circumstance, thought, or in this case, the book, that triggered those feelings so that you can escape the discomfort. In doing so, you deaden a part of yourself and your ability to embrace life fully. You push those intense feelings back into denial, close the lid on them, and act as if they don't exist.

As life goes on, you continue pushing the hard feelings in life down or away, shutting yourself off from the parts of you that feel those feelings. Little by little, you deaden one part of yourself after another. Of course, while doing so, you create yet another false self that pretends everything is fine, in order to keep going. As this self-protective process continues, you become less and less authentic, less real, more in denial, and less available to experience life fully. You have to create more false selves to replace the parts of yourself that are in denial.

I often hear, "That's in the past, so why bring it up?" Or you might say, "That just brings me pain, so I don't think about it." Or, perhaps you're one who says, "What difference does it make if I don't tell my family? It would only hurt them." Your motto for living life becomes, "Just don't go there!" **So, you leave people, circumstances, feelings, challenges, and careers. You leave relationships, families, and growth. You leave yourself, and ultimately you leave your own sense of aliveness and life itself.** Every time you leave feelings without healing them, you become less of who you are, and you feel less alive.

The unresolved issues inside you make you feel even more vulnerable. It's as if you have Swiss-cheese holes inside yourself into which people and circumstances can poke their fingers. **Each time you push some new feeling into a state of denial, you have added to your list**

**of people you can't be around, feelings you can't face, and circum-
stances you attempt to avoid.** You hesitate to go forward into creating
new relationships, or taking steps toward a sense of connectedness in
the relationships you currently have. **It's easier, you tell yourself, to
just maintain the status quo and not rock the boat by trying to create deeper passion, communication, and real connection.** So the
chasm between you and your true self, or between you and those you
love, remains huge.

Before you know it, as life goes on, you have created greater fear,
anger, guilt, and pain, but mostly you create denial about all these feelings. The more denial you have, the less you're able to be fully present
with yourself. You live life as an observer instead of as a participant. I
know people who can never be without some activity or an other person. They fill life up with anything that prevents them from feeling
themselves. They are never fully with anyone because they are never
fully with themselves. Activities, serial relationships, and other people
are simply the Band-Aids that make it possible for them to keep life at
an arm's length, rather than embrace love or life. All the while, these
people blame everyone and everything else for their lack of happiness.

If you're one of these people, your anxiety and fears grow because
when you're not *with* yourself, you become even more vulnerable in the
world to getting triggered and hurt. When you're disconnected from
yourself, you can't access your inner wisdom or your personal power. All
your denials make you miserable, either consciously or unconsciously.
Good people, good relationships, and good families fall into this trap.
Some never get out. Those who do look back and say, "If only I had
known then what I know now."

Healing does require emotional courage, the willingness to look at
what has been triggered. It requires looking at the parts of you that are
not real. What motivated you to create those parts? It may be something from the past, or present. Was it a lack of safety, a sense of not
being seen, honored, or respected? Was it a breach of boundaries, a
hurtful label or discounting remark? Was it the energy you felt from a
friend or family member that reminded you of your past? Was it your
own judgment that you are not enough, not lovable?

When one of those vulnerable places inside gets triggered, it tells
us we are still holding some old unresolved pain that needs healing. It's

a signal that there's work to be done on ourselves. It tells us we still have a place inside that feels powerless to act on our own behalf. Therefore, we move away. After all, we are never affected by what others say unless we fear it could in some way be true.

The answer is to stay present and *stop* creating false selves, starting right now. You are no longer a child, and there is no reason for you to be anyone other than who you are. If you're in a relationship where all these issues are coming up, believe it or not, you're probably in a great relationship! You have found enough safety to feel yourself and what you are holding inside in denial. If you're pretending to be someone you're not so you won't have any issues to deal with, then you are not in a relationship at all—not with yourself or your beloved. Instead, you're playing at the game of relationship, and ultimately you will fail or live life not fully alive to your experiences. The good news is that because you're now an adult, you get to do this healing in small pieces, and at a pace that feels safe to you.

Some of you will say, "I've been working on this stuff for years and I'm sick of it." I empathize. Some part of what you have been working on, however, is still unresolved or the issue would not come up again. Remember those times when you really resolved an issue? Wasn't it over and done with once you got the answer? Respect yourself and your inner wisdom enough to refrain from judging yourself or being impatient. You may have done so much work that you have finally reached the last piece of what you need to address.

## Everyone Experiences Fear

The first place to start dealing with your issues is simply to be emotionally courageous enough to admit that they exist. **It's also important to remember that *you* are not your issues.** You're something so much greater, a wondrous individual reflection of Spirit. Well, you say, if we are not our issues, what is it that we are afraid of? Very good question. Ask it of yourself. Once we have acknowledged and owned the fear, breathed it out and brought light to it, it becomes less dangerous.

There is *nothing* in your red wagon that can kill you. You have already survived every feeling that you hold there. You're alive and well and reading this book. Do not hold on to the illusion that you can be destroyed by your own feelings. You're much greater than your feelings. Feelings are intimidating only when we are in denial about them. Learning to use them instead of moving away from them or getting lost in them is an act of mastery. Instead of remaining limited by the fear held by our small self, we can tap into the strength and courage of our spiritual self. Healing these feelings brings us closer to ourSelves. It teaches us that we can trust ourSelves. We can honor ourSelves and resolve those issues that prevent us from being ourSelves. When you get to red wagon issues, say that you have reached that place, name it for yourself and the other person, have a good laugh, grab your sense of humor, and jump on in! I can often be heard saying, "Oops! That came right out of my red wagon. Sorry, let me try that one again."

## Relationship Red Wagons

You will know someone's, maybe both, of your red wagon issues have been encountered in relationships when neither of you can hear each other, understand what the other is feeling, or find a way to negotiate a compromise that is right for both of you. You have thrown up your hands, decided you no longer know what to do, and have nearly given up. People don't deliberately start out to cause divorces and kill relationships. Who among us starts out in any relationship with the intent to create breakup and grief? It's the unresolved pain and denial in red wagons that cause divorces and kill relationships.

The vast majority of us do not want to cause each other pain. We want to give and receive love. But without the understanding necessary to recognize our own pain and come out of the destructive cycles of self-protection that we create, we give up and leave. We often say, "So-and-so didn't understand me. We're just too different. We don't want the same things." My all-time favorite denial is "Well, who needs him or her anyway?" You do! We all need each other. We need to be loved and to give love. But we also need to learn how to navigate through our fear and denial and reconnect in loving ways before the relationship is too broken to save. Think of it this way: How many people do you know who are fully conscious, aware? Well, unless you're fully conscious, you have feelings in denial, and denial means you have a red wagon. We are all still in denial to some degree. In fact, the better your relationship is, the more fears and denials you may discover. This is to say, we usually don't allow ourselves to feel deep feelings until we are in safe relationships.

I can't count the number of times clients have related that they were doing "just great" and then suddenly the bottom fell out of their relationship. Stunned and depressed at their inability to communicate or get off the destructive cycle, most people walk away, adding to the statistics of commitments that don't make it. In addition, let's not forget the thousands of broken relationships that fall by the wayside on the path to that commitment.

When couples and family members come to therapy, I immediately congratulate them for being safe enough to have encountered intense feelings. Once they have the tools for healing and *start to use them*, aliveness and safety return to the relationship, and they experience deeper intimacy, more passion, better communication, better sex, and more successful negotiation than before!

The tools you are about to receive in this book have helped 95% of my clients to stay together. Those relationships that failed did so because one of the partners or both were not open to change. They came into therapy for a safe way to break up. The rest were willing to change and found immense joy when their relationships finally began to work.

*Once you are able to see Spirit in one you love,*
*there is nothing else to see.*

These clients have healed their families, relationships, and themselves by having the courage and willingness to see what was keeping them separated from themselves and those they love. The payoff is insight, awareness, and aliveness. You will be able to safely do the same.

## Spiritual Red Wagons

There's one more type of red wagon we need to discuss before we move into acquiring some tools. These are of a spiritual nature. They are the ones we experience between ourselves and the awareness of a loving universe, Spirit. No matter what your belief system or religious convictions may be, to feel cut off from Spirit is painful. Feeling cut off from the beauty in the earth, the magic of nature, or the blessing of spiritual energy, creates the greatest isolation of all. That separation is a direct result of the self-judgments we carry inside us. Spiritual red wagons get created because we are afraid to believe what the Divine has told us over and over: *There is nothing in the universe except love.* Even fear is love seeking itself.

*We can only reach as far out to each other and as far out to the Divine as we have been willing to reach into ourselves.*

The very same fears, judgments, and denials we hold inside about ourselves also prevent us from feeling connected to Spirit, the universe, the earth, and one another. If I am not real, authentic and honest with myself, how can I profess to be any of those things for or with you? If I am not trusting of myself, how can I trust you or Spirit? It can't be done, because I have no reference point until I have connected fully and lovingly with myself with trust and honesty.

## Why Heal the Denial in the Red Wagon?

To answer that simply, that's where love is. In fact, that's where *you* are, right there underneath all that denial. When was the last time you looked into the eyes of a beloved partner, family member, or friend and saw in them a deep appreciation and understanding of exactly who you are? Have you ever felt a person so completely present with you that you knew she understood your specialness, your gifts, and your exquisite, unique qualities as a divine human being? Not lately? I hadn't either until I reached middle age.

I grew up in an emotionally empty room. I felt miserably alone and longed for some real sense of connection to someone or something so I could feel myself and know that I existed. It's nearly impossible to know you exist until you have someone who, at the very least, appears to be alive enough to reflect your aliveness back to you. My mother was an alcoholic and my father was emotionally abusive, so neither of them felt very alive to me. As I watched them abuse themselves and each other, my denial grew. I denied my pain, my childhood, and my worth.

As I grew into an adult, intuitively I knew there was some mysterious key to creating meaningful relationships. I longed for the kind of connections that touched and changed my soul, the kind that breaks through to a new reality. I watched others in life who had that. Couples who were so bonded that anything less than complete integrity would have been unthinkable. Mothers so fully present, who touched their children with such sweet gentleness that they imparted a sense of the sacred. Friends who spoke together softly of intimacies in an environment of trust and belief. Each person discovering who he or she is through the blessing of relationship. Could I find a way to discover who I really was? Would I ever experience being so close to another human being that I could literally feel the real man or woman I was facing? Could I allow people to be so close to me they could feel the real me? Not just the physical me, the person people see. The real me. Would anyone ever know the person I am inside as a teacher, a friend, a Pisces, a sexual woman, a mother and grandmother, a psychotherapist, a psychic healer, a soul, and, yes, even a spirit? That's how deeply I wanted to know and experience the important people in my life, and that's how deeply I was willing to share myself. I had no role models for how that looked, so how was I to create that in my life?

I knew if I could find out how to discover myself and move through the incorrect messages, the lies, I had been told as a child, I would reach a greater understanding of myself. I wanted to share the real me, but I also wasn't even sure who the real me was. I could envision myself *out there*, about an arm's length away, strong, wise, mature, loving, kind. And yet *here* I stood, still filled with childhood issues that I judged should have been resolved by now. Here I stood still afraid, still small in so many ways and still not yet actualized. In between *the me that I presented to the world* and the *me that I longed to become* was a red wagon filled with all the protections, false selves, and defense mechanisms I had created as a child in order to survive.

I also knew at a deep intuitive level that understanding and resolving separation in my life was a spiritual issue, a critical means through which I could evolve my own soul. I pictured myself moving into it, meeting one little neurotic false self or another saying, "Thank you for helping me survive. I see how hard it was for you, but, truth is, I no longer need you." Poof! It would dissolve, and I would be one step closer to the real me. I pictured that all right, but my fear was greater than my ability to face my false selves. Each time I came upon the opportunity to give up that part of myself that kept me from being real, I recoiled in fear. My ego stopped me. I didn't have the tools or safety I needed. Perhaps you're feeling exactly the same way.

If so, you're about to make a wonderful discovery, just as I did. The simple decision and act of being connected to your feelings, perhaps for the first time, creates a degree of natural resolve and healing. With it comes insight, flashes of understanding, and new awareness. It's a process. **Enlightenment is the process of bringing light to these dark places and replacing fear with love.** You too will discover and create the kind of experiences that happen as a result of being deeply connected to yourselves, life, or another person. You will be able to break through to rich new information about yourself that changes your limited, self-critical perceptions. This healing begins the instant you're willing to resolve some of the denial that continues to steal the quality of your life.

Ready? Here's your first assignment. Your very first step is simply to become more aware. Begin to listen, notice, and get curious about coincidences, insights, thoughts, fears, and repeated patterns in your life. Start to question from where those repeated thoughts and events come. Turn off the car radio or put on music without lyrics and listen to your own thoughts and inner messages. Does this idea scare you? If so, you have already started this process and can be curious about why you feel afraid. Check how your body feels. Are your shoulders tight? Is your stomach in knots? Do you feel as if you have a band around your forehead? How deeply does your breath move into your body as you breathe? You have a world of information available to you, right now, which can give you insight to the issues you're holding inside. These are the issues that keep the love you so deeply desire at a distance.

I want you to follow each thought as if it were a clue on a treasure hunt taking you deeper into the truth. With each clue you uncover, go deeper—under it. It might sound like this: "The thought of doing this work feels scary." (Go deeper.) What feels scary about doing this work? (Look for what is under each thought.) "What if I discover something that really hurts?" What if you do discover something hard? "Can I deal with it?" You probably already have dealt with it and survived or you're dealing with it at the moment and it's time to heal it. "What would I do if it was a friend hurting?" You would take care of her. "Am I capable of taking care of myself?" Yes! Good then, now what makes you afraid? "Nothing. I can do this."

Get the idea? Don't stop until you hit the very bottom of your emotional ladder and have answered each question for yourself. Don't let the fear become an excuse to stop your healing process. It's just a feeling, which most of the time is not based on present reality. I will promise you something, right here and now. Under all of your fear lies a magnificent being who can deal with all of your issues. It's time to find him or her.

Since we are emotionally layered with denial from years of avoiding these issues, you may have to dig for the truth a bit. My favorite exploring words for myself and my clients are, "What's under that?" If you keep saying to yourself, "What's under that feeling?" you will be able to go deeper into the core of the feeling. But, more importantly, there is something under all that feeling that you must find. Somewhere at the core of your self, there is a wise, radiant being that is untouched by all these emotions. She is calm, knowing, and undeniably connected to Spirit. Once you reach her, you will find you are connected to Spirit in such a way that you cannot help but have a direct experience of your own divinity. And you will find her if you follow your fear to the very center of yourself.

My clients often describe this core place as filled with a calm state of grace that is neither anything nor nothing and at the same time has a connected sense to everything. It's as if you have reached a place inside that is so expanded that you're able to realize your connection to All That Is. It's from this place that you begin to understand that you are not your feelings, your abuse, your body, or your role in life. You're not anything other than perfect, exactly as you are. Reaching this place inside is a priceless gift from the universe. And it's why love must come from the inside out. That is where love resides, at the core of your being. It's your being. It's you.

It's also your partner. If you're able to reach that place inside each other, the result is truly divine union. It becomes impossible to leave, betray, or abandon each other once you have connected spirit to spirit. If you're able to reach this place with friends and family, you will have relationships that result in a spiritual family built on love, growth, and the awareness that all relationships are a sacred trust. You will reach a peaceful place of saying, "I'd forgive you if there were anything to forgive," because you will be able to see that we are all in the process of trying to get to this truth of who we are. That awareness alone brings great compassion to your process, for yourself and for all those who are courageous enough to be on the path with you. All you have to do is follow where love is pointing: directly inside.

## Where Does All This Pain Come From?

Most childhood pain comes from the lack of a deep sense of bonding with our caretakers. Not having had this bonding, we go through life bereft of it, seeking it in many costly or inappropriate places. In many cases, we may even be unaware that we have never experienced deep bonding because we have no reference point for it. Have you ever had an experience where someone looked deeply into your eyes and connected so intensely that you had to look away? Of course you have. Why were you so uncomfortable? Because you're not used to having people profoundly present to you.

Often we can't even name the thing that is missing in our lives, but we are aware that *something of great importance is missing,* and on some unconscious level we long to find it. Incredible numbers of people spend thousands of dollars and inconceivable amounts of time in therapy, seminars, 12-step or self-help programs. What are we looking for? We are desperately looking for an experience of *connection.* Many people become dogmatic, religious, and devoutly holistic. We seek out unhealthy relationships, spiritual highs, or become workshop junkies, but no amount of money buys the ecstasy we seek. In fact, during all the time we spend seeking ecstasy elsewhere, it patiently remains hidden, waiting inside each seeker.

## Relationship Is Your Finest Tool

Now you can learn how to recognize the pain or denial you hold inside and get to that place of profound presence with yourself and those you love. You will learn to see the opportunities for healing, embrace them, and then with perfect ease and comfort, you can create healing opportunities with someone you trust. You will start breaking through the walls that keep you from feeling love and giving love without hesitation. You will begin to make new choices, based on love for yourself and others.

You will not have to spend thousands of dollars for therapy simply to experience a deep sense of connection in your life. You will not have to go around the world to mystical places of divine inspiration. I think it's wonderful if you're fortunate enough to have those opportunities; however, most people don't. You will not have to seek out another whom you perceive to be more aware than you are. You will not have to stop your ordinary life to become a visionary. Do I dare tell you that you already are a visionary? Well, all right, we'll wait on that one. Let that idea just hover somewhere out there, off to the side of your awareness. But I will tell you that in your process you will learn how to use your current ordinary life experiences and every relationship as your precious workshop, the one you use to evolve your own soul. You will learn how to sit in safety alone or with those you love and create these trips into expanded hearts and consciousness.

It's so simple! **Stay present. Be honest. Make your decisions out of love, not fear.** Every time you resolve a portion of the pain or denial, you have more room for love and safety. **If you are in continual emotional and spiritual pain, you are probably consciously or unconsciously refusing your own healing. You're in conflict with yourself and your own spirit.** Now you can change that, take control of your healing process and make this experiment in aliveness as habitual as breathing.

## Gifts

Relationships and the deep connections they offer are the best gift the universe has given us. They demand that we get real in order to get the most from them. They offer us the best, most loving means to intense deep healing. And they give the most back in the way of information, love, and insight that helps us to be more of who we are.

Conscious relationships are the pure gold in life. They offer the kind of healing that results in the windows of your mind and spirit opening up with searing new truths, truths that carry such impact that you will never be the same again. No other process can provide such a gift. Do you know the kind of truth I mean? Relationships offer you new information about yourself. The kind that reverberates through you like the sound of fine crystal, or brings you a long-awaited "I love you." The kind of truth that acts as a wake-up call for the dark side of the psyche, like an unexpected siren in the middle of an intersection. It's the kind of truth siren that leaves you with the knowledge that you almost spiritually did yourself in, through a lack of awareness or selective blind spots. Think about what you could be missing if you're not conscious to this opportunity.

We have all met people who seemed to have found peace of mind. Didn't you wonder where they had found the missing key that enabled them to return at will to their own schools of enlightenment? They appear to experience a greater harmony and far less anxiety than most people. Did they go to some mountain where insight about the real meaning of life became available to them? Don't they seem more peaceful, more whole? You know what? I'd be willing to bet most of them would tell you that all they did was resolve the denial that prevented them from living life fully. They found themselves. And in doing so, they also found a profound sense of Spirit.

Will every one of you who reads this book achieve this same depth of healing? No, **only those who are willing to read the book, become still, and act on your desire to be deeply connected to yourself or those you love.** You have to make this a priority. Harry Emerson Fosdick once said, "If you want to know what your priorities in life are, look in your checkbook." I will add that you must also check your calendar. Where are your time and money, both of which are different forms of energy, being spent? **If you want meaningful relationships with yourself or another human being, you must devote quality time and focused energy on creating them. You can decide right now to make your own healing a priority.** Those of you with a courageous Spirit and a commitment to yourselves will get to amazing spiritual places and be astounded by what you achieve. And all of you have a courageous Spirit, even if you're in denial about it. Is there anything in your life at the moment that could possibly be more important?

*Any direction you take away from your true self and your Spirit goes nowhere.*

A state of grace exists the moment one decides to do the kind of deeper work of being present to yourself or another human being. This decision alone creates a magical opening into each other's heart and mind that permits exploration and understanding. In fact, if you stopped reading this book right now and just became present, your life would take a whole new turn, and you would heal in spite of yourself, holistically, without doing another thing. But don't do that, because you're about to receive some tools that will make your trip infinitely easier.

## Now Is the Time—Don't Miss Your Chance

Most of us miss the opportunity to experience healing because we don't recognize the opportunity when it presents itself. Or perhaps we are too afraid to try. Some of us are not willing to be that vulnerable or work that hard. We'd rather feel *safe*. But the refusal to heal does not bring safety. And even if you're able to create an illusion of safety, it will deaden your aliveness. Safety deadens a relationship. We say we want this connection to ourselves, our beloved, life itself, but what we often don't say is that we are afraid to do the work. It takes intent, motivation, awareness, and a courageous spirit to be willing to sit in the presence of another without your protective barriers. Few people really understand that this place of vulnerability is also a place of immense power. Only when you're vulnerable and authentically who you are, without your false protections and defenses, can other people truly have an effect on you, or you on them. Unless you're willing to allow others to have a deep effect on you, you cannot grow. There is little growth to be had while bumping around in an empty room—or inside your protective façade.

*Growth means becoming vulnerable enough to embrace all of life with love. Therefore, vulnerability is a place of great power.*

This is the only work worth doing, simply because our external world will not and cannot change until our internal world is healed of pain, hatred, and judgment. We can't heal the pain that creates distance between couples, families, cities, states, cultures, nations, genders, lifestyles, or countries until we are willing to heal the pain inside each of us individually.

This book is written for you. Merely by the fact that you felt drawn enough to this subject and are reading this book. Something inside you is seeking deeper experiences, more growth, or greater intensity in love. You have your own lab at home, right there in the center of your being, in the center of every relationship that you're in, no matter what the form. In it you will discover wondrous new things about yourself and those you love. I have included dyad exercises at the end of each chapter that you can do with your partner. These are exercises you do together to put you in touch with deeper feelings.

Each of us has an inherent right to experience ecstasy, divine union, total connection with those we consider beloved. Perhaps for the first time you can now experience the safe and exciting steps in this book to help you reclaim that right and fulfill that need. In the next chapter, we'll look at what being present means and how you can begin to do exactly that. Before you start it, let's do another meditation together.

■ ■ ■

In a moment, close your eyes and see yourself walking along a beach, sun on your face, water making soft sounds as it kisses the sand, birds flying overhead. Look ahead and see your spiritual self. Together, find a quiet place to sit, commune, and visit. Talk about your fears of becoming authentic, honest, and real. Take all the time you need, and when you're finished, ask your spiritual self to step inside your body and become one with you. If there is hesitation or fear, take all the time you need to resolve that before you continue. Once you have been able to do this and you feel your spiritual self inside, take as much time as you need to walk along the beach, play, or just get used to being one.

# Dyad Exercise

At the end of each chapter, you will find an exercise that you can do with a partner. Let's begin now with our first one. Choose a partner with whom you can begin this work. If your mate is not yet ready or you're single, choose a friend or family member. Sit across from each other and adjust the distance between you so that you are both comfortable. **As you do this exercise, one person begins and does the entire exercise before the other person begins.** Once the first person has completed his or her exercise, stop, take a moment and share how it was to be the listener and how it was to do the exercise. Before you begin, make sure you both can agree to confidentiality and respect. Nothing shared in your growth process together is ever shared with others without permission. You may talk about the process but not about the content.

1. The most real person I have ever known is:

2. The qualities/attributes that made him or her real to me are/were:

3. The way those qualities and attributes made me feel was:

4. In my house, as a child, being real was:

5. In my house, when I was a child, feelings were:

6. In my house, when I was a child, being connected meant:

7. My biggest fear about being real and connected is:

8. The most real thing about myself that I offer you now is:

9. The most real thing that I honor about myself is:

10. The thing I would ask of you, if I become connected with you is:

11. The gifts I would get from being more connected are:

# CHAPTER TWO
# The Freedom in Staying Present

*Freedom*
*is not the choice between one repetitive*
*thought after another.*
*It's the spontaneous expectancy*
*of the new and unknown.*

*It's the creation of*
*a space within*
*which one can stand in silence*
*and excitedly wait to see*
*what Spirit has in store.*

*Freedom is saying,*
*"I am no longer who I once was*
*and I am open*
*to becoming who I can be.*

*With certain courage*
*I stand at the end of the old*
*and the beginning of the new*
*in the timeless space of now."*

There's an art to staying present that happens on many levels: the physical, emotional, and spiritual. The more conscious to Spirit you become, the more aware your relationship becomes. The first and most obvious place we must be willing to be present is on the physical level. First we have to physically be in the presence of another person to have a relationship. After that, staying present, if you want a conscious relationship, means making the decision not to leave out of fear or denial. That means not leaving oneself, first and foremost, and then it means not leaving those we love out of fear or denial, even temporarily.

## Leaving Physically

How is it possible to leave ourselves physically? We do it all the time. We do it by not treating our bodies with respect and love. We do it by using substances. A person standing in the same room with you who is loaded on alcohol or pot is not physically present to himself or herself, or to you. We leave ourselves physically when we stop listening to what our bodies tell us they need or when they request through discomfort or illness that we stop ingesting harmful foods. It's the, "I know I shouldn't eat this, but," syndrome. We leave each other physically when we encourage behaviors in our partner, out of our own addictions, that are not in his or her best interest. How many times have you encouraged your partner to lose weight for the sake of his or her health, but when you got hungry for sweets, you came home with a grocery bag full of them? How many packages of cigarettes have you bought for your partner, who has expressed being ready to quit, because you were not yet ready to stop smoking?

We also leave ourselves physically when we move into denial about a physical sensation in our body that is trying to tell us something about an emotional issue we are experiencing. What are headaches, stomachaches, neck, back, and shoulder pain trying to tell you? We leave ourselves physically when we continue in the self-hatred that arises when we are not able to met society's standards for how we *should* look or behave, especially as gay men and lesbians. We leave physically when we stop believing in ourselves and our ability to work through issues that arise in relationships. We simply walk out the door. In other words, you and I leave because we do not trust ourselves, or the Divine, to have the answers. It's *never* about the other person. You don't leave because of what anyone else says or does. The truth is, you leave the process of negotiation or finding resolution when you lack trust in yourself.

*The universe pours into us whatever we need,*
*if we are not first filled up with need itself.*

## Leaving Emotionally

You leave yourself emotionally when you act as if your feelings have more power than you do. They don't. You're not your feelings and you have a choice about how to respond to your own feelings. Most of us will do anything *to avoid* feeling our real feelings. We label our feelings as negative, unhealthy, or not OK. Spirit knows you have feelings. Spirit gave you the ability to have them, all of them, even the ones you hate. Have you noticed that when you're able to fully acknowledge and then vent your feelings, that you are also able have a good laugh at yourself afterward? It's then easier for you to decide to do something constructive about them. When you shut down from the feelings you have labeled or perceive to be negative, you also shut down from your own joy and healing.

I remember the first time I allowed myself to admit that I really just wanted to kill someone. For years, I could never allow myself to have the full gambit of my angry feelings, because I had an emotionally abusive father and didn't want to admit I could be like him in any way. I was so repulsed and hurt by his behavior that I didn't want to feel the same things he felt. Well, the truth is, we all have the capacity to feel rage, to be outraged. It felt so good to finally just say it out loud. Afterward I had a good laugh at myself about how much power I had given that person to get me to the place of wanting to kill him. First I had to admit I had that feeling before I could laugh about it. People who stay in denial about their feelings are much more apt to act on them in destructive ways. Trust yourself to feel whatever you feel and stop judging yourself for being human. After I had allowed myself to feel the anger inside, I could also more clearly see some of the good aspects in my father and the gifts he had given me. Part of our gift of Spirit is that we get to feel everything, and then we have choices about how to deal with the feelings.

You leave each other emotionally most often when you assume you must take responsibility for each other's feelings. You fear you must fix your partners' feelings or do something immediately to get him or her to stop feeling. You and I even avoid hearing each other's pain, because we don't think we will have the answers. Probably not. It's not our job. You never have the answers for how someone else should do life. *The only thing you need ever do in response to another's feeling is understand how the other person could feel the way they do.* Don't fix it. Don't stop it. Any feeling that is fully felt will reach resolution and healing on its own.

In short, you leave each other emotionally first because you don't trust yourself to have all the answers, which has never been your job in the first place. And, secondly, you leave because you don't trust your partner's innate ability to find the answers for him or herself.

**Your only responsibility is to feel your own emotions fully and to attempt to understand what your partner is feeling. You don't have to agree with what your partner is feeling. You don't have to change or fix your partner's feeling. That's not your job.**

## Leaving Spiritually

We spiritually leave ourselves when we forget we are divine. We act without integrity or honesty because we do not believe in our divine heritage. If God is All That Is, are you not a portion of God? If you are, then how can you say you love the creator but hate yourself?

*When we are not there for ourselves,*
*it's impossible to know that Spirit's there for us.*

If you knew for certain, right now, that you are everything Spirit wants you to be—in fact, that you're a perfect reflection of Spirit—would you ever need to lie, cheat, or betray yourself or anyone else? Couldn't you let those shoulders drop a bit and take a deep breath and let go? Wouldn't we already be free from internal oppression? We can't afford to postpone this awareness any longer. We are doing and have done too much damage by denying our true Selves.

*When you realize you are Spirit manifesting as Itself,*
*it's difficult to see anyone else as less.*

There is not a single thing I am going to tell you in this book that you do not already know. I am simply going to write some truths in a way that you can understand and apply them. There is not a single thing in any book that you do not already know, yet you're too frightened to live the truth inside you. What are you afraid of? The universe is waiting for you. Your beloved is waiting for you. The child inside you awaits you. In the center of your own aloneness, you're waiting to accept this truth and you're frustrated. Nothing less than this truth will ever satisfy you, because anything less is a lie. You and I are not afraid of failure. We are afraid of our own divinity. When I first realized these truths, I was terrified I would be all by myself, no one with me on the journey. Guess what? Years ago I couldn't have spoken to a single person about the truth inside me. Today I cannot sit with a single person who is not seeking this truth or sharing his or her own truth with me. It's on *Oprah, Sally Jessy Raphael, Prime Time Live,* and *20/20.* It's all over the Internet. At my last count, there were more than 250,000 spiritual sites on the Internet. This business of being spiritual is everywhere, because it's time. Our choice as a gay man or lesbian is a spiritual choice. It's the fire in our process of becoming authentic, truthful, and honorable. We need to get conscious because we are running out of time. Take a good look at our planet. You will not be alone, I promise you.

We are living in a critical time, and the only assignment, the only thing that matters, is accepting this truth. Once we have accepted our own spirituality, everything else falls into place, including our choice to love each other. You will arrive at that previously elusive place where your heart longs to reside. Your right partner will also arrive. Those who can love you at the deepest levels you can imagine, as spiritual family, will also arrive. This healing work of being present to the truths we already know is the most important work in the universe.

Don't say, "I'll get to it after I find my mate." You will not find a mate that stays until you get to it. Don't say, "I'll get to it after I create my career." No career will satisfy you until you do this work. You can embrace all of life, including your relationships, your career, and anything else life has to offer you, and if you're doing this work at the same time, all of it will be richer, deeper, and more satisfying. Living life fully is not in conflict with becoming spiritually aware. It's, in fact, the key to all of it.

We stop being fully present and we leave physically, emotionally, and spiritually when we have forgotten who we are. We allow fear to take the place of the reality that we are capable, loving, and spiritual. Whenever you're not being completely present to yourself, your loved ones, and life, you function from fear. Some fear inside you has been triggered, and you have convinced yourself that you're not capable of dealing with that fear. No matter what excuse you may use, a lack of presence is nothing more than fear. We use a laundry list of excuses: "He or she doesn't understand me. She won't listen to me. There's no use. It doesn't matter. I don't know how. He won't let me and I'm trying." These are some of the myths and excuses we use when we lack faith in ourselves. It's not about your partner or your parents or society. It's not about your family. It's not about your friend. It's about you and your own lack of trust in yourself. Today, right now, you can stop telling yourself these lies and begin to heal the part of yourself that needs these excuses. You're worth it. You're about to have everything you need to do it.

## Your Gift Is Waiting

Healing is a gift only *you* can give yourself. Many people go from guru to guru, partner to partner, seminar to seminar, and book to book, waiting for someone or something outside themselves to do it for them. No matter how smart or enlightened the teacher, we must be willing to do the work ourselves. No matter how many tools provided in a book or seminar, you must be willing to use them. Many of you seek people outside yourselves in the hope of consciously or unconsciously making them responsible for your personal healing. You will soon feel abandoned by your partners, disappointed by your gurus, and betrayed by your friends, all of whom will ultimately find the task impossible and will eventually resent you for your unrealistic, uninvited assumption. When that happens, you will end up isolated and alone again, creating the opposite of what you say you want.

Even those of you who have found a guru and sit in subservient adoration are still not living in truth. You're still sitting in a sense of separation. A true master calls forth the master in each of us, and once you have truly found the truth of your being, you cannot feel any separation at all. If your teachers are living truth, just as Gangaji, Ram Dass, Gandhi, Christ, or any master will tell you, they simply reflect back to you the truth of who you are. They are doing that for you, just as each of them is reflecting the truth of who the divine source is. It's all one. When you sit with truth and a master who is living truth, you will find he or she reflects back that you too are a master, as great a Spirit as he or she is, even in the midst of your denial. As Gangaji once said to a student, "When you're really in truth, there is no separation or difference between the student and the teacher and that which is taught." I have often heard her say, "You are myself and I am yourself."

*Nothing external can make you whole.*
*Wholeness begins within and moves outward.*

## Healing: A Discovery Process You Give Yourself

Staying present is your personal opportunity to prove to yourself that you are courageous, trustworthy, and compassionate. Some of you may not trust yourselves to be any of those things. That is why authentic healing *must* come from the inside out. This is why this book is so important. We need to begin trusting ourselves to create the experiences that make it possible to do deep healing, without being so afraid of our feelings. **In 16 years of doing healing work, I have never lost a client to a feeling. I have, however, known several people who died of cancer, ulcers, heart attacks, and other illnesses because they never learned how to feel or express their feelings.** When you're willing and able to take control of your own healing process, you begin to discover wonderful qualities within yourself such as strength, courage, wisdom, and compassion, initially in tiny steps and then in quantum leaps. The act of staying present is the opportunity life gives you to find those qualities within yourself. This is what being present means, the willingness to be with your feelings and those of your partner so that they can surface and naturally resolve themselves. It means being present to joy, ecstasy, pain, and fear, knowing all of it's transitory and all of it's safe. It means being proud that you're gay or lesbian. And you will feel all of it. It's the gift of being human, this process of flowing from one end of the continuum of feelings to the next, knowing that in the next breath, just behind the grief, joy is waiting. You will also learn that behind every feeling is the real you, the you that is inviolate, divine, and never changing or disturbed by any of the feelings.

You're the artists painting the landscapes of your own lives. You each decide if the colors will be vibrant and alive or dull and lifeless. I believe arriving at the realization that we each have the capacity within us to create profound change and be empowered is actually the major assignment of this life. In essence, we are going to "life school," trying to graduate to that very awareness. We are trying to get to the awareness that we already are, and already have, everything we need and want, waiting for us to discover it. This is the truth of our being. Until we get there, we continue to blame life, Spirit, our parents, our partners, our children, our bosses, our teachers, and society. We blame everyone but the person who has the most control: ourselves.

*Enlightenment is the realization that you're*
*the only one who deprives yourself of anything.*

There are many things we come here to learn, and this issue is one of the required courses necessary to becoming loving human beings. Blame is simply a way of distancing your own empowerment. It's a game we will discuss later. It has no value. Now just breathe.

## Stay Present—Fulfill Your Purpose

No matter what age you are right now, once you have stepped into the empowering realization that you alone choose the quality of your life, your life takes a dramatic turn for the better. You feel a strange sense that you have finally begun doing what you came here to do. All the years and trials you may have endured while finding this awareness become like a mother's labor pains. They fade and are less important than the joy of the end result.

I remember sitting in my therapy room with one of my clients, a woman, 53 at the time, who had just discovered that she had been a brilliant child, caged for most of her life by her father's narcissistic insecurities. Her discovery brought her out of that cage to a place where she could begin to live her life free from the fear that she would ultimately be found somehow unlovable. In the instant she discovered her father had lied, the whole world opened to her. She could never retrieve the lost years of her childhood, but she could live her life to the fullest extent from that moment on, and she did. She exemplifies many clients who have shared their own journeys with me, some young, some 40, 50, 60, and 70. All of whom will tell you that one moment of life fully lived has the capacity to diminish years of pain. I would be the first to attest to that myself. Actually, I discovered that truth accidentally. Some of the most powerful healing experiences I had didn't happen until I too was a middle-aged woman. It's never too late to begin living life fully.

*When you give yourself permission to live life fully,*
*you become the light of your own experience.*

I also understand how easy it is to move into denial. We use denial as a defense when we feel we cannot survive without it. It has been one of our most important survival tools, so be gentle with yourself. We need to have great compassion for ourselves and understand that denial has acted as a self-preservation tool in the moment of crisis. You just don't need it anymore. If your fears and needs remain in denial, you begin to function and make life decisions from that fear base of the past. We will speak more on that issue later.

## Healing Happens Naturally

In my work with clients, I discovered that if I was fully present, willing to connect with the deepest part of their soul from a place of vulnerability in my own, our energy shifted into a deep connection. We moved together into rich ground that offered opportunity for healing that changed the fiber of our being. It was simply about being fully present to the moment, to myself, and to them. It was like a dance. If I began to go into that place of connection to myself, to them, and to Spirit, all of who is one and the same thing, they followed.

I want you to make a decision not to continue being satisfied with "just getting by." Make a commitment to yourself to get present, to learn everything you can about your unique responses to life and about your potential. If you do so, you will bring excitement and vivid aliveness back into your life again or, perhaps, create it for the first time through your new awareness. It's as simple as listening to yourself in the very next breath.

Behind the everyday mundaneness of life, our ordinariness, is a rich terrain of mystical surprises waiting to be revealed. When your ego steps aside and releases its tenacious hold on the familiar patterns it believes to be safe, your soul or Spirit steps through the denial and takes its rightful place as the directing force in your life. You can count on that.

## Staying Present Creates
## Your Private Mystical Experience

When you're willing to be present, the mysticism and healing opportunities of ordinary life and relationships become the gold in your process. Your first step is to realize you're now standing across from yourself. "Can I," as the Sufis ask, "be who I am before I was?" We live *here*, on this side, where we are driven by fear and attachment. Often we aren't even aware that we are not being who we really are.

Over *there*, on the other side, is the real us, just an arm's length away. There is the individual whom we long to be and who in some ways we already are, or we could not envision ourselves. Between the spaces of *here* and *there* are the fears and pain of our childhood, the illusions of our adulthood, held tightly by our ego. That ego, in turn, constantly warns us not to go forward. It says, "Maybe being gay *is* a sin. Maybe your parents were right and you're unworthy, unlovable. What if you become who you really are and then misuse your power? What if you step into being empowered and then you're isolated, alone? What if you accept and let yourself be who you are and then others leave you? What if you really are not courageous, not strong, and not wise? What if you won't like who you really are? What if you're kidding yourself? What if you're nothing? Better stay back, be safe, and remain with the familiar. Don't go there."

## Who Are You?

Most of us don't really know who we are. Years ago I had a client who always came into my office in some flamboyant dress or outfit, making large, sweeping gestures with her hands, flipping her skirt above her knees as she sat down. She began each session by telling me in long, exaggerated sighs how disgusted she was with the people in her life who just couldn't be real. I listened to the litany for weeks, and then finally I said, "Why do you think this is such an issue for you? Could it be that some part of you is not feeling very real? Tell me about you, and who you really are inside."

Within about five minutes, not ever having been asked that question, she was in tears. She began telling me how painful it was that she had been raised to become who her dad and mom had wanted her to be, but she had never felt as if she had permission, or support, to just be herself. Inside, she held years of denial and fear that her parents were right, that she was nothing. We made an agreement that each time she was in my office, if I felt that the parents' impostor child was there, I would say so, and so would she. That would give her a moment to examine some of her deep fears. Why was she was not being who she was authentically? She could make a shift inside and perhaps make a conscious decision to be more real.

She did this for several weeks, becoming more and more aware of when and why she slipped into her false self. Before long, the false self she had been forced to create in order to survive was no longer the one who came to my office. A genuine, caring, nonjudgmental woman took her place, and both the client and I felt gratified that this real person had an opportunity to step through and be herself.

The majority of healing took place for this client outside my office. In fact, it took place when she was alone. Everywhere she went and every time she was with other people, she made it a point to check in on her own level of presence and authenticity. She moved from her false self into being her real self. She checked to see if she felt fully present in her body. She checked to see what she was feeling emotionally and mentally. She checked to see when she was accurately telling her truth, embellishing her truth, holding back. When she felt she was not emotionally, physically, or mentally present, she asked herself what denial or fear had surfaced that made her check out.

Little by little, she saw a pattern of *leaving* whenever she felt she was about to be judged or when she judged herself. By understanding what made her leave originally (i.e., her parents' judgment and the fear that they would stop loving her), she became able to comfort herself and consequently become more safe and real. She became present to her fears and found the strength of spirit to change them. The process became a Zenlike experiment of asking, "Where am I, what do I feel, how present am I right now, and if I am not fully present, what have I begun fearing?"

After checking in with herself, she would then decide if her fear was valid, at which point she would address it directly with whomever had triggered her fear. When she felt the fear was not valid, not about a present situation, she would do some self-talk about how her life is different now than it was for her as a child. In essence, she was comforting the scared child inside herself, dealing with her own denials about who she was. She was asking the child inside to honor her adulthood. She stayed present to herself so that the child was no longer living life for her.

This entire dialogue took place in the privacy of her mind, and within a short time, she became so good at it that it took her only a few moments to analyze each situation and get more present. Each time she did so she created a healing for herself. Her body, mind, and spirit experienced new and more frequent periods of safety. Soon she no longer needed her false, flamboyant self.

## A Little Emotional Courage...A Big Payoff

Committing to this process of being present requires some emotional courage and a willingness to allow for some frustration and delayed gratification. Most of us reach for a cigarette, look for a new lover, or go to the refrigerator or the mall the moment we become aware of uncomfortable feelings. **What I am asking you to do is simply stop for a moment and look to find out where the uncomfortable feelings are coming from. Then ask yourself what you can do to resolve the feeling instead of reaching for some temporary fix to divert yourself from experiencing your feelings.** Ask yourself which untruth this feeling is based on. See if you can move to the truth behind it.

# It's Easy

Start with just five minutes of self-examination. Take little steps. As soon as fearful, angry, or separating feelings come to the surface, take a breath and simply ask yourself, "What am I feeling and why?" Stay present. Five minutes of focused attention may resolve the issue. If not, at the very least this process will begin to tell your mind that you will not be decimated or overwhelmed by exploring your feelings. This awareness greatly increases your courage. You will discover your feelings can't get you.

If you don't get an answer in the first five minutes, simply tell yourself you owe it to yourself to work on the issue more. At some point, turn off the television, stop running here or there, and sit with the feeling again. You will get to the answer that you need, but you may discover it's layered with all the false messages you have given yourself throughout the years in order *not* to deal with the issue.

"Why am I afraid to be who I am?"

Ego says, "Well, if you were who you are, your family wouldn't like you."

"OK, so if I stop using my family as the excuse, why am I not being who I am?"

Ego says, "Well, you could never be who you were as a child."

"OK, I'm no longer a child, so what's stopping me now?"

As you dig deeper, you will get to the answer. When you do, you'll know it's the right one, because your entire body will feel a sense of relief. It may be that you're afraid your parents were right, and you really are nothing, bad. Or you may be afraid that if you are who you are, your partner will leave you and you'll be all alone in the world. There could be a multitude of individual different reasons, but whatever your reason is, it's *only a fear* and not a reality.

If, by some chance—and I mean a very rare chance—your family would actually leave you if you were more real, or out, frankly, your family was never with you in the first place. Their love was conditional. You're trading away your life for what you perceive to be safety. It's an illusion of safety. The result is spiritual annihilation. How much safety is there in pretending to be someone you are not in order to maintain the status quo? You will never be safe under those circumstances, and you're in denial about the fact that your relationship with them needs mending or is already over. The real *you* is not even in it. What is more often true, despite your fear, is that your family, mates, and friends would be delighted to see you be more real, more present. In all the times I've counseled with clients who were afraid to come out or be fully who they are, there have been only two instances in 16 years where families did not ultimately come around and eventually allow that person back in the family. Try to keep from going into disaster or crisis thinking about what your answer might mean and just be focused on discovering the reason for your feeling. What you do with the information is another step. Your first task is simply to understand yourself. Once you have the information that helps you understand your fear, you have already taken a major step forward.

Let's be excruciatingly honest for a minute. No circumstance or person can *make* us feel anything. We respond in certain ways to people and circumstances in life because of our beliefs or past experiences. When your fears get triggered, you say to yourself, *I have to leave because Mary makes me feel stupid*. Actually you begin to feel stupid because Mary triggers some feeling from your past that you have not healed, and you allow yourself to feel stupid. Mary is simply the triggering agent in the moment for some unresolved fear, but you give her the blame and choose not to be around her so as not to feel the discomfort. Right? Be truthful.

You continue to do that with many people and circumstances, withdrawing more and more from life. If you were to stop the denial and address the issue, you might say to Mary, "As a child I was made to feel stupid, and when you address me in that way, it triggers those feelings. Therefore, I would prefer you not do that." Or you could simply say to yourself, *I need to heal the part of me that still feels stupid when I am around people like Mary. It's about you, not Mary.*

## Fear: A Lack of Trust in Yourself

In the majority of cases, you'll find you're holding on to your fear because in some way you don't trust *yourself*. It's never about anyone else.

*We always resist what we most fear.*
*Facing the fear has the most to teach us.*

If your parents gave you negative messages when you were a child, chances are you still believe them. If you're in a relationship with someone who needs you to stay disempowered, you may not trust yourself to deal with him or her in a way that leaves your relationships intact. In other words, *you* may not trust that you can be who you are and that your partner will still love you. If you're holding yourself back in your career, you may not trust yourself to be successful, deal with money appropriately, or have good business sense. Learning to do these things is exactly that—a learned process. You may not have all the skills you need, but you cannot go about learning them until you get past your fear and admit you have the power to make positive changes. Could what Saint Catherine of Siena said be true? "We arrive as soon as we depart."

*A master is what you become when you refuse to perceive failure or doubt your power.*

In the space behind your fear, you will find Yourself. You're not your fear. You're standing behind it, between the words you were told as a child and the life experiences that have created your pain. The real you is the part of you that longs to step forward and be who you really are. The part of you that longs to be present to yourself and others. You already know what I am saying is true. A million times in your life you have said to yourself, *I know what I should do, I just don't know how to do it.* Some part of you knows the truth, wants what is best for you and those you love, and wants to step forward.

## Become an Explorer: It's a Life—and Death—Issue

You have the safety and personal freedom to become an explorer into the rich recesses of your heart and psyche. Unless you need to continue suffering, you can opt not to wait until life has passed you by to realize you do not feel intimately connected to much of anything. You can realize now that you're not present to your own feelings or anyone in your life. We literally break up inside ourselves when we are not connected to our feelings.

Our bodies break up, our minds break apart, and our connection to life breaks. It's time to stop the continuous cycle of breakups that occur inside you, in your relationships, in your families, between siblings, between parents and adult children, and even between friends. It's time to break through the frustrating cycles that create isolation and pain, and get to the deep connections that bring you joy and love.

It's time unless, of course, you need the suffering. If you have not yet gotten to the place where you're aware enough to know that your life is not working, you may need additional suffering to get to that awareness. There is no judgment in that, because that is what free will is all about. You have everything you need to make change right now, so you have nothing to fear. If you choose not to grow, because you want others to be responsible for your life and happiness, ultimately you will be left alone. Regardless of the motivation, you may postpone your own empowerment as long as you like. You may experience as much pain with that postponement as you wish, until you're willing to come out of your denial and into your own greatness and courage.

## The Lesson of Suffering

Most of us do everything humanly possible to avoid suffering, and yet *we* create most of the suffering. We do that in two ways. First, by our own refusal to grow. When you refuse to grow, it's as if you have been stuffed into a box that is one tenth your size and your mind, body and spirit rebels with sickness and discomfort. The world bumps up against you with issues and confrontations, trying to wake you up. You cannot and must not be contained. Suffering is not spiritual. There is no limit to who you are, but still you contain yourself with your refusal to be who you really are. Have you ever seen the roots of a tree that is too large for its own space? Ultimately they surface and break through the ground, the sidewalk, the planter, but no matter what they continue to grow. So will you. You can *break through* and experience your own growth in difficult destructive lessons or you can give yourself support, room to grow, and an environment of comfort and assistance.

Secondly, we try to avoid suffering by demanding that people or circumstances be different than they are. We often see these dynamics working together in relationships where one partner wants her mate to make her feel lovable, and yet she refuses to deal with her own insecurity. We see it when a partner refuses to communicate with his lover and then blames him for wanting too much from him, instead of learning how to communicate. Most of the time, however, suffering comes from wanting something from our partners that we are not willing to give ourselves.

Very often when I tell this to clients, they balk with comments such as, "Well, if I could do it all myself, why bother to be in a relationship?" I'm not suggesting you become an island, live alone, or stop wanting relationships. Relationships are the finest gift Spirit offers us, and wanting them is perfectly natural and healthy. What I am saying is, you will never get from your partner things such as security, safety, respect, a sense of being lovable and desired, unless you're willing to deal with the blockages you hold inside that prevent you from feeling these things about or for yourself.

When you begin to feel insecure or afraid, some issue inside you needs to be resolved. If you're able to stay with that feeling and explore it, what you will find right inside is that you have exactly what you're seeking so voraciously from your partner.

Let's say that you begin to feel unattractive. Have you ever noticed that is the time when you also develop "perfect body" antennae, and suddenly you feel as if everyone in the mall, the bar, or on the street looks better than you do? Not only do they look better than you, but you also suddenly feel as if your lover is doing a visual inventory of their body parts. You start dropping hints and trying to get compliments from your mate. Your mate, who has played this game with you ad nauseam, knows this dance and tries to convince you that you are her Julia Roberts for life. The result is that no amount of assurance from her will convince you that you're attractive anyway. The compliments you solicit appease you momentarily, and soon you're again faced with your fear of not being attractive. So what have you accomplished? Why not stop the fear, aggravation, and anxiety right in their tracks? You have a wonderful gift waiting for you if you choose to do that.

Try to just be with your anxiety, sit in the middle of it for a time, enlarge it, and make it the size of the room you're in. It has much to tell you. In the midst of your fear is some circumstance or belief that you developed from some past event that needs healing. That's why it keeps coming up. Let's say, you grew up in the shadow of your attractive sister and felt less than her. OK, now go into that and sit with it. Once you experience what you have been trying to avoid feeling, you will get to a space in the center of the discomfort that is expansive and incredibly freeing. There is a truth about you right in the middle of that fear. Once you have reached the core of it and begin to get to the truth of who you are, you can breathe deeply and have directly experience your own beauty. Your own radiance. Your own attractiveness.

Even if you do not perceive yourself to be physically attractive, once you get to the core of your being it will become irrelevant. If you can get there, what you will experience is a beauty that goes far beyond the physical and connects to your own divinity. You will experience yourself as you truly are—unique, precious, and lovable. In that instant, you will know for certain there is nothing about you that is less than anyone else. You can release your need to have your lover constantly assure you, and you have given yourself exactly what you were trying to get from her—acceptance and love. Doesn't this sound safer and more satisfying in the long run? Of course it does, because it's your natural state. A state of wholeness.

This refusal to see your own greatness is a life-and-death issue. In essence, when you choose to stay in denial, you're refusing life. If you refuse life energy and change energy long enough, your body will interpret this refusal message as a desire to die. You will begin the death process physically, emotionally, or spiritually. I don't need to explain that statement because each of you has had the experience of feeling at some level inside as if you were dying. You already know what I am talking about. If you allow this refusal to go on too long, your mind, body, and spirit may not be able to gather the energy necessary to turn your choice around and sustain your life in this incarnation. You know people who are dying physically. You also know, or know about, those who have chosen emotional or spiritual death. The vast majority of you are nowhere near that level, but neither can you afford to waste any more time by choosing to remain unconscious. This is the opportune time to make a new decision. Right now.

Some suffering in life will always be necessary. When we lose a loved one to death or when life's circumstances create unavoidable tragedy, we will suffer. But imagine for a minute how much suffering you could save yourself if you stopped trying to change others and worked on healing your own issues. Would you say 75%, 50%, or 25%? My guess would be 90% of the suffering in your lives could be avoided by taking personal responsibility for your own healing and by releasing the need to change those you love to get your needs met. Think it might be worth it? Well, by the time you finish this book, you will have the tools.

## Your Feelings and Therapy

Part of the problem, in our quest for consciousness, meaning, and intimacy, is that in the past we lacked the necessary tools for getting connected to ourselves and others. Without them, venturing on a journey of self-discovery feels frightening. Those who have taken the leap of connecting with themselves have probably had the experience in therapy or a therapeutic process of some kind where they had assistance and support.

Unfortunately, in today's society therapy is no longer readily accessible, even to those who wish to take advantage of it. Most health care providers and insurance companies now limit the number of visits each insured may have for counseling about any given issue. All too often those decisions are dictated by cost rather than need and made by an administrator rather than a caregiver.

Using therapy as a spiritual journey by which to enhance one's life is a luxury not afforded to most. Even when therapy was more readily available, most people found the idea too threatening. The concept of sharing one's innermost feelings and fears with a stranger felt threatening and kept most people out of therapy until they were met with a crisis. Only after having entered the process, often out of dire need, do people begin to understand the benefits of therapy and lose their fear about the process.

Therapy is a gift, a spiritual journey one gives to one's self. But I am acutely aware that because therapy is becoming more difficult for people to obtain, we must find ways of healing ourselves, both by ourselves and with others. It time for you to become your own therapist.

*When you do not hear Spirit within,*
*it's because you have chosen not to listen.*

You can create nonthreatening, nonjudgmental spaces for yourself in which you can safely explore what you feel and why you feel it. You can embrace your feelings and come out the other side safely, having healed the pain inside just by being present. The human spirit's an amazing thing. Over the years I have discovered that most of the time, after we have become willing to be present to our true feelings and have discovered why we feel certain emotions, negative or fearful energy is simply diffused. Our perspectives and actions change automatically. They change naturally, holistically, out of our new awareness. Have you ever noticed how a plant placed anywhere in a room automatically reaches for sunlight? That is what you're doing in this process. And because change and healing are natural states, you will be pleasantly surprised how easily they occur, once you're present to yourself. Understanding is the key to change. If you have a good therapist, you can process the issues you discover with him or her as well.

However you choose to process your feelings, it's critical that you stop judging them, even if you have what you perceive to be terrible thoughts, such as *I'd really like to kill that person*, or *I think my partner is stupid*. It's better to accept a "terrible" thought and explore it than to deny it. Remember, anything you deny will ultimately become more powerful and surface in another way. It's much more healing to say, *OK, I feel like I'd like to kill her. So what's going on in me, and where is this coming from?* Accepting your own feelings and thoughts gives you permission to explore and heal them. Otherwise, they stay in denial, and they will get you, one way or another, later.

Guess what? All those nasty little thoughts are inside your head. No one can see in there. No one needs to know your thoughts but you, so stop judging them and just be intent on healing them. All of us have negative thoughts we'd rather not have. It's part of being human. Those negative or painful thoughts tell us where our personal work needs to be done. They are little red flags saying, *Over here! We need some work done on this issue*. They are nothing more than reminders, so stop judging or fearing them.

## About Relationships

This book is about relationships, the first of which is the one you have with yourself. I am always amused by the response I get when I begin a workshop and ask, "How many of you are in relationships?" Inevitably, about half the audience raises their hands. I have to chuckle, and then I ask, "Are the rest of you alive and breathing?" I explain that in our society we are not perceived to be in a *relationship* unless we have a mate. We do not place as much value on our relationships to ourselves, our siblings, our parents, our children, our friends, or our planet. We have not learned that these relationships provide incredibly important opportunities for healing ourselves.

Now add the relationships we have with associates, the stranger in the grocery store, or the driver in the car ahead of us on the freeway. Our opportunities for learning about ourselves become limitless. So in this sense, **even when you're doing this work alone, you're really working on yourself by using your responses to life and the world around you as the material of your healing.** How you respond to and receive life is the grist for your mill. From the moment you arise in the morning, your first thoughts about your day give you insight into how receptive and positive you are about life. Even when you're alone in your room, right between you and your response to life is a world of information.

*Once you understand the creative nature of the universe,*
*you will see that everything you do matters.*

The many encounters we have in life bring us into *relationship* with other human beings. Every response we have teaches us something about ourselves. You can heal so much simply by becoming conscious to your own thoughts and responses. You can still be in an active, productive healing process, even when you can't be in therapy or in a mate relationship. Some times your own issues may feel too threatening, and therapy may be the only safe place to do your work. However, a great deal of healing can and should occur for all of us with or without a therapist as we *relationship* with ourselves and the rest of life.

## Staying Present *Is* Awareness

Staying present involves the times in our life when we become aware of some new piece of information about ourselves. Staying present brings new understandings that change the way we see the world and how we behave in it. For example, say you're walking out of a grocery store and you see a man who is a minority, shabbily dressed, looking frazzled, approaching you. The dialogue in your mind becomes fearful. You hold your purse tighter, watch where he is heading, and make a beeline away from him. After passing him, you realize you forgot the most important item on your list, and you return into the store. You turn around, and you see the store manager smiling, with his arms around the very same gentleman that you were afraid of, and you hear him saying, "How's that new baby, Paul?"

In that instant you realize you may have some unfounded fears about minorities or that you have a tendency to make snap judgments based upon a person's attire. You leave the store feeling a bit guilty, but in reality you have just had a healing experience. All the emotions you felt and the thoughts that came rushing up to fill the space between you and that man are rich with information about you and your inner world of experience. If you're conscious and aware, or, in other words, if you grasp the potential of this moment and use the new awareness in it, you will probably make a commitment to yourself to be less judgmental. At the very least, you will be less quick to make snap decisions about who is safe and who is not.

If you're not conscious, not present to your feelings, you will, no doubt, have exactly the same response the next time a similar situation occurs. In fact, you may have had that same old tired response most of your life. Most adults are victims only to our memories. Those memories hold us hostage and dictate the same destructive behaviors. We can use our memories creatively, to our advantage. They teach us about ourselves and free us from the past, instead of keeping us chained to it.

We are not our memories. We are in the silent places between them. We are in the silent places between our fears and our repetitive responses to them, waiting to come forward and reclaim our lives. We have a responsibility to evolve, first for ourselves, and then to offer the same gift for the sake of all human beings. Our Spirits are calling us to it. We have forgotten our sense of connectedness to ourselves, to one another, and to our source. This sense of separation is killing us, and it's killing our planet. It's certainly killing the sense of aliveness we feel inside.

Take a breath and get connected to yourself right now. What do you feel? Overwhelmed? Anxious? Bored? Distant? Uninterested? Doubtful? Well, if you are feeling any of those things, you're in denial, because what I am talking about is how to enhance the quality your life. And since you haven't read this entire book or tried any of the ideas in it, chances are, you zoned out because you became afraid in some way. What I am saying to you is the truth. If you're having difficulty connecting to it, you owe it to yourself to find out why, because that denial is stopping you from living life fully. This is not just another one of *those* books! This is your chance to make incredible change in your life. You have read this truth in a million places, and still you refuse to take it in and make it your own. Ask yourself why you need to distance yourself from the very thing you say you want? What are you afraid of? Here's your chance to start being present right now.

## Your Responses Are Your Key to Awareness

At any given moment, on any given day, you're having thousands of responses to life and everyone in it. You're having responses as you watch TV, as you write a book, as you read this one. Whenever you enter into a relationship with something or someone else, you have entered into a field of feelings and emotions in the space between you and the "other" that is rich with information. Instantly, you can access information about your life as a child, your beliefs as an adult, and even how well your own soul is evolving into a conscious, loving human being.

When you're in the grocery store, even without speaking a word, you're in relationships with the other shoppers. Like it or not, we are in a relationship to everything and everyone around us. You're in relationships with coworkers, employers, and even your estranged family members. Every thought and response we have about those circumstances and the people we meet are rich with information about our childhood, our belief systems, our level of safety, and our soul's evolution.

Most of us allow this rich terrain of responses to go unnoticed. We simply continue to respond with the same old patterns without question. As Deepak Chopra says, "We have approximately 60,000 thoughts a day and 90% of them are the same as the ones we had the day before." We have the ability and the privilege of changing our minds and increasing our conscious awareness. Even when you're standing alone on top of a mountain, your response to the universe and the wonders of nature tell you a great deal about yourself. Can you be fully present to the moment and the beauty before you or are you thinking about the million things you have to do at home, driven by the fear that there is never enough time?

These kinds of opportunities for healing happen to us all the time, but because we are not trained to recognize them, not present, we lose their benefits.

At the other end of the continuum, in the pages to follow you will read about experiences when your mind is so expanded that you see the whole world and your own reality differently. There are healing experiences in which you see a family member or partner in a whole new light, and there are those during which everything you once believed about yourself gets called into question. This rich process of discovery begins with your decision to become present to and conscious of your own feelings and responses. You must be willing to question where those responses came from and whether they are still valid for you. You're about to open your own treasure chest of tools, your red wagon, which you can use to evolve your soul.

If you're not yet in a mate relationship, don't despair. There is great power in healing alone. Doing so gave me the courage to begin the process of healing with others. It will do the same for you, and it may even help you find the right mate. Until your partner arrives, staying present to yourself and doing this work on your own will give you the courage to do it with others as well. Healing with someone else is a gift of a different kind. For me, healing with friends became a gift of luxuriant moments of feeling so connected to another human being that the isolation of my childhood became only a memory. Healing with others provides new ideas and perspectives, and increased capacity for compassion. Both processes are valid and will become necessary to your healing when you are ready. I encourage you to begin where you are most comfortable. The tools for creating both experiences are in the chapters that follow.

## Working Alone

Some of you may be beginning at the beginning. That is, you may be at a place where your first appropriate and least fearful step is to get present with yourself. Your first step may be simply getting acquainted with your own feelings. You take a giant step when you start that process and become curious about why you feel the certain unique feelings you experience about people and circumstances. So here's your first giant step. Ask yourself:

- What makes me afraid?
- What makes me feel open and free to be vulnerable?
- When do I close down and emotionally withhold?
- How safe do I feel about learning new things?
- How intent am I about creating intimacy with friends, lovers, children, and work associates?
- What fears do I have about intimacy?
- Where did they come from?
- What do I feel passionate about?
- How safe is it to become passionate about anything?
- Why is it safe or not safe to feel life fully?
- What patterns keep emerging in my life?
- What are the things I don't know about myself?

Working alone requires that you become aware of your feelings and that you understand them. If you don't know what they are, how can you heal them? Most of us spend lifetimes deliberately avoiding our real feelings because we don't trust ourselves to handle them. Once you begin listening to the millions of thoughts you have in a single hour or a single day, you will see patterns emerge, patterns you may want to question. "I feel intimidated every time I walk into an expensive store. My mom always told me nice things were for rich people. Is that a truth, or is that just something I was taught by Mom?" "I drop my lover's hand every time we go to Mom's because I know she will hate me if she sees us." Is that a truth or is it your fear? Begin to question your beliefs.

## Staying Present Is Simple

Staying present may sound like a monumental task, but *it's so simple*. All it requires is that you listen to yourself and watch your own responses. Don't get stopped before you even get started by making yourself feel as if you must make massive changes in everything that you feel all at once. Change is created slowly; it's a process, and most of the time change occurs holistically. Often, just becoming aware of your feelings and responses is all you need to create a change.

> *Enlightenment is the realization or remembering of who you are*
> *and all you already know.*

The woman who made the snap judgment about the man entering the grocery store was changed the moment she had insight. All she had to do was listen to herself. You can do that too. As Ram Dass says, we are all works in progress, all in the process of becoming who we are. There is no end to the process.

Most of us go through each day repeating the same old 60,000 or so thoughts from the day before, and the day before that. Ninety-five percent of what we think is the same as what we have thought most of our lives, and yet we never stop to question how much of what we believe still serves us. How much of what we fear is still valid? What you now fear may have been valid when you were a child, without the cognitive ability, the physical size, or the mental ability to care for yourself. You may now be reacting in the same way you did as a child to an issue that is no longer fearful or valid.

Most of us don't know how to create intimacy; therefore, we fear it. That is, until we get into the process and begin to see that intimacy grows gradually. Each step we take strengthens us to take the next step. We assume that creating intimacy is dangerous. Where did that assumption come from? Perhaps it came from watching your parents argue or from one parent using intimate details of the other's life to hurt him or her. It comes from a million different individual life experiences. Thanks to those old experiences, you may prevent yourself from even exploring your own feelings because you believe you can't trust yourself to deal with them. That's not true.

## It's Probably Not Even About *Now*

You may still be operating from an old belief that intimacy is dangerous, even though you are now living with a loving partner or living alone with great friends in your extended family. I would venture to bet that many of the people in your life would love to know you better, get closer, and create a deeper relationship with you. No doubt they honor your need to stay at the level of intimacy you currently have because they too are afraid. That's why they are your friends. We always seek out people who are like us; therefore, you can be sure most of them also long for something more.

There is immense power in the process of being present to and exploring your own feelings. By doing so, you're giving yourself the message that you're safe and able to determine what is best for you. So what if you discover something that feels less than perfect? No one will know but you! I often hear patients tell me, "I don't want to tell you about that feeling. It's just silly, and it makes me feel stupid." With a little assurance from me that I don't see any of my clients' feelings as silly, they become willing to tell me. And inevitably we find this person's feeling came from an experience or event in his or her life as a child and wasn't just a stupid response without foundation. Your feelings cannot kill you. What happens in your life—or to your body, because your feelings are unconscious and unresolved—might end up killing you.

Once you become aware of your responses and feelings, you can explore how you came to feel a certain way.

1. When was the first time you remember experiencing that feeling?
2. What were the circumstances?
3. Who was there and what took place?
4. Are your current circumstances different from when you first began to feel this way?
5. How would changing this feeling impact your life?

A whole world of information is waiting for you, and you can explore all of it by working on your own, in the privacy of your own mind. Don't be afraid to laugh at yourself in the process. We are all holding on to many beliefs and feelings that may seem silly until we discover how they began. Don't judge yourself. Just make a conscious decision to change your responses. If you can develop compassion for yourself, you won't have any trouble having compassion for those around you who are still operating within their old belief systems. Unfortunately, to some degree or another that's what we are all doing.

This process of working on your own reality and level of awareness is an ongoing lifetime process. Just accept it in the way you accept that tomorrow, and the next day, the sun will come up.

*There is no place at which to arrive called enlightenment.*
*There is only the joy of the process and the gift of*
*becoming enlightened.*

Allow your learning process to also become a way of life. There is no end to becoming more enlightened. Every time you get to another level of awareness, there is yet another level to which you can go. Fall in love with the process, starting right now, and don't get caught up in expecting some final result. With each step you take, the quality of your life will improve, and your process will become addictive in a good way. You'll be delighted with the new things you find out about yourself and thrilled to feel yourself growing. You will have opened back up to life.

*As you gradually go from some love to more love,*
*you will also go from smallness to greatness.*

## Working With a Partner

As you become safer with the process of examining your own reality, you may wish to practice the art of being present with a partner. My clients have discovered the joys of entering into this process with someone they trust, because it brings the added dimension of someone else's perspective into their awareness. They get great benefit from that experience. Not only do they find that those they love are dealing with many issues similar to their own, but they also learn from each other's process. Most of my clients work with their mates, some choose their best friends, and others work with family members.

When you work with a partner, the field of energy and life experience between you becomes even richer. Many gifts are given and received in the process. You will develop an increased capacity for compassion as you hear your lover talk about his or her life experiences and the ways in which he or she learned to survive and deal with their challenges. Once you understand why your partner is the way he or she is, you can afford to have much more patience, tolerance, and understanding in dealing with the issues that arise between you. You may even change some of your own behaviors because you're better able to understand how they affect your partner.

## When You Are Present, Everything You Think and Feel Becomes Part of Your Workshop

From the moment you sit down with another person, every word of dialogue in your head and every feeling in your body becomes your work in the process. It's all about you. What makes you feel closed off emotionally? When do you feel the most open and caring? What feels frightening about what your partner is saying? How is what they are telling you similar or different to your own life experience? What can you learn from the information he or she is offering? When do you find your mind wandering and why? Is your inability to stay focused due to a lack of caring for your partner or is he or she triggering an unresolved feeling in you? Do you feel you have all the answers about what your partner could or should be doing? What is your investment in having the answers rather than allowing your partner to have his or her own process? Are you invested in your partner taking certain actions because you benefit in some way from them? Is your ego invested in your partner changing?

*The unconscious believe they must do.*
*The conscious know they must be.*

If your relationships with the people in your life have been painful in the past, you will want to take it slow and make definite contracts about how you want to work with each other. Suggestions follow about

81

how to make the process safe for you. Remember that you are in control of the pace at which you go and the depth of sharing you feel appropriate. Each tiny step you take toward each other and deeper into yourself gives you the strength to take the next step. Don't expect to jump immediately into deep issues or deep sharing. Take it slowly, and prove to yourself that you and the process are safe.

Whether you decide to experience the power and joy of getting present and doing this work alone or doing it with a partner, do it! Do it for yourself, and begin as soon as you finish this book. No, on second thought, begin right now. Do the exercise that follows to see if you can identify the things you're aware of that make you afraid or uncomfortable. Then see if you can discover why.

## Personal Inventory of My Fears and Responses

1. The circumstances or people I avoid, who intimidate me or make me afraid are:

2. The reason I have this reaction is because:

3. These people or circumstances are similar to the following people or circumstances from my past:

4. The belief about myself that was created from my past is that I am not able to:

5. If I choose not to believe that about myself any longer, the scary thing that might happen is:

6. The positive thing that might happen is:

7. A new message I could begin telling myself in order to get stronger is:

8. Some of the fears or negative beliefs about myself that I want to resolve are:

9. The pattern or theme in these fears or beliefs is:

10. The issue I can begin to work on inside myself is:

11. The thing that scares me the most about being present is:

12. What I need to remind myself in order to feel safe is:

Put that last reminder on your mirror, on your refrigerator, or in your car, and say it to yourself as often as possible.

Now that you've tried this process, you can see that it's not as scary as you may have thought. I'll bet you have already learned something new for yourself. Imagine doing this all day and the gifts that will come from it. The more often you're able to be present, the greater the number of gifts and the more profound they become.

## The Gift of Staying Present

I know you have had an experience, perhaps even more than one, that dramatically altered your perception and forever changed your way of being in the world. Maybe it was just finding out you were gay or lesbian. Although you may never have spoken of an experience like this, you, like most people, no doubt had a secret moment of magic that turned your world and belief systems upside down. Maybe someone made an offhand remark that shuddered through you with a new truth about yourself. Maybe you were deeply touched by some miracle of nature that helped you see the bigger picture of your oneness to the earth. Maybe you sat with someone as they died and felt the strange, unbelievable peace that surprisingly comes to them, and you, with that transition. Perhaps you experienced an unexpected moment of tenderness or flash of soul-deep understanding that put your priorities back in order. Those experiences were a direct result of being present and connected enough to yourself to see the denial and then resolve it. And it happened naturally. You did it naturally.

## How We Developed the Fear of Being Present

An experience of deep and complete bonding or connection should be provided during infancy by your parents or caretakers, but unfortunately it's often missing. This bonding is critical to your life. It becomes the needed reference point for your ability to create unions based in love. It's the basis for how intensely you're able to experience connection to yourselves and others. If you felt safe and nurtured as a child, your experience of union becomes a positive one, and therefore, you will seek out those who can provide ongoing positive connections with you.

If you did not feel that anyone connected in a loving way with you as a child or if others abused you during those connections, you will fear this bonded state or choose people who are similar to your abusers, because that is the kind of person who is familiar. You fear being connected because all of your negative experiences and feelings about it are still making you afraid.

Like the ripple in the pond that extends outward, this childhood experience of connection to yourself and others affects the way you embrace all aspects of life. Learning to stay present to yourself, nature, and others is vital to your healing process. Your very sense of aliveness depends upon your ability to do so. **Your ability to stay present is directly related to the amount of unresolved pain you carry and your willingness to release it.** The more pain we carry inside, the more we move into denial and the more we are apt to act in unconscious and unloving ways toward ourselves and others.

Now the good news: The more you get present, the more old pain is resolved and new space is available for feelings of union and love. As old pain is resolved, the armor that protects you becomes less necessary, and you're able to be more available and present to opportunities for deep relationships.

What we have been doing is unconsciously holding back or holding down the painful feelings so as not to feel them. It's a natural response to avoid pain, emotional or physical, by constricting. Have you ever seen a cat blow up and hold onto itself when it's frightened or is in pain? We do the very same thing without even realizing it. It's called the "flight or fight" syndrome. Many of us live in it. Then at some point when you become willing to be present and connect deeply, perhaps because love or some other moving experience of beauty has arrived at your doorstep, you open yourself up. When you do, all the old original pain immediately floods to the surface. At the moment of opening, you naturally contract or close down again to avoid or postpone experiencing past pain again. You stay in that contracted state, prevented from connecting deeply with others, which is the thing you desire most. Many of us stay in that contracted state for the rest of our lives. We never get fully present to ourselves or each other. Some people get to difficult feelings, experience them, and even if they discover they feel better afterward, they decide never to do it again. They assume experiencing difficult feelings must mean something is either wrong with life or wrong with them. Not so. Difficult feelings are a part of life. When you experience them and allow them to naturally heal, you will always feel better.

## My Difficulty With Getting Present

The most intimate moment I ever had with my mother was when I left her womb at birth. The most intimate moment I ever had with my father was when I buttoned his shirt after he died. By the time I was a toddler I was already frightened and holding onto myself. Until I was about 8, I didn't realize how frightening my life had become. One night while sitting at the dining room table, my father said, "Why don't you kids try mom's dinner? Go ahead. You take the first bite."

My mother looked at him in disbelief, as if someone had slapped her across the face. With determination, she took a big bite of the food herself and then instantly left the table in tears.

Later, I heard them arguing. My mom said, "Why in the world would you pull a stunt like that?"

My father replied, "I thought you might have poisoned the food."

I heard my mother catch her breath, aghast at his response. Holding the volume of her voice down she asked, "So you were willing to let them eat it instead?"

That's the way it was at my house. My father spent his life creating separation between himself and his wife and between each of us. Who wants to be present to that?

Even though I adore my sister and brother, the moment that our conversation gets deeper than a tissue, the minute we approach deep feelings, one of us does something to take us out of the process and away from the intensity. We never talked about my being a lesbian. They knew but would not discuss it. We couldn't go near truth, the past or realness. A look away, a change in subject, a break with a quick aside comment was all it took. Getting too close reminded us of the pain and betrayal we felt as children and still held inside. We anticipated real feelings meant separation and pain. We consciously and unconsciously used distance, religious differences, and lack of time as excuses for not connecting deeply. The risk of going deeper was too great. In our household, when we were children, deep connections equaled abandonment, betrayal, and pain. If we never experienced intimacy and love as children, how would we know how to practice that with each other as adults?

Only years later, after deep work on myself, with my children, and with my own extended family have I been able to experience the deep, loving connections that I longed for with my family.

*Profound change takes place only when we give up
the need to change anyone other than ourselves.*

## Your Relationship Is a Gift

Your decision to look at your feelings, one small step at a time, creates transformation, a change in consciousness, a spiritual awakening. By becoming present to yourself and others and doing this work, you can create healing opportunities during which you can take the most base, common emotions and transform them into an experience of enlightenment. You can fly.

We are presented with an opportunity to become alchemists, magicians, and Merlins turning apathy into fire. The gift of being fully present is vivid insight, spiritual awakening, correct advice from our inner healer, deep clarity, and inner knowingness. Relationships and the opportunities they offer to be real can bring the release of pain and a deep experience of connection to our purpose, or something greater: Spirit, Buddha, the Source, the Tao, the creative energy of the universe.

The process of being fully present may feel magical. It provides an opportunity for transformation, the potential for being our own heroes. It does so not because of what we go out and *do* in the world, but, rather, because you and I become vital and filled with aliveness, connected to ourselves and our own divinity. We become our own healers. The choice to heal emotions allows us to live momentarily in the center of our own frustrations and questions about life, which in turn makes it possible for answers to arise holistically, from our own inner healer. This process contains aware consciousness and internal action that allow appropriate change to occur naturally. *It's the process of becoming the answers instead of just hearing or knowing them.* It's the difference between *being* and *doing*.

You will begin to understand the defense mechanisms you created as children. You'll get clarity about what was happening in your life that required those defense mechanisms. For instance, if you find that as an adult you "check out" and stop listening when someone yells at you, you can bet that when you were a child, someone you loved was verbally abusive, deliberately or not. When you are a child and you have neither the cognitive skills nor the physical strength to make an adult stop abusing, you may choose to survive by "checking out." That understanding alone often provides resolution because judgment is removed. With the resolution of pain and judgment comes greater aliveness and the ability to become fully present. We must learn to approach the fear we are still holding with profound compassion for ourselves.

Being alive and feeling aliveness is like enlightenment. Aliveness is on a continuum, and is experienced in degrees. It's not a black-or-white, all-or-nothing proposition. The possibilities for aliveness are infinite, and conscious people cannot tolerate lack of aliveness any more than they can tolerate lack of water. Once you have tasted living life fully present, you will become invested in having more, knowing more, being more. Our society has forgotten that it's our heritage to be all that we can be to our fullest potential—every one of us. To be Spirit realized. Real healing refreshes your memory and ignites your desire to begin that precious process of becoming again, just like the plant that reaches for sunlight.

We are all partially alive. **You cannot have aliveness from what you do or from doing more. Aliveness comes only from being more of who you are and resolving the denials you hold about your true self.**

In our society we have confused this issue. We spend our lives *doing* in order to become someone or be who we are. We *do* to *be*, instead of *being* in order to *do*, as one of my spiritual mentors, Naunie Batchelder, forever reminds me. Not having had the nurturing I needed as a child, I often forget that I do not have to do anything to be worthy. I was born worthy of being loved, and so were you. If you have any doubt about that, go and stand beside the crib of a newborn, and ask yourself whether that baby, even in its most vulnerable and needy state, is worthy of being loved.

## Relationships Are Our Teachers

You learn about how far you have come, who you are, and how much unresolved pain you're still holding by being in relationships with others. The extent of your ability to bond deeply with others is a barometer to the amount of aliveness you allow in your life. By doing this work, you will find out how far you've come toward being fully alive. You'll know because you can reach out spiritually and emotionally toward someone you care for only as far as you have reached spiritually and emotionally into your our own emotions. Facing your denial offers opportunities to see ourselves and others more clearly.

## Getting Present

When you decide to get present to yourself or another person, a literal energetic process happens. You create a connection of energy that provides a sacred sort of workshop. It's similar to the difference you feel between being in lust and being profoundly in love. You experience the energy of your connectedness to life, your connection to each other and to Spirit. This energy is a holding space that offers a state of "enough time," or a sense of timelessness and a "reunion with the feeling of oneness with another," so that you may release pain safely. It gives back that lost sense of oneness you should have felt with parents and with your greater source. Can't you remember the times in your life when you and someone you loved were so connected and together that for a moment in your process you lost a sense of time and space? The only thing you felt was each other. It was as if you had an eternity and you lost all sense of time. This is what this process of staying present feels like and brings.

It's one thing to say, "I am with you," and another to *experience oneness*. When you're in that connected space, you will also experience a reunion with an awareness of the divine energy inside yourself and your partner. You feel that universal energy that connects us with each other. It's not about religion, dogma, or doctrine. It's about the spirituality of life, love, and aliveness. It's about positive power, nature, synchronicity, coincidence, and reclaiming our divinity.

We have become a society bereft of, and therefore addicted to, the search for this state of divine union. That is what is creating this unmet longing in each of us. In truth, that is what we are all trying to find—the union with Spirit that we once knew. From the instant we had to disconnect from caregivers or life in order to protect ourselves, we also disconnected from a sense of safety with a higher power. Since that childhood disconnection, we have voraciously sought this state through the use of substances such as sex, food, and the altered states achieved through drugs, technology, or unhealthy relationships.

Our search, though sometimes in the wrong places, may also reflect our wisdom, a higher sense of inner knowing that without this ability to deeply be present to ourselves and each other, we remain isolated and alone. Unfortunately many of us search for this connection in promiscuous sexuality and serial relationships. This never lasts. It doesn't work, and after it's over we hate ourselves. Still, we know that without this deep presence to ourselves or someone else, it's next to impossible to face what we are holding. Now we can make the decision to connect more deeply with each other to ensure that others do not inherit our legacy of a world of separation that breeds contempt and war.

*When you attempt to see those you love as if it were for the first time,*
*it may indeed be so!*

As long as you and I remain willing to avoid our deepest fears and denial and live in our aloneness, we disrupt the cosmic sense of harmony and unity. We don't take our rightful place in our families, in our partnerships, or in society. It becomes easy to perceive our fellow human beings as an "other," separate and not connected to us, and therefore dispensable in war, poverty, homelessness, or crime. We've disconnected so much so from each other that abuse, dishonesty, and lack of compassion are accepted ways of life for many. These things fill our television shows, our movies, and our music. We are functioning out of pain and denial, instead of out of our Spirits, our hearts, and out of love. Relationships offer us a bridge across this sense of isolation into deep healing. If I'm present to myself, I can perceive you as part of myself, connected to me, and vitally important. Once I get there, there's no way that I can abuse you, dismiss you, or become immune to your pain. Once I am truly connected to you, I cannot help treating you as I wish to be treated, with respect and love.

*It's only possible to see the smile of God in the face of each other.*

## Staying Present to a Sense of Connection

In any given instant, you and I are united in some way. Perhaps it's simply because we are two human beings. Or, more likely, we have *called* each other into our lives to teach each other something. Something about you is also a reflection of me; otherwise, we would not have attracted each other.

For instance, if I want to be taken care of, no doubt you're a caretaker. If I am feeling powerless, no doubt you seem to have greater power. If I refuse to express my anger, no doubt you're expressing the anger for the relationship.

We may not have discovered these things about ourselves until we are in a relationship, until we turn and face each other and stand in the place where we connect. Once I am present to myself, I can move into the space where we get present to each other, and that is the terrain of possibility, the doorway to right, safe, deeply committed union. This is the connected space where healing is created. We learn about ourselves from this state of oneness. This is the only place from which we learn about fluidity, change, acceptance, and compassion. In this space we become safe enough to let down the barriers and armor that prevent us from feeling each other. In this space of being fully present we become willing to be affected by each other and each other's pain and joy. In this space we can feel ourselves, feel what we are holding individually, and feel how to release our pain. Notice I said *feel* these things. **Healing does not occur from thinking. It can occur only from direct experience, feeling.** It must occur from direct experience, like enlightenment, love, and divine union. This is exactly why people stay in therapy for years, talking about their issues but never healing them.

Memory is held at a cellular level. It must be felt in order to be released. Your willingness to feel your feelings is your greatest tool for healing. It's also why our relationships are critical to our enlightenment. Those feelings arise only when we are in relationships. They are a product of our connection to ourselves and each other.

## We Crave This Fully Present State

Some people seek this feeling of presence and connection through orgasm and the "in love" state. They feel a "divine" sense of unity. Some people seek it by communing with nature and animals; others through spiritual or emotional growth processes. Healing results when one is present to oneself, whether the catalyst is another individual, a mystical experience, or a connection with nature.

Scientists have proven our cells contain memory. Therefore, each time we allow ourselves to become more present, a new connected level of energy is held and sustained, and we gradually become more able to be in this aware state of bonded intimacy for longer periods. It's like taking your first steps. Soon after the first one, you try again and hold the position until it becomes natural.

I remember a time when I stood alone on a cliff, near the ocean, above an expanse of deserted beach in Cambria, Calif. It was the first vacation I had taken in years. I took deep breaths of cleansing sea air. The longer I stood on the cliff, the more at one I felt with the ocean. As my breaths grew deeper and I took more of the energy in, the exhaustion in my body flooded to the surface and tears streamed down my face. I kept breathing until I was sobbing out the tiredness I had long repressed. As the negative energy left my body, I became filled with awareness of how little nurturing time I allowed for myself. How much I was giving out and how little I was letting in. I stood for a long time, allowing myself to feel how important this kind of experience was, and I made a commitment not to wait so long to address this need. By the time I left that place on the cliff I felt filled up, refreshed, and had a greater understanding of my own limitations. I have never forgotten that experience. In this space, my connection to the energy of the earth and to myself provided safety that allowed me to face my own resistance to just *being* and taking in nourishment for my body and soul.

Since that moment at the ocean when I discovered a new level of peace and relaxation, I now know very quickly when I have waited too long to take time out and get present to my feelings and needs. It's almost as though every cell in my body begins to long for that space again.

## Staying Present May Feel Odd

Initially, your body or mind may be unable to sustain this present state of awareness for long because the experience may feel strange or disquieting to you. It may feel new, unfamiliar, or odd. The remembrance that you are able to create this state of awareness can be blocked, traumatized, or inaccessible to the conscious mind. You can miss chances for this opportunity by not recognizing it. Immediate fears of abandonment or engulfment may arise. Guess what, those fears come from your red wagon. When the exhaustion began to leave my body on the beach, I grew frightened. There were moments when I felt I might be consumed by the exhaustion, and I wanted to disconnect from that feeling. When you have not allowed yourself to love deeply because of old pain, the moment you open your heart to love again you can expect the old pain to come floating up.

We are unaccustomed to feeling the intensity of living life in a fully present state. For this reason, it's perfect for you to do this slowly. Unless, of course, you immediately love it so much you can't imagine living any other way. Each time I went back to that special state, I was able to stay in that sense of oneness for longer periods of time. Another layer of exhaustion surfaces, and as I became familiar with the process, I could allow the exhaustion to leave and allow myself to become filled up more easily.

## A Process of Gradual Integration

The experience of becoming fully present to yourself is a magical state. This state is reminiscent of your original state of oneness with the divine or universal energy. If you do not perceive of God or that which I call Spirit, the divine, then this state for you may be reminiscent of your most connected moment in or out of the body of your mother or in the arms of your father or in nature. It's an intense connection and energy. If you don't have those kinds of connection with your parents, perhaps you have that connection with music, the ocean, exercise, writing, or painting. Most of us cannot honestly say we feel fully connected to the energy of the universe. Most of us, as children, did not even feel that connected to our parents. In many cases we are not fully connected to ourselves and our own feeling states, hence our disconnection with each other. For the majority of people, once these feelings of connection are experienced, they are found to be similar to the experience of opening gently to the sunlight after years of being in a darkened room.

*When you are the channel through which divine energy flows,*
*you become an ocean of greatness.*

This experience is so important that you even sought it unconsciously as a child. When you were a child, from the time you were born you would stare intently, gazing deeply into the eyes of a beloved parent or sibling. As a child, you were already familiar with this state and comfortable in it. You knew it was vital to your existence. It was only after years of being unable to experience this connection, or feeling abused during your process of finding it, that you gave up hope and pretended it no longer mattered. Secretly we all still long for it. Unconsciously, you are still looking for it.

## A Profound Connection

When you become fully present to yourself or someone else, the energy you create is immense. If we were able to measure the healing quality in the energy when we are really in that state of connection, we could compare it to:

- the most healing energy of nature,
- the most exquisite moment of orgasm,

- the most profound of intellectual "aha"s,
- the most electrifying moment of emotional feeling or release,
- or the most transcendent mystical instant.

Think for a moment about how you felt the last time you stood watching a sunrise, basked in the ocean air, or immediately after an orgasm that came from true *love*making. No doubt you felt a peaceful sense of wholeness and calm. This is because there is an alignment or similarity in the healing energy of these natural circumstances that speaks to the innermost sense of well-being inside each of us. When we deliberately align with or focus on that healing energy, we have, in fact, merged with energy that has little or no dissonance. This is the exact feeling of being fully present that is so helpful to resolving denial. In this connected, energetic state we become aligned with, and connected to, the natural healer in each of us, and dissonance is transcended. You're able to experience your oneness with yourself and another. Out of that union comes understanding and healing. Out of that sense of connection to yourself comes the strength and courage to deal with whatever is inside. When you're not connected and present to yourself, it's impossible to access the inner healer in you that has the answers. It's impossible to even know that one exists, and therein lies most of your fear.

Everything you experience as emotional pain is, in fact, the result of an internal and/or external disconnection from the experience of the One or love. **Pain can result from our longing for this union, our seeking a loving connection when there is a lack of it.** The original source of all emotional pain can be traced back to that moment when you experienced isolation and abandonment. That pain can be resolved only when you have once again moved from the separation of being two back into one. It's about becoming present once again with heart energy. Without the bonding that comes from a healthy heart energy connection, you're left without the experience of oneness with another and your surrounding universe. Getting present to you once again allows for that heart energy connection and a safe space.

This "feeling"—rather than "talking"—type of healing also assumes that your inner healer, with all its wisdom and healing ability, will emerge and direct the process. The most important task for anyone attending the process is simply to **stay fully present, be connected to**

**yourself and the process.** As you will see, the inner guide in each of us knows exactly what is needed. With the information that follows, you will be able to determine for yourself when you have authentically created healing.

One of my clients, Ellen, expressed it this way: "The point when we became profoundly present and shared that intense energy flow between us is hard to describe because the experience went beyond words. It was like zeroing in, being on the same wavelength, tuned into the same channel of total awareness. I experienced a unity and perfect wholeness totally contained by that space. It was as if the two of us were one. The energy that flowed between us was one energy. It was the same. It was as if we shared the same space, and that was scary because there were no walls between us. No walls meant I was more vulnerable than I ever remembered being. More vulnerable and yet more safe than I ever remembered.

"As trust began to build," Ellen continued, "there seemed to be a giving up or a letting go of self-conscious feelings. I began to just be there without defenses. Like a bridge that began to form, we seemed to come together. The you out there and the me inside somewhere connected, and our time became a journey we took together."

Ellen had never before felt this sense of presence with another human being. If you take a moment to think about it, I'm sure you have gotten to the edge of this kind of connection in your own life. Maybe you came right up to the edge and then retreated. Maybe you went fully into it and experienced the healing. Or maybe you saw it coming and went the other direction. These opportunities for connecting deeply are what bring us to the edge. As soon as we are open to being fully connected to ourselves or another person, we experience fear. If we feel we can not safely deal with the denial and fear, we close back down. There are opportunities to create deep healing all around us in everyday life. Take this quiz to see for yourself. Check off those experiences in which you remember this deep connection. Then you will see you already have a reference point for the connected state I am talking about. Answer yes or no for each question.

- Have you ever had a moment with another person, during which you connected so deeply that you felt you had known each other before from a previous time?

- Have you ever looked at some beauty of nature and felt over-whelmed or filled up?

- Have you ever taken yourself out of a conversation that felt like it would bring up deep emotions about your past?

- Have you ever had a moment with someone in which the exchange that took place forever changed your perception of that person?

- Have you ever been alone thinking on an issue when a stream of enlightenment about the subject flooded your body or your mind?

- Have you ever felt fully connected with someone without words?

- Have you ever had a moment when your consciousness suddenly shifted and you saw things differently than you had a moment before?

- Have you ever *known* something about someone before a person told you?

- Do you ever feel what's going on with someone who's not in the same vicinity as you?

- Do you have certain commitments to people that result from some kind of *connection* you don't talk about?

- Have you had an experience that you can't explain that enhanced your life in some way?

- Do you remember instances in your childhood or as an adult when you lost a sense of time and space?

- Have you ever heard someone say something or seen something that suddenly took you from one belief you had held most of your life into a new and different belief?

• Have you ever just given up on an issue and suddenly found you had the answer you needed?

If you answered yes to any of the above, you have probably already experienced being deeply present. You can see this work has already been a part of your process. Now you can learn to create this kind of presence at will and use it fully in your healing process.

## The Costs and Risks

I have told you some of the wondrous things you have in store and can expect to experience when you enter this process. And although each of your experiences will be different, they *will* be filled with great joy, I promise you. Now it's only fair that we also discuss some of the risks and costs of this process.

Sometimes you may discover parts of yourself that you are not proud of and may not like. Again and again, just when I have felt I have gotten to a place of sure footing in my process, I have found yet another saboteur within me. She makes herself known when she has nearly done me in with some unkind act, some unconscious response, or some place of blind denial that abruptly gets unearthed from deep in my unconscious. These discoveries may take your breath away, make you want to throw up, and embarrass you to tears. They do me. They can make you feel bad about yourself, and if you let them, they can discourage you. Don't let them. First of all, if you were not growing, these hard issues would not be surfacing at all. You'd still be in the denial. The difference is that once you're healing, the underpinning of this discovery is always one of greater freedom and increased understanding. Although you may not believe it yet, it does feel good to feel so bad, when you know feeling bad is about your own growth not your denial or self-sabotage. Just take deep breaths and keep going. In every single instance in my life, with only two exceptions, I have been able to go to the person I have inadvertently wounded, and together we have been able to forgive these unconscious acts and discuss how we both contributed to the process and what we both learned. In the instances where this is not possible, you must simply let go, forgive yourself, and understand that you may not be able to reach resolution with the other person. This is especially true if they have not yet evolved to a place of understanding the importance of this kind of healing or feel able to do so. When this happens, reach resolution inside yourself.

Don't continue beating yourself up. This is not healing. Once you have learned what you need to learn about your mistake, commit to doing it differently next time and move on. You wouldn't continue to punish your child after he or she has learned a lesson, so don't punish yourself in that way either. It's neither loving nor helpful. We are all products of our environment, and we will all make mistakes in our process. No one is immune from this. Anyone who cannot forgive you still needs to learn some lesson about his or her own fear or anger. Let it go once you reach a place of complete understanding *for yourself.*

You may also experience some difficulty, when you encounter some people who are not delighted that you're growing. Some may be envious, some may get angry, and to be truthful, some may even leave your life if they are invested in your remaining the same. No matter what anyone else's response to your process may be, you cannot give yourself up for anyone else. Ultimately you will grow to resent them and hate yourself for the decision. It's your right to become enlightened and have as much love in your life as possible. Do not think for a moment that *anyone* else should be more important than you. Not your mother, not your lover, not your child. No one. If you do not put your own spiritual and emotional growth first, you will not have everything you want emotionally or spiritually to give to those you love. Trust Spirit to clear the way, and if this person is meant to be in your life and truly loves you, he or she will eventually come around and accept you as you are.

What you may discover is what I found to be true in my own life. The more I stood fast in my own truth, the more others were able to do the same for themselves, and the closer we became. The more I healed, the more love I was capable of giving and the more understanding I could extend to those who had none. It took a long time for some members of my family to come around. Be patient. Trust your process and the Spirit within. Remember, anything that you give up to become more of who you are is always replaced with something better.

Without an ounce of hesitation, I can promise you this is true.

Finally, there may be times when you feel lonely. In one way, however, you will never again feel lonely, because not only do you find yourself in this process, but you also find Spirit. You may, though, feel lonely at times about the number of others who feel as you do and are as committed to their own growth. Unfortunately, there are no lists in our community of those who are living spiritual partnerships to whom we can go for support—yet! But more and more groups of spiritual partners are being started. At one point, not too many years ago, Ram Dass said only 10% of the world was awakening. Now the numbers are much higher, and you will have many more people with whom to play. Do not stay in that loneliness. Get on the Internet. Believe it or not, there are more than 250,000 spirituality sites and too many personal growth sites to count. Find a local organization that provides spiritual support. Attend a conference, seminar, or workshop where personal and spiritual growth is the focus. Trust yourself to take what you need or leave if it does not fit your needs. Buy local magazines or newsletters that list events in your community. In other words, be with other people who, like you, are dedicated to their own growth and unfolding. Walk this path with them and support each other. Do not get attached to any dogma or doctrine or teacher. These are not truth. Truth is found only in your personal relationship to Spirit.

In the next chapter we will look closely at the process of being present. You will learn how to recognize your denial and your reasons for fearing the idea of being fully present. You will also learn to move into it and through it safely. An important step in your process is to be willing to *not* have all the answers immediately. Stay in the process! Be patient! Everything you need and want to know will come to the surface if you're doing your work. Let's take a minute to do the following exercise, so you can begin to identify your family patterns and explore some issues that may arise about becoming fully present. If you find it difficult, do it a bit at a time and be kind to yourself. You have all the time you need. The important thing is not how quickly you do it, but rather how deeply you're willing to explore for the answers.

# Being Present: Identifying Family Patterns

1. In my family, communication was: (open, nonexistent, guilt-laden, etc.)


   Secrets were: (prevalent, forbidden, used against us, etc.)

   Disagreements were dealt with by: (violence, verbal abuse, discussion, etc.)


   My opinion was: (valued, discounted, belittled, etc.)


2. If I had to describe my parents' relationship, I would say it was:


3. If I had to describe my relationship with my parent/s, I would say it was:


4. In my family, intimacy was: (nonexistent, followed by anger, etc.)


   The only form of intimacy I ever experienced was: (broken boundaries, occasional encounters, verbal, physical, sexual abuse, etc.)

My response to the idea of becoming fully present to myself and others is:

5. The ways that my partner could help to make that a safe experience are:

The thing I would never want my partner to do is:

For now just be aware of some of the issues that may come up in your process. As these issues arise, your inner healer will provide the answers you need for resolution. Good, now you have the ability to stay present to yourself, so let's see what we need to be fully present to each other. But first, a quiet meditation.

■ ■ ■

For this meditation, close your eyes and imagine yourself in safe surroundings. This can be at the beach, in the forest, or wherever you feel safest. This place can be imaginary or real. Check inside to see that you and your spiritual self are still one with each other. Take a minute to create a small pond, beside which you decide to sit for a moment. Ask your spirit to show you, in the reflection on the still water of the pond, what future you are going to and who you will become. Take all the time you need to see how this "future you" acts, talks, thinks, and feels. Once you have come to know this future you, take some time to see which part of you fears stepping into this vision and becoming it. Take all the time you need to commune with your spirit and resolve the fear. Have your spirit tell you which kinds of support you need and how to give it to yourself. When you're finished, try to make a commitment to yourself to become this "future you," one day at a time, one decision and action at a time.

## Dyad Exercise

• The person/people in my life who abandoned me are:

• The ways in which I now leave myself are:

• The ways in which I leave myself emotionally are:

• The reasons I began to leave myself as a child were:

• My belief then about what could happen if I did not leave myself was:

• The ways in which I leave you emotionally are:

• The reason/excuses I use about leaving you are:

• My belief/fear about what might happen if I were fully present to you is:

• The tools I have to deal with that are:

• The benefits I would get from staying fully present are:

When you're finished with this exercise, take a break. Don't discuss the content you shared. Just leave it intact, undisputed, and leave the space as a safe place to which you can return for future exercises.

# CHAPTER THREE
# The "B" Word: Boundaries

*At the same moment*
*that I am fully present*
*and one with you,*
*I must remember to be*
*fully present and*
*one*
*with me.*
*When I am able to do that,*
*the space between us becomes*
*a fertile, spiritual ground*
*for healing.*

Where do you begin and end and what exactly is your job in relationships? Ask a thousand people, get a thousand answers. This confusion is so pervasive that it extends all the way into our relationships with Spirit. We don't know who we are. We don't know exactly what our job is in reference to each other or Spirit. We are either entirely enmeshed, working from the concept that we must give up everything and all of ourselves—or we are scared to death and totally disconnected, afraid we could lose ourselves if we get too close. One of the reasons we have trouble creating successful relationships with each other or with Spirit is that we are afraid to be fully present because we don't know where we or our responsibilities begin and end. So we just don't go there. We don't get present. And we won't until we can clear up this incredibly important issue and feel safe. **The biggest obstacle to staying present—to ourselves, to each other, and to Spirit—is a lack of information or massive confusion over the "B" word: boundaries.**

We cannot love each other with an open hand and heart unless we understand that each of our individual processes is a sacred path to Spirit. It's not our job to change each other. It's not our job to take on each other's lessons. Your process is as sacred as mine and must be honored just as I honor my own. I cannot take your spiritual lessons on as my own, nor can I pretend to have your answers. I can only love you as you heal your own issues and find your way to Spirit. You are not here to make me whole, nor am I here to make you whole. We are here to do our individual spiritual work together. Without boundaries this is nearly impossible.

In many relationships, couples believe they must be joined at the hip. The U-Haul pulls up after the fourth date. Or, at the other extreme, one or both individuals may be terrified of intimacy. Both of these responses to being present are about the lack of healthy boundaries. That same lack of healthy boundaries can also make it difficult to connect to your own feelings, especially if they are intense. Without healthy boundaries, you cannot feel safe, whether you are doing your work alone or with another person. That's why we are going to give focused attention to this issue. Having healthy boundaries can be likened to having a sturdy boat with which to row to the center of a great, expansive lake. When you have a sturdy boat you trust, you can go further into your issues, deeper into the experience of being connected, deeper into intimacy. When you trust yourself and know how to exercise healthy boundaries, staying present becomes easy and you can create deeper intimacy without fear. When you know who you are, you can give yourself completely to your partner or to Spirit without losing yourself or the reason for your journey.

Spirit has given the perfect prototype for respectful boundaries to us through the gift of free will. Have you noticed Spirit never demands that you grow? It does not set your schedule for you. It does not ask that you feel the same as It does. It does not even demand that you adopt spiritual principles. It simply offers information and, without judgment, allows you to partake as you feel ready to do so. Spirit trusts your process and knows that every lesson you create for yourself is a valuable learning tool that will eventually take you where you desire to go—to the truth. This is a perfect example of unconditional love and the perfect prototype for how you can be with those you love.

Most of us want our partners, friends, family, to think as we do, love as we do, act as we do, give what we give, and, in essence, be exactly like us. We want that because of the illusion that if someone thinks, acts, and loves as we do, then we must be right. It makes us feel safe. However, you are not safe.

Sameness does not create safety. We need to learn how to give each other the freedom, the free will, to be exactly who we are, with all our attendant emotions, feelings, fears, and doubts. We need to become safe enough to allow the full expression of each other's feelings without judgment or control. Then and only then are you really safe in your relationship, because you are both being real.

*Who you are being will always speak louder*
*than what you are demanding.*

## Trusting Yourself

People who don't trust themselves to express anger, rage, grief, or pain do not have healthy internal boundaries. The feelings that can arise about being "out of control" "overwhelmed" or "taken over" are all about a lack of boundaries. With healthy boundaries you know you can feel your rage and yet feel confident that you will not act in a way that is hurtful to yourself or someone else. If you have healthy boundaries, you are also aware of your inner strengths and, therefore, can allow yourself to feel your grief or pain and know that you won't be engulfed or overcome by it. If you don't have healthy boundaries, there is no way to have a sense of who you are or what your strengths are. If you don't trust yourself to feel your own feelings fully, it will be impossible to trust your partner's full expression of feeling.

This subject is not dealt with early in our lives, so there are many ways in which good boundaries failed to get formed. Few people have understood the importance of boundaries. Many people feel they were never abused or never had their boundaries broken, and yet those same people may also have difficulty with self-esteem, self-respect, and self-love issues. Why? Because we were not respected in the ways that help us create healthy boundaries. Low self-esteem and a lack of self-respect are also boundary issues, as you will see.

## How Did We Get Here?

When was the last time you felt safe and secure inside? When I was a child, there were guidelines for living, social etiquette, if you will, that made us feel safer. The world and life seemed simpler, more manageable. We felt safer in dealing with each other. Children played under street lamps at night. There was less crime, less struggle, and there appeared to be more emotional reward from our endeavors.

Then social boundaries became too limiting, and we explored how it might feel to live without them. We stopped looking to our parents, our churches, and our government for acceptable guidelines for living. We struck out on our own to explore and establish our own limits. Hence the women's—and then the gay and lesbian—movement. We began pushing at the edges, breaking away from these old traditions and social mores until in the 60's, in bright, living psychedelic color, we blew open the windows of our minds, and we blew off the traditional boundaries that offered both the illusion and the reality of safety.

Since the 1960s, we have excitedly explored new realms of consciousness. But we have still not yet felt safe, nor have we been safe. We haven't felt safe because we don't know where our limits are. We haven't felt safe because we live in a world where all too often there are no limits. We have begun to behave as if we are drunk, bouncing off the walls of our environment, each of us dancing to a different tune, bumping into and walking all over each other. Often we feel freedom equates to pushing the limits past our own safety.

We are desperately trying to find the balance between exploring our right to be fully who we are as individuals and learning respect for one another and the ailing planet on which we live. It has not been easy. Obviously, we have not yet found many of the answers. Families feud with each other. Breakup rates are climbing, and we are still at war in many parts of this planet. We haven't yet found the way to balance our free will with the principles of truth telling and an ability to act out of love and not fear. In our communities, men are still at odds with women, and we have interpreted being powerful as making the same mistakes as our heterosexual role models.

Parents feel out of control because kids are out of control. Drugs, weapons, and unwanted pregnancies are on every campus in the country, starting with kids in grammar school. Kids feel parents are out to lunch, and neither group is doing much talking to the other. We don't know where to begin. How do we tell our kids what to do and also allow them the space in which to find out who they really are? How and when do we let go of adult kids, allowing them to have their own path and process while providing necessary guidance?

*When you treat yourself or anyone else as if they were all they can be, they will become it!*

More than half the relationships in this country end in breakup, for as many reasons as there are people. In the gay and lesbian community, the statistics for long-term, committed, monogamous relationships are becoming worse, for an endless list of reasons. First and foremost, there are fewer visible role models and more stress due to survival issues. Today we are dealing with economic survival and beyond that physical survival due to all the violence in our world. All of these issues are about poor boundaries.

*Weakness occurs when we are out of harmony with ourselves. Strength arrives when we return to center, and to Spirit.*

Can you even remember the last time you sat with a close friend or family member and had an intimate, meaningful conversation that left you feeling more alive and connected? We fear being deeply affected by each other so much so that we avoid meaningful connections altogether. We leave before *real presence* can even arrive. God forbid you should want something from me! What if I don't want to give it? What if your fears and feelings awaken fears and feelings in me that I don't want to feel? What will you do if you know too much about me? How will you use that information to hurt me? Where will I find the energy, time, and interest to deal with your issues, when I feel so overwhelmed with my own? *We are missing something critical to our process of staying present.*

With the hundreds of couples and families in my practice, we go round and round until eventually we get to the real issue creating the problems in most relationships—people take a hike, emotionally, physically, and spiritually, because one major element is missing: the "B" word: boundaries.

# Boundaries

Most of you have some idea of what I mean when I talk about boundaries. You may have read a paragraph or two on boundaries in your last self-help book. That's about all most authors include. You could have heard a comment or two about boundaries from your therapist. Most of your therapists studied the issue of professional boundaries when they were in school. They learned when it is legal to release information about you, when they have to refer you because issues are out of their scope of practice, when to intervene if a client is at risk. However, many therapists weren't taught about personal boundaries. They may role model firm boundaries in their process with you, but often they don't discuss this issue. When they were children, no one taught them either. There is no "Boundary 101" class. This issue is so important because it is the very foundation for our ability to relate to each other successfully. Yet it is given usually only cursory attention.

This issue is also critical for safe voyages into healing your own issues. One of the main reasons we don't heal the issues in our past is because we are not sure we can take care of ourselves, survive our feelings. Learning we are capable of dealing with our feelings safely is also about having good boundaries. Without healthy boundaries, you can't trust yourself. Working on your issues should not make you feel overwhelmed or out of control. You may give yourself—hopefully you *will* give yourself—permission to experience your feelings fully. Get angry. Shout if you want. Hit pillows if you wish. Do all the things we will talk about that help you vent rage or sadness. But even in that process, if you have healthy boundaries, you will have the process under control and feel safe. With healthy boundaries you will experience that same kind of safety in developing deep, meaningful relationships.

In our relationships, boundary issues are even greater because we are sitting across from someone who is the same gender. We expect them to feel the way we do, want the things we want, and behave as we would behave. We are dancing with such a similar energy at times that we lose a sense of where we begin and end.

This chapter will help you become aware of boundaries. It will help you clarify how and when boundaries are respected or not respected, and it will teach you how to set stronger, more healthy boundaries for yourself. Boundaries are your most important tool for learning to stay present. Although this book may magically open your eyes and mind to some important issues, it will not do the work of creating boundaries for you. It is your job to put this information into practice.

At the beginning of your process, it may seem as if you must set and reset your boundaries a hundred times a day. That's normal, and in fact, it's exactly what you must do to successfully create boundaries. When you have lived without boundaries for most of your life, it is not uncommon to lose your awareness of them in the beginning stages of your work. You can start out with them firmly set in the morning before you go to work, yet the minute your boss steps over one of them, they will appear to have vanished. It is not that you are doing anything wrong—you may be doing it exactly right! It's just necessary to set boundaries again and again, until they become internalized and strong enough to remain naturally in place. Then you will begin functioning with them, automatically and unconsciously, without having to be so diligent or defensive about making sure they are in place. It takes time to create solid boundaries. Although you may read this chapter and instantaneously become aware that you don't have healthy boundaries, creating them is a process that takes time.

All too often we get into a variety of relationships, whether with a mate, guru, therapist, doctor, or anyone else we perceive to be in authority, and we expect that person to make life safe for us. We want him to make our decisions about our bodies, our minds, and our futures while we stand by waiting to express outrage when he makes the wrong decision or adulation when he is right. Do you think I'm kidding?

Do you know what's in your medical records or the contents and possible complications of the medications you regularly ingest? If you are in a relationship, do you know exactly what your financial status is, what your investment portfolio consists of, and how much insurance you and your partner have purchased? Do you believe a lover will always take care of you? Do you take responsibility for your own healing by understanding how your body and mind function? Or do you walk into a doctor's office or a therapist's office once you have become ill and hope he or she can fix you? Do you think drug manufacturers, government agencies, food manufacturers, and health care givers all have your best interests at heart? If you do, let me tell you, those are dangerous beliefs.

**One of our biggest boundary challenges is to take back responsibility for ourselves, in every area of our lives.** No other individuals are a greater authority than you are, even though they may have good information to offer you in your decision-making process.

Think about how the simple process of establishing better boundaries and becoming more informed could avoid many lawsuits. Today we are living in the age of the victim. The TV made us do it. The therapist made us do it. Our parents made us do it. Our lovers made us do it. The devil made us do it. No one made you do it! You have a right to be treated in an honorable, respectful way in the world. But **no one other than you is in charge of making sure that happens. No one other than you is responsible for your decisions, including the ones you make not to be respected and the ones you make to give your own power over to someone else.**

*It is almost certain that the most important communications
are those we have with Self in silence.*

Remember the last time you were in a bad relationship? From the very beginning, some small—or loud—booming voice inside probably told you to keep on looking, but you decided not to listen. No doubt you discounted your own intuition and went right along for the ride. And no doubt you cleaned up the mess for months, possibly years after. No matter the circumstances, there is always some voice inside that has our best interest at heart. There is always some voice inside that has the right answers when we are listening. **We break our own boundaries when we refuse to listen to that voice.** We must learn to stop blaming the "professionals," spouses, parents, and friends in our life when we refuse to listen to our own inner wisdom.

*Most answers are received long before they are heard.*

The process of listening to yourself and establishing firm, healthy boundaries is exciting. You stop being a victim to circumstances or a victim to others, because you take power back and respond from your own center of truth. This is especially true in regard to drugs, sex, and other addictions. No one but you is responsible for treating you as a sacred, precious human being. If you are not treating yourself that way, why should society? Having boundaries gives you greater joy and a deep sense of empowerment. **Safety always comes from inside— not outside of—you.**

In this chapter, exercises will assist you in your process of creating positive internal boundaries. Having firmly established boundaries will ensure that your healing process is successful. Before you get started on these experiential exercises, however, take a minute to complete the following quiz. In doing so, you may discover that your boundaries get tested every day in ways you had never thought about.

The purpose of this quiz is to help you think about your boundaries and how they get broken in ways you might not have considered before. Doing the exercise might trigger some of the feelings you had when your boundaries were broken in the past. That's OK. Just notice the feelings, take a deep breath, and tell yourself you will deal with those feelings in time. As you read the questions you may find some circumstances in your own life to be a little different. If so, change the question in your mind and mark it if you feel the concept is similar enough. The quiz is a tool to help you begin thinking about your personal circumstances and the ways in which your boundaries get broken. Obviously, no one will fit perfectly into any category, but you will get a general idea of where you fit. Respond with your first impulse or first answer. Don't edit. Your first answer is normally the right one.

If you don't fit into any of the categories, ask someone you trust to take the test for you and mark those answers he or she feels apply to you. Then reevaluate your previous responses and see if you can agree. There may be so much denial that you are unable to see the ways in which you respond out of fear. Be gentle and loving with yourself during this process. Remember that denial has helped you survive.

Even if you do not consider any of the things that have happened to you to be abusive, you still have issues about boundaries. We all do. Parents are not provided with parenting classes that include this issue. There are no grade school classes teaching us about boundaries or how to respect them. There are no high school classes for creating internal boundaries. Chances are that even if you have been in therapy for a long time, you may not have discussed the issue of boundaries because many therapists, being human, have boundary issues themselves.

If you have already done extensive work creating boundaries, you may find you are in a category with fewer checked answers. If so, congratulate yourself for having done some fine healing work.

No one needs to see your answers but you, so be honest with yourself and watch out that you don't try to make things appear better than they actually are. Many people dismiss their hardships or abuse because, never having experienced a different way of living, they simply see these hardships as typical family conflict. One of the ways you become able to tolerate painful issues is by diminishing the pain in your mind, by pretending it really doesn't matter or is not as bad as it seems.

Take a moment to answer the following questions and see. Don't worry about checking lightly so that you can erase the answers later. You won't want to give this book up anyway, so just be honest. You can buy another copy for your friend.

1. _____ I believe other people should know what I want and give it to me. If you have to ask, it's not worth getting.

2. _____ I don't understand why others can't give back the way I give to them. I am often disappointed when others don't show up for me.

3. _____ I accept food, gifts, and even a friendly kiss that I don't want, rather than tell people no and hurt their feelings.

4. _____ I always hug or touch everyone to let them know I care. Or, hugging and touching even those I love is uncomfortable.

5. _____ I never look a gift horse in the mouth. I'll take anything you give me. Or, I often try to get others involved in making money pursuits that benefit me.

6. _____ I would never make a major decision without (your mate's name)'s permission. Or, I make every major decision myself, even when I am in a significant relationship.

7. _____ I abuse myself in one or more of the following ways: food, alcohol, drugs, cigarettes, abusive relationships, unsafe sex, compulsively working, cleaning, or being constantly busy and on the go most of the time.

8. _____ I am very open and tell people whatever is on my mind, even if it's hurtful. Or, I never share my real feelings with anyone.

9. _____ I feel an intimate bond with people the moment we meet.

10. _____ I often or have often in the past gone to bed with people on the first date.

11. _____ I don't enjoy sex, but I do it for my partner.

12. _____ People can walk all over me before I realize they are doing it. I expect them to be as nice to me as I am to them.

13. _____ People often tell me I expect too much from them.

14. _____ I often feel people take more from me than they are willing to give.

15. _____ I often get close to people only to have them leave. Or, I feel that I often need to leave.

16. _____ I often discuss negative feelings about my lover with a friend—or about one friend with another without having gone to him or her directly first.

17. _____ There are many kinds of information or teachings that I refuse to consider for myself.

18. _____ If (your mate's name) says I was being needy, (rude, weak, sexy, etc.), then I must have been acting that way.

19. _____ I often don't know if I have the *right* to do certain things or feel certain ways.

20. _____ I often feel I have the right to meddle in my lover's affairs or other people's affairs, even though they are adults.

21. _____ I can be convinced to support or tell a lie even when it hurts me inside to do so.

22. _____ I feel parents, employers, friends, lovers, spouses, adult children owe me, so I expect them to treat me in special ways they don't treat others.

23. _____ When something is going wrong, I often feel that I am the one who creates the unhappiness or problems.

24. _____ Like a dog with a bone, I obsess about problems until they are solved.

25. _____ My level of fear can be overwhelming and uncontrollable. Healing issues from the past is a terrifying idea.

26. _____ I often tell people what they should be doing.

27. _____ When bad things happen, I always feel guilty.

28. _____ The idea that someone could love me just for me is foreign.

29. _____ I often feel as if I am not "in" my body.

30. _____ I can emotionally "leave" when things get tough.

31. _____ I am known as either a rescuer for my friends or as unavailable and cold.

32. _____ A lot of my friends are into activities of which I don't necessarily approve.

33. _____ I have been physically, sexually, or verbally abused a number of times.

34. _____ I usually get very close to a person quickly. I then have to take space or I feel engulfed.

35. _____ When an authority figure tells me to do something, I always do it. Or, I always feel defensive or resentful.

36. _____ I have accepted unwanted lunch or dinner invitations from people rather than tell them no and hurt their feelings.

37. _____ I am friends with some people just because they want me to be their friend, not because I like them.

38. _____ I have given money to people who spend it on things of which I disapprove.

39. _____ There is someone in my life whom I enable to be an alcoholic, a drug user, or an abusive person.

40. _____ I often make commitments to myself I don't keep.

41. _____ When I make commitments to others I often have to change them, cancel them, or I arrive late.

42. _____ I allow my family to treat me or my lover in disrespectful, dishonoring ways. Or, I treat my family in disrespectful, dishonoring ways. After all, they are my family.

43. _____ I often lie and tell people things such as I'm busy when I'm not, I'm not home when I am, or other white lies that make life easier.

44. _____ If criticized, I crumble inside and feel terrible. Or, I become defensive and respond with anger or distance.

45. _____ Some part of me always feels like a failure, a bad person or the guilty one in difficult circumstances.

46. _____ My lover/significant other knows little about my real feelings.

47. _____ I am seldom able to find time to do the things I love to do most.

48. _____ When I am not the center of attention I feel rejected. Or, when I am the center of attention, I feel scared.

49. _____ I get my greatest sense of self-esteem through work, sex, my looks, or achievements.

50. _____ I can hurt myself or allow others to hurt me physically and dissociate from the pain.

Once you have taken this test, ask someone close to you to take it for you as well. Then compare your perception of yourself with the perception others have of you.

Count the number of checkmarks and see if any of the categories below apply to you. Remember, no one fits perfectly into any category because we are all so different. No matter which category you fall into, everyone can learn to establish boundaries. No matter how badly yours may have been broken, it is still possible for you to heal.

## 0-6

You have a pretty solid set of boundaries and a good sense of yourself. Congratulations. Since you know how to respect boundaries, you can help those people in your life who have boundary issues by being a good role model. Most importantly, share your knowledge with others through your actions, especially the young people around you so they don't have problems as adults.

## 6-11

You may have grown up in an environment in which one or more parents was dysfunctional or emotionally absent. This could have been due to hardship or simply because they did not have the tools for being good parents. You may have gotten very few messages, or confusing or conflicting messages, about your value or worth. Your parents were not as emotionally present as you needed them to be. In some ways you may feel you lost your childhood and grew up too fast, or perhaps you feel you are still trying to grow up, now as an adult. You may be trying to make yourself feel safe by being in control of your external world and everyone around you much of the time. The tools you are about to get in this book, which your parents probably wished they had been able to give you, will make your process much safer and more exciting.

## 12-20

You may have grown up in an environment with alcoholic or otherwise dysfunctional parents. You learned to get what you want and avoid any conflict by diligently being aware of everything that was going on with everyone else all the time. You learned quickly to put everyone else's interests and needs first. In fact, it's hard for you to know what you're feeling, even when asked, because you are focused so intently on others and their needs or feelings. You can deliberately "zone out." You may do anything to avoid conflict. It may feel as if it has been difficult for you to even want to be here in the past. Don't worry. You will get the tools you need now to feel safe in the process and get the focus back on you.

## 21-30

You may have been raised in an abusive environment, even if you don't call it that. You seldom tell anyone your real feelings, and deep, connected intimacy may scare you. You often take space, or leave either physically or emotionally before you can get left. Intimacy may seem frightening because your first intimate relationships with care-givers may have resulted in your feeling abandoned or being abused. You may feel it's safer to be a loner and keep your feelings to yourself. Secretly you may long for someone to be fully present with you, yet the prospect feels frightening. This conflict may feel constant and ongo-ing. Now you will be able to create safety for yourself, perhaps for the first time. You will soon have the ability to create deep intimacy and meaningful relationships.

## 31-40

You may have survived abuse over long periods of time, perhaps continuing well into your childhood and adult years. Since adulthood, you may have selected abusive people as partners. You may feel as if you could actually die when people leave you or when your relationships end. You may be terrified of being alone and at the same time terrified of being too close. You may even tell yourself relationships just aren't in the cards for you this time around because they are just too hard or dangerous. You no longer have to hold on to that belief. With the tools you are about to receive, you too can have successful relationships and loving intimacy. If you are a man who has been sexually abused and have not worked to resolve the anger, you may feel your rage or a need to distance, especially after intimacy, and not understand why. If you are a woman with unresolved abuse, you may feel you are obligated to be sexual, even when you do not wish to, or you may choose not to feel anything when you are being sexual.

## 41-50

You may have survived extreme abuse verbally, emotionally, physi-cally, or sexually, beginning in infancy and continuing throughout your childhood and adult years. It's hard for you to believe that you really have rights or that healthy relationships are possible. You hide your feelings and are secretive or fearful most of the time. You too can learn to create healthy boundaries and begin to have healthy relationships in your life, perhaps for the first time. You may owe it to yourself to do this work with a qualified therapist who can support you in resolving some of your past. The fact that you survived tells me that you are creative and intelligent and deserve the best support possible. Consider giving that support to yourself in the most loving way.

Everyone can learn to create healthy boundaries. So no matter what your score, you are about to make a great discovery about safety. Boundaries are your key to safety. If you did check some of the statements, congratulate yourself for being honest, and let's work together to help you understand boundaries and create some new healthy ones.

Now take a deep breath and blow it out. Knowing that you have boundary issues is the first step toward fixing them and creating deeper connections, deeper healing, and more love in your life.

## Understanding Boundaries

We live in a world full of boundaries. **Boundaries are lines, seen or unseen, that define the limits of things.** Cities are divided by city limits or boundaries. Borders or boundaries also divide states and countries.

In human terms, we are obliged to respect certain boundaries at work. The number of hours we are required to spend at work or at school is a familiar boundary. The home we live in is considered a residential boundary, because it establishes the limits in which we dwell and we expect them not to be violated.

Sometimes dates and times can be used as deadlines or boundaries, such as in the case of our taxes being due by April 15 or your lunch break ending by 1 P.M. Judicial or legal boundaries and limits of jurisdiction bind courts of law. Certain principles or standards of ethical conduct bind different professionals. All of these limits, both seen and unseen, can be considered boundaries.

Boundaries also allow us to see each other as individuals, separate from each other with different paths to spiritual oneness, different lessons, and different purposes. Boundaries were created by Spirit based on free will. Spirit respects your boundaries by allowing you to make your own choices about your growth and process. Boundaries help you and me accept differences. They allow each individual to travel his or her own path, as he or she sees fit, just as Spirit does for each of us. This model set forth by Spirit says we each have a right to our own choices and processes, and that no one, not even God, should make those choices for us. To do so would steal our personal opportunities for growth and the joy that comes from our individual choices. Would you give up a single lesson you have learned in life, even the hard ones? I think not. Even the hardest lessons have brought us to the place, the person, we are now. They have given us valuable information about ourselves and how to live life better.

*Everything is in your best interest, including the hard lessons!*

## How Boundaries Start Getting Broken

For us to grow into healthy grown-ups with healthy boundaries, we need a few basic things. We need parents or caregivers who provide a caring, nurturing environment in which we can explore, establish, and expand our own limits. We need encouragement, support, and validation for our growth and accomplishments. We need a space in which we can express our intelligence and creativity and receive support, positive mirroring, and appreciation. We need kind, consistent, continuous guidance that sets healthy, respectful limits and boundaries without shame, blame, or humiliation. And we need to see parents, teachers, corporate leaders, and public figures around us living in ways that provide good role models for these principles. In other words, we need role models who have good boundaries and who respect ours.

In this kind of healthy environment we begin to internalize healthy boundaries. It's as simple as this. If you were loved and respected as a child, you grow into being an adult who both expects and gives love and respect. If you were abused as a child, you grow into an adult who either expects or seeks abuse, or you abuse yourself or others. Every message you receive from birth instills some belief about yourself as to whether you are valuable and worthy of respect. Society's judgment of our lifestyle is a boundary violation. That judgment implies that we do not have a right to exist as we are, love who we wish, and be respected by our neighbors. The implication is there is something inherently wrong with us and our choice. That is a spiritual violation of our right to be exactly who we are and love whomever we choose.

## Boundaries Get Broken at an Early Age

Each day, from the moment of our birth, as we grow, thousands of new messages about boundaries come to us from caregivers and parents. If we have loving caregivers, we will learn that certain boundaries are for our own protection. For instance, we may not be able to play in the yard or walk across the street without someone to accompany us. We may be asked to swim in the shallow end of the pool at first.

Parents who need to establish firm boundaries can do so by implementing a system of choices. This, again, is exactly what Spirit has offered to us: choices, abundant choices, all of which have results and consequences, not punishment. Spirit does not punish us; It never has. Spirit allows us to experience the consequences of our own choices so that we may learn to make better ones in life.

"David, you can go to that movie you wanted to see this weekend, provided you spend either tonight or tomorrow night cleaning your room. You decide."

Notice that boundaries are set for David—you can go if you clean your room—in a nonintrusive manner that doesn't break his boundaries or spirit. Instead, they honor the free choice of the child within healthy limits. Compare this to parents who barge into their children's rooms, start throwing toys out, and yell at them for being stupid and sloppy.

We create positive internal boundaries every time we are encouraged, as children, to make choices for ourselves. Those choices can be about when to clean our room, what to wear, or which toys we play with. Then, if those choices are encouraged and respected, we get the message that our choices and, therefore, our boundaries, can be respected and trusted.

*True masters teach all whose lives they touch that they too are masters.*

Mom and dad may get angry with each other, and yet, they love us and make it very clear their problems are not our fault. By making sure they don't let their anger spill over into their transactions with us, we learn we are not responsible for other people's feelings. Parents can get upset and still love us. This is how we learn that feelings need not be dangerous.

From these positive life experiences we learn it's OK to have feelings. Feelings are safe. We also learn feelings that are processed from within healthy boundaries are not destructive. Our space, body, and emotions are worth respecting. In other words, we start internalizing more healthy boundaries. Healthy boundaries are those that respect and honor ourselves, our feelings, and our needs. They also respect and honor the other person, his or her feelings and needs.

*The creation of boundaries provided the first experience*
*of honoring through free will.*

Children don't have to get their way to have their boundaries respected. For instance, if you tell a child, "I know you really want to go in swimming today and it's making you very sad that you can't. Maybe it will be warmer in a few days." The message is that it's OK to have your feelings even if you can't have your way.

If your caregivers are not so loving, you begin to learn from the *lack* of boundaries in your environment that the world is not such a safe place. For instance, when mom or dad is unable to control their feelings of anger, no matter who they may be angry with, and they hit you or scream at you, you learn about the lack of boundaries. You learn your boundaries are not to be respected. Unfortunately, after you grow up, sometimes even without meaning to do so, you pass those same messages on to your own children or partners. Because your boundaries were not respected, you grew up without training or the proper role models for how to respect your children's or partner's boundaries. If your example was one of disrespect for boundaries, that is what you will take with you into your own parenting process, because that is all you know. **Children whose boundaries are broken grow up to be adults who either break the boundaries of others or who allow their own boundaries to continue being broken until healing occurs.**

On and on, generation after generation, the vicious cycle is perpetuated. So here we are today, living in a world without respect for boundaries.

You may be someone who is not even sure what a boundary is or when your boundaries are being broken. Don't feel bad about being confused. There's a good reason for your confusion. When your boundaries have been broken often, your sensitivity to this issue becomes deadened, and it's easy to get confused.

Some of you might not even feel safe unless someone is breaking your boundaries, because that's what you were accustomed to experiencing as a child. The intimacy created through broken boundaries, such as during sexual abuse, might be the only kind of "closeness" you've ever experienced. You might not feel safe unless you are in an abusive situation—you know how to handle that. There is a vast difference, however, between the kind of illicit, secretive intimacy created during abuse and the kind of healthy intimacy that respects you and your boundaries. **Having boundaries does not mean you will be less close to those you love. In fact, you will be able to create even deeper intimacy because you have solid boundaries.** Boundaries make it possible for you to feel safe about exploring deeper connections. When you have healthy boundaries, you won't feel concerned about being engulfed or abandoned. Healthy boundaries make it possible for you to feel safe about exploring your feelings and denials.

## What's It Like to Be Without Boundaries?

Without boundaries, you have difficulty telling which emotions belong to you and which belong to other people. It's no wonder the idea of being deeply connected in a loving relationship could be frightening. For instance, if someone you care about cries or feels sad, you may immediately feel sad as well. You actually *feel* your friend's feelings and process her emotions for her. This is not a healthy, empathic understanding of what she is experiencing. Rather, this is called "being enmeshed" with your friend and her feelings. An empathic understanding would allow you to *understand* her feelings and *be supportive* while she processed them and worked them out *herself*. Without boundaries, you cannot separate yourself from the pain of those people you love. Their pain feels like your pain.

Without boundaries, you also have confusion about which issues are yours and which belong to other people: You do not experience a healthy separation between yourself and others. For example, your friend Angie is having a fight with her sister about being a lesbian. Angie's sister yelled at her and told her she is no longer a member of the family. Who wants to rush over to Angie's sister's bright and early the next morning to tell her off? Not Angie! You are the one who takes on Angie's battle. This inappropriate response is your boundary issue.

People who do not have good boundaries often fight other people's battles for them or get involved in other people's business without being invited. People without good boundaries are unable to keep confidences; they are not trustworthy. Some people have difficulty containing their own emotions and keeping their own personal information and business private. I am always able to tell which clients have had their boundaries broken on their first visit to my office. Without even knowing who I am or whether I can be trusted, they immediately launch into telling me the most intimate details of their life, without a second thought.

Boundary issues are also rampant between adult parents and their adult children. Many adult children feel responsible for the difficult times their parents experienced as young people. Many of us feel responsible for the grief and self-judgment our parents feel when we tell them we are gay. We carry the guilt and feel as if we must make up for those hard times. Some of us feel the fact that we even exist made our parents' life harder. So now, as adults, we feel responsible for making sure our parents are happy and have all they need. This guilt response is reflective of misplaced responsibility. Wanting to give to your parents because you love them is one thing. Uniting as a family to help provide for, or add to, the quality of life for your parents is a great gift. However, trying to make up for the fact that you were born, or gay, or that your parents endured certain hardships is about your own poor boundaries. Those choices were theirs, and so are the lessons.

On the other end of this continuum are the parents who refuse to stop running their adult children's lives. They feel they have the right to comment on or become involved in every decision their children make. Let's be clear here. Once a child reaches the age of 18, parents are no longer in a position to *demand* anything. You can *offer* a great deal, including advice—if that advice is requested. You have 18 years to fill up your child and share with him or her all the things you know. As parents, you have already had your opportunity to learn from your process and choices. Adult kids also need the space to find their own way. Yes, you can give support. But from the moment your child turns 18, spiritually you become a guest in their lives, and they a guest in yours. They have made a choice to learn all the blessed lessons about having gay parents, and they get the gifts. You should act as a guest offering your knowledge out of love, not out of a sense of entitlement or misplaced responsibility.

I remember the day I came to that realization. I was worried about my son, who was going on a dune buggy trip in the desert. During a phone conversation before he left, he made some enlightened statement, as he often does, about an issue I was dealing with. Suddenly I had the overwhelming feeling that the person on the other end of the line with me was not just my son. He was an incredible spirit that I had been entrusted to raise. His spirit was no doubt as ageless as my own, and from that moment on I have always seen my adult children as equals who are due great honor. My children and I respect each other's boundaries, and we feel blessed to have chosen to be in each other's lives.

In extreme cases, without boundaries, you may even find it hard to tell which life is yours. That is, without boundaries, you might believe you could literally die if someone you loved died because you have become so enmeshed with him or her that you no longer seem separate.

We each have several kinds of personal boundaries:

- **Energetic boundaries** define our space.
- **Psychological boundaries** involve our emotions, mind and thought processes.
- **Physical/sexual** boundaries involve our body and sexual activity.
- **Spiritual boundaries** involve our spirit and right to be valued for who we are.

Even if you feel you did not, as a child, experience extreme boundary breaking, this information is important because at some point you are likely to encounter someone who did experience this kind of abuse. With this information, you will have the tools to lovingly honor his or her process and create a safe space in which they may heal. Unfortunately, I believe at least 70% of women and 45% of men have been abused in some way if you include issues of neglect. Your partner, your friend, your parent, or even your sibling may have experienced some form of abuse, even if you did not. And even implications that we are somehow damaged or broken because we are gay is a core violation of our boundaries.

## Energetic Boundaries

You have an **energetic boundary** that defines your space in the world. Have you ever stood in line at the grocery store when the man or woman behind you pushed so close as you wrote your check that you felt agitated and perhaps even violated? Without ever touching you, the person was encroaching on your energetic boundary.

You hide when Aunt Jane comes over because she talks right in your face, too loudly. She interrupts, acting as if you don't exist when you speak. Your mother implies, without ever directly saying so, that your perceptions or actions are somehow incorrect. These people are not respecting your energetic boundary or your special space. No one wants to be crowded out or treated as if he doesn't exist. All of us know people who behave this way.

You'll feel this kind of boundary being broken when you speak and the other person doesn't listen, when you feel crowded out of line or bumped into by some unconscious person. You'll feel it when people say things about you behind your back to people you know, secretly hoping you'll hear it.

I have a friend whom I like a great deal, but I choose not to spend time with her because whenever we talk, she is always on the run, on her cell phone en route to some appointment or on her way to some meeting at her office. She treats everyone this way. It is impossible to create a meaningful relationship with her. She has obvious boundary issues that are reflected by packing her day so full of appointments and meetings that no one in her life gets treated with dignity.

I once saw a couple who came into my office for therapy. One partner sat down on the couch, and his lover invariably sat so close to him that he was nearly sitting on top of him. He never even noticed his partner was backed completely into the corner of the couch trying to make room for himself. Do I need to tell you this man was feeling totally engulfed, constantly caught in the feelings that he repressed? And their issue was about? You guessed it, boundaries.

Your energetic boundary defines your space or place of existence. Respect for this boundary helps you feel you have a right to exist in the world. That's where the expressions "back off" or "give me my space" come from.

If your energetic boundary or space was not respected as a child, you probably internalized that lack of respect as a message about your lack of worth. Not being noticed or respected made you feel invisible, as if you didn't count. Today you probably have difficulty asking for what you need from others or from life. You may have difficulty feeling you deserve to have better things in life, better career positions, better friends, and a good mate. You might feel like others have more rights than you do. Perhaps you give up easily when it comes down to fighting for what you want or need.

When your presence is not acknowledged in a positive way, you have no way of knowing you are valued or important. You have no reference point for how you should be present to others or how to treat others. You become a person who has no awareness of how to respect another person's presence and space. When you first begin a relationship with someone new, energetic boundaries are the boundaries that usually get tested the most, because you are learning to live together and *share* space. Actually, this is true even if you don't literally live together, because you are still learning where each of your personal boundaries is in regard to the need for time together and the need for space apart.

## Psychological Boundaries

You also have **psychological boundaries**. If you were somehow negated, discounted, or ignored, you had your boundaries broken by emotional/psychological abuse. You might have been told, "Stop crying, or I'll give you a reason to cry," or "I don't care how you feel, do it my way." " Stop acting like a sissy." "You have to wear dresses and act like a girl." If you and your emotions were constantly put down or negated, you may never have had the opportunity to develop self-esteem. Self-esteem, self-respect, and self-love are all generated from within us individually, as adults, but they must be first role modeled by our caretakers.

Your parenting may have included threats of punishment or retaliation. You may have been confined until you were made to agree. You may have been tricked or put into double-bind situations about your gayness or you were abused with statements such as, "If you tell, it will hurt your mother." Or even if there was no abuse, you may have been told not to cry, express your feelings, or ask to have your needs met because it might upset one parent or the other.

You may have been in a situation where no one said bad things to you. It could be that no one said anything to you, and through sheer neglect you were devalued and emotionally dismissed. Your presence was not reflected back to you in a positive way, and, therefore, you had no way of knowing you were valued and important. You may have been a wonderful, talented kid, but if there wasn't anyone in your life to let you know that, you are probably still fighting with issues of self-worth. This kind of neglect results in the disintegration of any trust in your own worth and value.

If your emotional or psychological boundaries were broken, you may get confused about whose fault it is. You might feel it's always your fault and doubt your own truth or reality. Perhaps you discount your own feelings and emotions or get fragmented when under fire emotionally. Maybe you emotionally check out when you feel over-loaded or  overwhelmed, or you simply choose not share your thoughts, ideas, and perceptions. You might be overly critical of others' feelings and thoughts or feel unsafe to the point of experiencing ongoing terror.

If your psychological boundaries were broken, as an adult, you may choose friends and partners who do not value or respect your feelings. As adults, you may seek the same kind of people and treatment you experienced as a child. You might find you instantly feel bonded to people, as if you have known them forever or are irresistibly drawn to them. This attraction may be an unconscious draw on your part to a person exactly like one or both of your parents. The comfort you feel may simply be that his or her energy is familiar to that which you experienced as a child. The result can be that you enter a relationship and create a dynamic similar to the one you experienced with your parents.

Some people seek mates who are the exact opposite of their parents, so as to avoid repeating the same family scenarios. You may mistakenly feel you are safe because the person you choose is nothing like your parents. In some cases this is a good choice. If you aren't careful, however, you could be choosing a whole new set of problems.

If your psychological boundaries were not respected when you were young, you might not even know what your own feelings are most of the time because you are usually focused on everyone else's feelings and needs. You become "other directed." You may have learned this as a survival tool. By keeping track of what everyone else was doing, saying, and feeling all the time, you may have been able to stay safe or avoid crisis. You are an excellent caretaker for everyone but yourself. This is how we become codependent. We take care of others in the hope that if we just give enough, do enough, they will in turn give back to us. In almost every situation you feel bad and wrong and know that if *anyone* is at fault, it is no doubt *you*.

## Physical or Sexual Boundaries

If you were physically or sexually abused, your **physical or sexual boundaries** were violated. Since this is not a book about abuse, I will not spend a great deal of time discussing or describing these different kinds of abuse. It's not that the issue is unimportant, but because there are many good books already written on this issue. I will, however, say one thing I believe with all my heart. In the gay and lesbian community, we often perceive the sexual interaction of an adult with a young boy as an acceptable introduction to homosexuality. It is not. There is a power differential between a child and adult that precludes equal choice in these situations. Children do not have the cognitive ability, language skills, or emotional ability to process sexuality at a young age. Instead, without this maturity, they fragment, and the pain left inside directs many of their decisions in life. Because choice is not an element of the process, many men grow up to believe they have no choice when it comes to sexual expectations from partners. In addition, because sex is introduced to many children out of the context of a committed relationship, they have a difficult time as adults understanding the need for or the gifts of monogamy as a path to deep spiritual intimacy.

To help you understand how to deal with childhood boundary violations such as abuse, it's important to realize that today, as an adult, you may have trouble tolerating loud noises or rapid physical movements from others. You could feel hypervigilant about who's in the room and where they are at all times, or never feel safe or let down your guard. You could numb out in order to stop physical pain or leave your body when you feel at risk or during sexual activity.

Sexual abuse includes any manual, oral, or genital sexual contact or any other explicit sexual behavior that a person imposes on a child or adolescent. This includes making sexual movies or taking pictures of children, talking about sexual details in front of children for gratification, and inappropriate nudity or sexual acts in front of children. It even includes emotional sexual abuse, such as when a mother sexualizes a relationship with her son by encouraging him to be provocative or a spousal substitute. It also includes circumstances in which a mother or father seeks sexual admiration or activity from a child.

## Spiritual Boundaries

Some of you, as children, had your **spiritual boundaries** broken through degradation and humiliating attempts to break your spirit. This differs from psychological or emotional boundary breaking, during which your emotions and feelings are invalidated. When spiritual boundaries are broken, your very existence is in question or jeopardy. Perhaps you had parents who were jealous of you, hated you, engulfed you, or made you their reason for living. Maybe you were told you were the reason mom and dad's bad marriage didn't break up, or, worse yet, you were the reason for mom and dad living. If it hadn't been for you, they would have left either their marriage or the planet long ago. In other words, **you existed only for their needs and were not valued just for being you.**

As an example, Alison's father was an alcoholic, and her mother was weak and dependent. When Alison was a child her mother kept her at her side constantly. Fear and denial ruled her mother, and she never went anywhere without Alison. Nonverbal messages let Alison know that mom was afraid to be alone with her partner. Alison believed she was responsible for her mother's safety and was terrified to leave her even to go to school. She never developed her own sense of self-worth, growing up to be a woman who committed to another woman who abused her emotionally, just as dad had abused mom.

Throughout her adult life, Alison felt disaster was imminent whenever her partner left town on business. Just like her mom's, her life was controlled by fear. Until she was able to clarify and resolve her issues in therapy, she was sure that if she was not at someone's side, either she would cease to exist or something terrible would happen to her loved ones. Her sole job and reason for existing as a child was to make mom safe. Now, as an adult, she seldom experiences her own safety or that of the people she loves unless she is right at their side.

Some of you may have received conscious or unconscious abusive messages from your parents. For example, they may have wished that you didn't exist at all. This message came from your parents' insecurities or perhaps jealousy about the attention you received from one parent or the other. In this case, children learn to draw into themselves and disappear. They do so because they feel their very existence or presence is a threat to either their own survival or the emotional survival of one or the other parent. I have watched many clients who literally lose their breath whenever they are near their mothers and fathers, whom they experienced as trying to suck the very life out them when they were a child. There is a visceral response in their bodies that is as if they believe they must stop existing in the presence of their parents in order to survive. They unconsciously stop breathing normally. An example of this is the sexually abused daughter who withdraws into nonexistence when both mother and father are in the room. The fear is that mother will become aware of the abuse and hate her or the father will see that she is there and abuse her. The message is "don't exist—don't even breathe."

If Mom and Dad had no boundaries and made you responsible for all of their good or bad feelings about themselves, no doubt there has not been a single person with whom you feel complete trust or safety. From the moment you realized your environment was hostile and trying to take the very spirit out of you, you have had to remain protected and closed down to life.

Using the role model of your parents, you may now make others responsible for your good feelings about yourself. When your lover feels good about you, you feel good about yourself. When your lover thinks you are wrong or feels bad about you, your self-worth disintegrates, and you also feel bad about yourself.

> *It is the mind and memory that rush forward to create chaos,*
> *not the reality of "now."*

Spiritual boundary-breaking is most heinous in cases of extreme abuse or ritual abuse. When a child is ritually abused (over and over in the same way) or abused during rituals, she is treated like an object and used physically, sexually, and psychologically for the gratification of others. The child is made to feel she is bad, dispensable, and in some cases, her very life is in danger.

## Positive Boundaries

When our boundaries are respected when we are children, we not only learn we are valuable and lovable, but we also get training right from the start on how to respect other people's boundaries.

Mom says to 5-year-old Annie, "I can see that you are too angry to talk right now, and that's OK. Just let me know when you feel like talking, and I'll listen."

The positive boundary messages in that healthy transaction are:
- You are a respected person who has a right to what you feel. I'm here with you. I understand your feelings.
- It's OK to be angry. Your feelings will be respected.
- No one will punish you or leave you because of what you feel. You are valued even when you are angry.
- You get to have the space you need to feel whatever you feel. I respect your space.

In other words, you are important and so is what you feel. **The message is: I respect you and your boundaries.** When these loving and respectful messages are internalized, they become the reference points for how we learn to respect another person's boundaries. Having your boundaries respected at home as a child has a wonderful impact on you in later life as an adult. At work you hear your supervisor, Davis, say he really hates the way you did a certain job. If you're an adult who has positive boundaries, you can then say, "I'm sorry to hear you feel that way. Why don't you tell me more about why you feel that way, and we'll try to correct the problem." Without good boundaries, you may slither away, feel you have failed, and start looking for a new job.

The terrific news about being a human being is that **it is never too late to begin learning.** As you continue to learn about and understand boundaries, not only will you feel safer and freer in the world, but everyone around you benefits as well. With a better understanding of your own boundaries, you begin to perceive everyone else's boundaries differently, and you give them greater respect as well.

*Controlling others is an act of fear, not love.*

## A Word of Caution

First, a little warning. As you learn more about boundaries, at the same time you will also begin to see how often other people break your boundaries. You may be shocked at how many times your boundaries are not acknowledged or respected. You will respond by getting very excited and happy about your new awareness. On the other hand, this new awareness could make you angry. Either way, you don't want to become overzealous about correcting people or telling them you don't like what they are doing, because they won't understand. They will just be acting in the same old way they have been allowed or encouraged to act in the past. In the gay and lesbian community, boundaries are nearly nonexistent because we have very few role models. In most states we don't have the luxury of openly proclaiming our love for each other through public ceremonies that tell the world we have committed to each other. Often long-term couples remain in the closet in bedroom communities where we don't see their successful relationships. So many people in our groups of friends have slept with each other that we lose a sense of real union. And we have moved into the mentality that serial sexuality is our way of life. We do not yet have the awareness that our families are as sacred as any other, and the boundaries of commitment deserve to be honored. We fight for the right to have our relationships, but we often treat them and our partners, both past and present, as unimportant and disposable. As we create better boundaries, the quality and level of integrity in our relationships will also change.

Just take it easy and remember that change comes slowly for most people, and it must come from the inside out, just like love. No doubt you want to make changes in your life in a loving way, both for yourself and others around you. Be gentle! Remember, up until this moment you had unspoken, unconscious contracts with people to let them break your boundaries. They've gotten used to it. Now that you are learning a new way of being in the world, you have to let those close to you know that you are changing those old contracts. You need to do that in a gentle, understanding way.

*Integrity is simply self being true to Self.*

For instance, you may have to tell your friend Mary, "You know, I'm learning some new ways to be more loving with myself, and it's no longer acceptable for me to make lunch engagements that get broken at the last minute. I need at least a day or two notice."

**Another important thing to remember is that boundaries are not walls.** Having walls that keep you from experiencing your own feelings and prevent you from feeling anyone else's is not the same thing as having healthy boundaries. **In fact, if you have walls, you probably don't have good boundaries or you wouldn't need the walls!**

When you have healthy boundaries, you will no longer respond to others out of pain. It will be easier to be present to other people's feelings and stay emotionally attentive without getting involved in unhealthy ways. Your healthy boundaries make it possible while you're hearing their problem for you to know you are:

- not the cause of the problem,
- not at fault,
- not required to fix the problem, and
- not required to take on someone else's pain or trouble just because you choose to be present.

In other words, you can be there for the other person without taking over or fixing his or her problem. Wouldn't you find it easier to be fully present to each other if you didn't have to feel so responsible for taking care of each other's problems? With healthy boundaries, you can be a compassionate presence to whatever is going on with your lover, friends or family. You'll be able to safely determine if it is appropriate to get involved with their issues and how to get involved in a way that is self-honoring and also honoring of their process. You can also easily determine to what extent you wish to be involved.

Having boundaries helps you to be a better friend, partner, and parent, and helps you create deeper and more meaningful healing. Once you have effective, healthy boundaries, you will not feel concerned about becoming engulfed or abandoned. **Boundaries are the number one tool to help you stay present.**

*You find yourself feeling fearful or anxious only when
you have lost trust in yourself or your partner.*

Now let's take a minute to do the following exercise. This exercise may be difficult to do, because I ask you to take a look into your past and see how your boundaries may have been broken as a child. If it is difficult, please be loving with yourself and take your time. If it feels too difficult to do the entire exercise in one sitting, feel free to do a little at a time until you finish.

If the exercise evokes deep feelings and you feel safe enough, just allow yourself to feel your emotions by writing about them, taking time to express them into a tape recorder, or just naturally let them resolve by crying or getting angry. Feelings are natural. If you allow them to surface and be experienced, they will naturally resolve themselves. **Expressing feelings will not make you sick. Not expressing them will. In 16 years of doing therapy, I have never lost a client to a**

**feeling.** When you hold unexpressed feelings in your body or mind for long periods of time, they will surface in the form of physical or emotional illness in an attempt to reach resolution or healing. When you allow feelings to just flow out naturally, they resolve naturally in the process of being felt fully.

*Healing has begun the instant fear is released.*

If you experience emotions that seem out of control or too big to handle, be kind to yourself and get assistance. You will know you have touched upon something very deep if you start to feel small, like a child, if the feelings seem scary or overwhelming, or if you feel afraid to deal with your feelings. Find a good therapist Yes! Shop until you find the right one, and begin working through the feelings that surface with support.

In every city are counseling centers that provide low-fee counseling so that most people who wish to get help can at the very least arrange a few visits. Find one of those centers if your financial considerations require sliding-scale help.

As you do the exercise, remember to breathe. Breathing is a wonderful tool that will assist you in accessing and releasing your emotions. When difficult or painful feelings surface, breathe it out or imagine them releasing on the breath. Stay present. When you want to focus on an emotion you are holding in your body, remember to breathe into it and expand it so you can bring it into focus. Many times, when you think you have nothing to work on emotionally, taking a few deep breaths will bring something to the surface. If you are flooded with intense feelings, stop deep breathing and breathe normally to help contain the feelings and slow down the flow and intensity. If you are working with a partner, take time for both of you to do the next exercise.

## Personal Inventory: Identifying Boundary Patterns

1. In my family, boundaries were: (nonexistent, respected, felt like walls)

2. Write down the ways in which your boundaries were broken as a child:

**Energetic Boundaries** (How your space and/or presence was disrespected or not valued):

**Emotional/Psychological Boundaries** (How your mind, thoughts, sexuality, and feelings were disrespected or not valued):

**Spiritual Boundaries** (How people attempted to break your spirit by invalidating your worth or making you their reason for living):

**Physical Boundaries** (How your body was hurt or not respected):

**Sexual Boundaries** (How you were abused or hurt sexually, including emotional sexual abuse):

3. How did having your boundaries broken as a child make you feel?

4. How have these broken boundaries affected you as an adult?

5. What my parents taught me about boundaries was:

6. The way in which I allow my boundaries to be broken today are: (Give up self or needs, do things I don't want to do, allow abuse)

7. The ways in which I have not respected others' boundaries are:

8. The ways in which you could begin respecting my boundaries are:

9. The ways in which I want to begin respecting your boundaries are:

10. The ways in which I am going to begin respecting my own boundaries are:

11. The ways our relationship will benefit by these changes are:

12. My new awareness about the issues of boundaries is:

Congratulations! The first step toward healing is being able to identify your feelings about what has happened to you and see your past as it was without denial. You have just created a successful healing process for yourself.

Remember, admitting to yourself that something was not quite right in your childhood does not necessarily mean your parents were bad people. Nor does it mean you should be angry with them. If you feel anger, that's fine, and if you don't, that's also fine. In most cases, if your boundaries were broken, it simply means your parents didn't have the tools they needed to be better parents. We are able to give our children only as much as we have been given. Parents who disrespected your boundaries were no doubt children of parents who disrespected their boundaries. You don't need to feel you are betraying your parents or you have to stop loving them simply because you have begun to look realistically at what happened to you. In fact, quite the contrary. You can see them as separate individuals, on their own path, trying to heal their own wounds. They too have a red wagon filled with denial and pain, and they are also on their own spiritual path, doing the work as consciously or unconsciously as they choose.

*We are all children, learning to be enlightened*
*and to manifest Spirit within.*

You have just gotten very present and taken the first step in your healing process of looking at your past without denial. Many of these issues will begin to resolve during your healing experiences. We are talking about them so that you can better understand your responses during your exercises. So now take a breath, blow it out, and let's get right to the job of creating healthy boundaries.

## Creating a Healthy Boundary

It's a good idea to ask a partner to do the following exercises with you, because working with someone often makes it easier for you to see and feel where your boundaries are and how they affect you.

Find a quiet place to work, and then settle into comfortable positions, preferably on a carpeted floor or bed. For the first few times, use a flat surface so that you can delineate definite boundaries. You do that by literally drawing or imprinting a circle around yourself that shows where you think your boundaries are located on the carpet or on the bed. Some of you may have no idea where or what your boundaries are or should be. Don't be discouraged. Draw an imaginary circle around yourself, and begin the process of creating a boundary. Just draw it with your finger. Make the imprint in the surface so that you both can really see where each of your boundaries is imprinted. This short exercise is going to teach you a great deal about yourself. Once you can literally see your boundaries, it becomes easier to envision them when you are doing your daily activities. The placement of your boundary, and how you respond to each other and each other's boundaries, can tell you a great deal about your dynamic together. It can tell you why you may be having communication problems or problems being respected. So each of you draws your boundary now.

OK, take a minute to learn some things about yourself in this very first step. Doing this exercise may have felt a bit contrived or uncomfortable, but it is the first step to creating healthy boundaries.

Is the imprint of your boundary nearly invisible, very light, or hard to see? If you are not sure where your boundaries are, how will it be possible for others to respect them?

Have you drawn a small circle around yourself right next to your body? Perhaps that's how you protected yourself as a child. You made yourself as inconspicuous as possible or got little and went inside yourself to be safe. As an adult, you are probably a person who still doesn't give yourself enough room to feel your own feelings. You still draw in on yourself to protect yourself. Others may have to get right in your face to have an effect on you.

Draw a larger circle and see how it feels to give yourself more space. Take some breaths and continue to adjust the size of your boundary until it feels as if you have enough space. You want enough space to feel your own feelings and enough distance to feel safe while you experience your partner's feelings. Don't be concerned with how your partner reacts to your taking more space. For the moment, just be concerned about yourself. Talk about the feelings that arise as you each adjust your boundary, but don't acquiesce to what your partner needs or give up what you need to feel comfortable.

*If your boundary is very close to your body, you may shut down or close in when you are angry or afraid.*

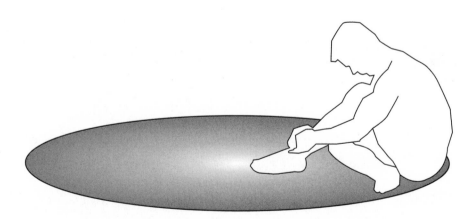

*If your boundary is very wide and expansive, you may distance yourself or leave yourself emotionally in order to feel safe.*

*A good boundary gives you enough space to feel yourself and your own feelings as well as those of your partner.*

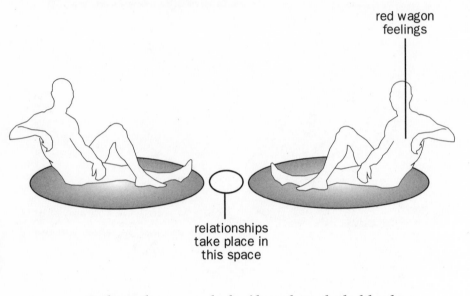

red wagon
feelings

relationships
take place in
this space

*Codependence or a lack of boundaries looks like this:*

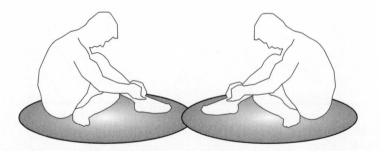

Without good boundaries, I can easily make you responsible for my good feelings about myself, my sense of safety, and my worth. This is not intimacy. This is enmeshment. If your partners leave, they take your good feelings about yourself with them. If they treat you as if you are not lovable, you begin to feel unlovable. Whole, healthy relationships are created by whole individuals who both have good boundaries. This enmeshed state can often be mistaken for being in love or being very loving, and we may erroneously think that is how it ought to be.

*This is called "your way or my way."*

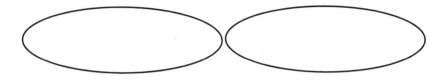

*This is called "I can't live without you." If you think I am lovable, then I feel lovable. If you think I am bad, I feel bad about myself.*

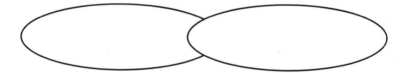

Did you draw a wide, expansive circle? Then perhaps you are a person who needs a lot of room in order to feel safe. Did you feel crowded or engulfed as a child by someone who had feelings or needs that were always bigger than yours? Did you feel there was never a safe space that was specifically yours? Adjust the space you've given yourself until it feels comfortable. Make sure you give yourself enough room to feel safe and yet you stay close enough to be connected to your partner energetically.

Did you draw your boundary right over your partner's space? Maybe you don't feel safe unless you are connected to or right next to your partner. Maybe you are not quite conscious enough about where other people's boundaries begin and end. This is how people who are codependent feel. **Codependency is nothing more than a fancy term for a lack of boundaries.**

A couple of words about the very confusing issue of codependency. People have begun to believe that if you simply help someone to do something in an act of kindness, you are codependent. Not true. **Codependency means "I am going to do something for you in order to get some need of my own met in an indirect way."** For instance, I will make a great dinner for you on Friday so you'll be in a good mood when I ask you to take me to the symphony in the park on Sunday. Why not just express your desire directly to attend the event on Sunday? This is a boundary issue.

Many people who have boundary issues or who are codependent seek mates who need fixing or are in some ways less evolved than they are. They think they will fix their mate and the partner will in turn be so grateful that he or she will never leave. In some cases, you may feel if you just give enough, be there enough, or support your partner enough, in time he or she will be willing to give back to you some of the good feelings and needs you never had met as a child. Usually this is not so. In fact, people who are always doing the giving seldom get their own needs met. In reality, it's one method of staying in control, but not a good way to create equal relationships where both mates have what they need. People with good boundaries don't need to be manipulative. They simply ask for what they need from an "I" space. People with good boundaries are not codependent.

Gaining understanding about your boundary during this exercise is a major contribution to real healing and helping your relationships work. Boundary problems are the first place where most couples and friends have issues that get them into trouble. Let's look at an example.

An overbearing, neurotic father whose needs were bigger than life engulfed Sally as a child. The only way Sally could think about her own needs was to leave the house and separate from dad. So, at a very young age, Sally began to reinforce her belief that the only way she could survive was to get away and be by herself very often. Sally then moved in with Paige. Paige's mom worked all of her life, and she could never get enough time or attention from her in order to feel valued and important. The only times Paige's value was reflected back to her were during the infrequent occasions when her mom took a few minutes to play with her at night after work. Even then she was tired and didn't have much energy. Paige's mom was emotionally drained and unavailable.

Now this couple moves in together, and guess what? Sally still occasionally needs to take some space in order to get her thoughts straight. Every time she does this, however, Paige feels abandoned and becomes clingy and insecure about her leaving. This kicks up all of Sally's fears about not ever having her needs treated as important, so she begins to feel engulfed, in the same way that she did as a child. This, then, makes her push Paige away even further. Even more of Paige's childhood insecurities are then triggered, and she becomes even more fearful and anxious. Feeling Sally distance from her, she reaches out for her with more intensity. Get the picture? They are both operating out of their individual denial in a vicious cycle.

This push-pull dynamic for attaining closeness became a major issue in Sally and Paige's relationship. In many cases, the individuals in relationships like this one break up, thinking their mate is too needy or engulfing. If this couple understood each other's boundaries and issues—how and why they exist—they could easily negotiate giving each other exactly what each needs. No one would have to leave. Let's see how that might look.

Pretend now that Sally and Paige understand their boundary issue, and let's see how they could handle themselves differently. Sally could tell Paige, "I'm not leaving. I'll be in the den for the next couple of hours to take some space, and after that let's have some quality time together."

Paige could then relax, knowing she is not being abandoned. She could support Sally's need for space, knowing it is Sally's own childhood issue and not about her at all. After some time Paige would probably stop needing assurance from Sally as she experiences her *not leaving*.

Sally, in turn, could understand and, therefore, support Paige, knowing her needs for closeness and reassurance are really not about wanting to engulf or control her, but rather about her own childhood wounds. She might say, "I'm going to take some space this afternoon, and then tonight let's spend some alone, close time."

Now let's get back to you. Where's your boundary in relationship to your partner's? Did you draw your circle/boundary right over your partner's space? Are you sitting close to your partner because you think that's what he or she needs you to do? Check in with yourself to see if you are sitting where you really feel most comfortable.

Next check to see if where you are sitting is also comfortable for your partner. Negotiate positions that feel comfortable to both of you. If that's not possible, for now just move to a position that feels right to you. Later we'll discuss how to give both of you what you need.

You may feel like asking your partner to move back a bit or you may want to adjust your own position. Remember, as adjustments are made, check in with each other to see what feelings arise as you change the amount of space and the boundaries between you. You may be like Paige and experience feelings of abandonment when your partner takes space for herself. Or you could be like Sally and feel engulfed if your partner sits too close. These are childhood issues you can each work on together or independently in your process, once you recognize and understand them.

If you were abandoned as a child, you probably cling to people and hold on to them too tightly. If you were engulfed as a child, you proba- bly push people away and don't feel safe unless you take a lot of room to breathe. **These are important issues and valuable information you can exchange in the first few minutes of this boundary exercise. These critical pieces of information can make a world of difference in your effort to create successful relationships and stay present to each other and yourself.**

Once you understand the kinds of issues you each bring to your mate relationship from your respective families of origin, you can be more respectful and supportive of each other's needs without feeling resentful.

> *The most important factor to achieving spiritual greatness*
> *is allowance.*

We all come to our relationships with a red wagon full of our issues. Once you understand this, you can stop taking everything so personal- ly and begin to negotiate what is best for each of you. Each of you comes into relationships with childhood hopes, fears, disappointments, and pain. Everything you hear and everything you say is filtered through your red wagon of pain and denial. In other words, if your part- ner tells you she is lonely and if you were made to feel responsible for everyone else's feelings as a child, you will automatically react to that statement as if it is your fault. It's not your fault! No doubt her feelings of loneliness are coming from some childhood experience in her own red wagon.

Let's look at another example. If you and three of your friends were each standing on a different corner of an intersection, and suddenly a lit- tle girl pulling a red wagon with a cute puppy in it stepped into the cross- walk and proceeded to cross the street, you would each have a different reaction. One friend might think, "Isn't that adorable!" Another might think, "My God, where is that child's mother?" Another might think, "Boy, I hope that puppy stays in the wagon," and you might run to the aid of the child in fear for her safety. Each response comes from some childhood experience of our own, and each is different. We can't know what each other's response is going to be, nor should we, because we each have different life experiences. A big mistake we make in relationships is to have the expectation that our partners should feel as we do. How can they? They have a different set of issues and whole different set of life experiences! They also have a different set of feelings and denials about those issues. Once you understand where your individual childhood wounds are, you can begin to heal these issues, which in turn brings you closer together. It's all about boundaries.

Amazing, isn't it? All of this new information can come from drawing that simple boundary around yourself, talking with your partner, and beginning to understand the nature of your own and your partner's boundaries. That's a lot to learn from one simple little circle! Now take a break and a breath.

## Taking Responsibility

We all come into relationships carrying both the joy and the grief of our childhood with us. It's all piled high in the red wagon we pull right behind us into the relationship. It is filled with all the pain and possibility that we take with us into every relationship. Sometimes we even try to make our childhood issues the responsibility of our partner. Very little spiritual work can be accomplished when this is going on. You may not think you are doing that, but if you are not working on your own issues—such as how you make yourself feel worthy through spending money, doing drugs or participating in other self-destructive behavior—you'd better believe your partner is cleaning up your mess from your childhood. In other words, **if you are not healing your own childhood issues, dealing with your own denial, your partner is dealing with the consequences.** He or she is dealing with the result of you making decisions out of your past pain rather than your healing. Let's look at an example.

If you were made to feel insecure and unsafe as a child and your adult partner now spends a great deal of time reassuring you, explaining himself, overcompensating and basing many of his decisions on your level of unsafety, guess what? He is doing your work! It's not his job to make you safe. It's your job to heal unsafety and insecurity and make yourself safe. What your partner can and should do is be sensitive to the fact that you are dealing with and healing this issue. He can understand, but he should not be doing your work. You will never be safe by manipulating those in the world around you. If and when those people leave, or make some human error, or choose to act on behalf of their own needs as opposed to yours, your safety goes right out the window. That's why it's critical for you to take charge of your own healing.

> *Before there can be freedom in togetherness,*
> *there must be the courage and faith to stand alone.*

This is a major issue in relationships. I have coached couples who felt betrayed if one partner so much as thought differently about an issue than the other. One European couple I worked with nearly broke up over this issue. The partner stated clearly before they were committed that he did not want children. The lover agreed that he did not wish to have children either. After several years together the lover decided he wanted to adopt a baby. The partner moved to a position of supporting his decision and assured him he would love the child. But because he was not elated and excited, the lover felt betrayed and unloved by him. He insisted that he should feel as he did, even though he was the one who was not respecting their original contract not to have children. All too often we enter relationships with the unspoken idea that we will change people, or that they will change their position on issues in time, because they love us. That's a boundary violation and a setup that is seldom fruitful. Most people don't change, especially if they feel they are being forced to do so for someone else. The rule of thumb should be, "What you see and what you are told is what you get." That way there are no disappointments. Be careful that your ego does not convince you that you have the power to make changes in another person. You don't.

*Love can only be disappointing
when you are expecting something in return.*

In this case, one lover had come from a huge French family of eight siblings where he was expected to give up his childhood, his dreams and wishes, in order to tend to the other children in the family. He was still unconsciously harboring the rage about having been asked to do that. There was more. Not only was he in denial about his rage, he was also in denial about his own desire for someone else to swoop in and devote himself totally to meet his needs. He perceived this desire to be the ultimate act of love because it was the very thing he'd never received as a child.

If we are to expect that others will respect our boundaries, then we must also respect the boundaries of other people. Sometimes that's not easy. For instance, if your grown child is making mistakes that you know will cost her later in life, you must still respect her right to make those mistakes. Or your partner wishes to complete a project she's doing in her own manner. Even though you know a more efficient or quicker way to do it, you must respect her right and her boundary of being able to do her projects her own way. Having good boundaries about giving advice means you set the table for your loved ones and put on it all your ideas, suggestions, and your wealth of knowledge. Then you step back and let them choose whatever they want without any pressure or personal investment from you.

*Nearly all anger is used to pressure someone into being who we want
them to be, not who they are.
Love is neither selective nor conditional.*

When you find that you are unable to respect the boundaries of another, it is *always* because *you* have some unresolved issue that needs work. It's not your partner's, your child's, or anyone else's problem. It's about *you*. Remember, if you are not doing your own emotional healing work, your lover, your family, or your friends are dealing with the consequences and cleaning up your mess. Let's look at an example.

Damon is in love with J.D., who has a very hectic job and many demands on his attention and time. He has explained to Damon that he would rather he did not call him at his office. In addition, J.D. told him that he must leave his apartment at reasonable times at night to go home, so that he can be rested for the following day, which begins for him at 6 A.M.

Damon still insists upon calling J.D. frequently at his office and continues to beg him to stay after they have spent the evening together. Damon hates himself for this behavior. His anxiety level gets very high each time J.D. prepares to leave his house at the end of an evening, or during the times when he has not heard from him during the day. He cannot control his need to cling to J.D. or make additional contact and demands by calling him on his cell phone or at home.

In therapy, he berates himself for not having better boundaries and being too needy. While in therapy, Damon is able to reflect back to his childhood to discover the last time he had similar feelings. He discusses how his dad left him at a young age and never returned because he was killed in Vietnam. From that time on, Damon felt disaster would befall the men he loved if he did not know where they were every minute. Consequently, Damon behaves in a needy, engulfing way that leaves him feeling terrible about himself. What is actually going on for him is that his unresolved childhood trauma gets triggered, creating great anxiety each time a man he loves leaves, even temporarily. This childhood abandonment issue ruined every meaningful relationship into which Damon entered because each man felt overwhelmed by having to constantly remind him to respect boundaries. In addition, the men in his life constantly acquiesced to his requests for contact because they felt his fear and frustration. Ultimately, they left because no matter how much they were present, it was never enough. That's because Damon wasn't dealing with healing his own inner fears and abandonment issues, and no amount of external safety could resolve them until he addressed it himself.

Many relationships fail because partners use each other like Band-Aids to soothe their own inner frustrations and fear instead of healing those issues for themselves. In addition, many people stay in destructive relationships because they cannot deal with the abandonment feelings that surface when they break up and are alone.

**Whenever you feel the intensity of the feelings that are coming to the surface do not match the current situation, you have triggered**

**an old trauma from your past that needs to be resolved.** If you don't resolve it, your partner, friends, or family will have to continue coping with your unrealistic level of expectation and need. It will show up as you create distance, become needy, or act out your frustration in other ways. We all do it. Our behavior is all about boundaries.

I have an elderly aunt who was abused as a child. Whenever we go to lunch, I can expect that she will change her choice of table locations several times to avoid drafts. She will ask that the air conditioner be turned down, ask to have the most simple menu items, such as pancakes, described several times. She will sit at the table long after I have departed. She will tell the busboy a number of times that he may not have her empty plate once we have eaten, and she will almost always send something back to the kitchen or ask for some additional condiment, even though she may not use it. She invariably arrives late and changes the date or some part of the social arrangement, even though she is an invited guest. She requires some special kind of attention no matter where we go for dining or entertainment. Unconsciously, she must take control in nearly every way she can in order to feel safe and cared for. Everyone around her pays a price and caters to her needs. If her needs are not met, she becomes angry, shaming, and disgruntled. This eventually creates separation, spoiling the evening for everyone else. But she has never been willing to face her need for control or the painful issues she still carries inside that drive this need. Instead, she continues to manipulate the world around her in an attempt to find safety, which, of course, she never can. Her safety can only be created from the inside, not the outside. Her lack of emotional courage is apparent to everyone and leaves her feeling abandoned and betrayed, as people, often exhausted, leave her life one by one.

When you have good boundaries and a sense of yourself, you can afford to be more flexible and able to go with the flow of things around you because you are apt to feel less threatened. It is not always necessary to have your every need met instantaneously or have everything your way. You do not need to deal with your frustration by obtaining immediate gratification or acting out with controlling behavior. When you have good boundaries, you can more easily respect the boundaries of others. With good boundaries, you can create the safety you need to deal with your own issues.

If you have been doing the exercises in this book to this point, you're off to a great start. Use the new awareness of your boundary from this exercise all week long, even when you are not with your partner. Make a boundary, either literally in the carpet or visually in your head, every time you talk on the phone, visit with a friend, negotiate with a coworker, or have a discussion with your mate. Make a boundary for yourself inside your imagination or literally in the carpet a hundred times a day.

Again, don't be surprised if you are solidly aware of your boundary and start to feel safe one minute and then suddenly lose that awareness the very next minute. This may happen because not having a boundary is more familiar state you are accustomed to being in. **This does not mean you are doing anything wrong, and neither does it mean the process is not working.** It simply means you will have to recreate your boundaries at least as many times as they were broken as a child. Could that be a hundred times a day? Ten times every hour? Whatever it is, don't be discouraged. Just go for it. It's worth it! Very soon you'll be acting automatically from within your internalized boundaries without having to think about them all the time.

Every time you create a boundary, it will become more internalized in your mind and awareness. Each time you remember your boundary, you are setting down a new track or belief in the topography of your brain. Believe it or not, this is exactly what actually happens. Soon that new track or awareness has enough energy to become an automatic way of functioning. Even if you need to set a boundary a hundred times a day, you'll soon be more consistently aware of it. Before long, working from within your boundary will become a habit as you go through each day.

Another word of caution: **Don't be surprised if fears of abandonment begin to come up as you get better at setting your boundaries.** After all, you are changing the very way you have dealt with people, and asking them in some sense to change the way they have dealt with you. In other words, you are shaking up the whole system of things. It's pretty normal if you were abandoned as a child to feel as if your partner might leave you if you honor yourself as an adult.

*In the middle of transformation, we are nowhere,*
*which is the first step toward going home.*

Whenever you leave where you are on your way to somewhere new, you must always go through a period of being nowhere for a short time. During your transformation, the old hasn't left completely, and the new has not yet fully arrived. In that space of nowhere, which usually lasts from three days to three months, you may become afraid that people will leave you. You may fear they might decide not to be there for you when you have arrived at your new way of being. That's a natural response because you may feel you're on shaky ground. Keep on going. These shaky feelings will pass.

Remember that truth and authenticity serve only to deepen your relationships. In the entire 15 years I have practiced the healing arts, I have never seen truth fail. The truth and your commitment to being authentic may shake things up—rather, will shake things up—but those who really love you will understand they can only benefit by your having stronger and better boundaries. Talk to them, explain what you are trying to do for yourself, and enlist their support. Most people will be happy to give it.

*When you refuse to risk and grow,*
*you cannot blame life for holding you back.*

Consistently choosing to make a boundary for yourself is a simple mind exercise that can have a truly profound effect on the quality of your life and your ability to create deep and meaningful connections with those you love and all your relationships. Before we look at the issue of boundaries and communication, take a minute to evaluate how this experiential exercise worked for you.

1. What boundary issue/s came up for you during the exercise?


2. How have those issues affected your relationships with others in the past?

3. What benefits would you individually get by having stronger boundaries?

4. How would your relationships improve if you had stronger boundaries?

By now the light inside your head may be going on, and you may be feeling a little overwhelmed. Great, that means you're getting it! Take a break and do something you enjoy. You've earned it. It takes tremendous courage to be honest and look at these issues. Congratulate yourself. Then, when you feel ready to continue, we'll look at how boundaries affect your communication. You're about to get the tools for becoming a better listener and learning to express your feelings safely. After you have taken a break, you and your partner can do the next dyad.

1. When I was a child, my boundaries were broken in these ways:

2. This is how I felt about it then:

3. This is how it's affected my life, our relationship:

4. This is how I can begin to respect my own boundaries:

5. This is how you can respect my boundaries:

6. This is how our relationship will benefit:

# CHAPTER FOUR
# Boundaries and Communication

*It doesn't matter if we speak*
*I cannot know who you are*
*until our Spirits meet.*
*A lifetime of words and thoughts*
*could not bring us together until*
*I get still and in the silence*
*I will find you*
*without so much as a*
*single utterance.*

## Boundaries and Successful Communication

Do you repeat yourself often? Do you feel like no one understands you? Do you think it's hard to express what you feel? These issues are about boundary problems in your communications with other people. Nearly every response you have while you are communicating is going to be based upon your childhood experiences. Everything you hear gets filtered through your red wagon. Everything you say comes right out of it. Everything your partner hears is heard through his or her red wagon. Everything your partner says comes right out of his or her red wagon. You got it! Everything you think and feel comes from your past!

You can't help but react out of the either the joy or the pain from your past. That's the only experience you have available to reference, since the future isn't here yet. Each of us has a red wagon full of our past experiences as children. If your past is still making you afraid of being abandoned, rejected, judged, humiliated, or engulfed, you'll find it almost impossible to listen objectively to your partner or to anyone else. Your own pain and fear will get in the way. Let's look at an example.

Jed and Dan have been together four years. They have a very difficult time communicating. Jed comes from a family that traveled constantly. He went to eight different schools before he was 13, and he never felt very connected to anyone for obvious reasons. On the other hand, Dan came from a family of overachievers. No matter what he did, neither he nor his parents felt it was ever enough. No award, no scholarship, no achievement ever satisfied his parents. Dan left home feeling he could never be enough.

A typical exchange between Dan and Jed looks like this. Jed says to Dan one evening, "God I'm feeling so lonely I could just die."

Dan immediately gets triggered, hears this statement and interprets it as a message that he is not home enough and responds, "I don't understand why you're so damn lonely. I've been home every night for the last month."

Instead of going deeper into the reasons why Jed is feeling so lonely, Dan has just cut him off and ended the conversation by his fearful response. Dan's fear of never being enough keeps him from hearing objectively and he takes Jed's statements personally. The discussion ends, and both leave feeling misunderstood and unable to talk to each other.

Now let's do that conversation again the right way. Dan and Jed both draw their boundaries and agree that whatever each says is not about them personally. Now, Jed says, "God, I'm feeling so lonely that I could just die!"

This time Dan is able to maintain awareness of his boundary and realize this is about Jed's issue and not about him. Dan responds, "Tell me what it's like to feel so lonely you could just die."

Jed says, "Every time I began to make friends as a kid, my mom and dad would uproot us and off we'd go to some new place filled with strangers. Today Allen moved to Colorado. Saying good-bye to him brought up all this sadness about all the times I had to say good-bye to people I cared about."

Jed softly begins to cry as Dan holds him. Since Dan is able to keep his own agenda and fearful feelings from becoming part of Jed's process by having a good boundary, he is able to be a compassionate presence to Jed's pain. They both feel more connected. Healing occurs that might not have otherwise taken place.

Once you understand that your partner's response is *never* about you, but rather about some old pain or issue from his or her own child-hood, you can afford to have greater compassion. And, naturally, all these great awarenesses spill over, enhancing and deepening friend-ships, family relationships, and all of your other relationships. And it's simply all about having healthy boundaries!

In addition, once you have established healthy boundaries and begin your process of creating healing sessions, you will be able to go as deep as you need to process your feelings effectively. That's when you have opened up a universe of possibilities. Think about what you could learn about each other. You could literally sit across from your partner for the next hundred years and not have learned everything there is to know about him or her. The person sitting across from you, whether she is family, friend, associate, or mate, is a multidimensional, multifaceted human being with a great deal to teach you about her and about yourself. She is a beloved and precious human being, if for no other reason than she has had the courage to enter into this process with you. Think of all the trials and challenges she has encountered during her process of coming to you. You should look at your partner with awe and respect.

*Whenever you meet anyone, it is a spiritual event*
*if you meet them with love.*

In today's world, we are so pressured we seldom take the time to really hear each other and be fully present to each other's feelings. We are so involved in the process of making a living, building a career, being a political activist, raising children, or pursuing other survival activities, including our constant avoidance of pain and fear. You must commit to setting aside time to do these exercises if you are going to be successful. Don't do the exercises in a half-present manner. You cannot provide deep compassion and caring while driving down the freeway or chatting over dinner. You may think you can create effective communi-cation in these situations, but it's really impossible. Oncoming traffic, off-ramps and other intrusions that require your energy and attention to go in different directions will no doubt interrupt you several times. You can-not be *fully* present to your own feelings, or your partner's, while doing other things. If you are not willing to make the time to do the exercise effectively, perhaps during your first communication exercise you can look at the reasons for your resistance. Instructions for it follow.

## Boundaries Versus Barriers or Walls

Couples who are just beginning to learn about boundaries sometimes come into therapy claiming they feel manipulated by what one partner refers to as his newfound boundaries. How can that be, if boundaries are so healthy? One reason for this might be that partner A is interpreting partner B's boundary setting as unloving or abandoning.

Another, more likely reason is that instead of using healthy boundaries, someone in the relationship has misunderstood the difference between boundaries and barriers or walls. He or she has put up inflexible barriers to connecting. Let's see how that might look.

Casey and Evelyn have a difficult relationship. Casey's mom was manipulative and controlling, and Evelyn's dad was abusive. Casey and Evelyn had been in individual therapy for several years prior to meeting, so they are aware of how they need to take emotional care of themselves.

On this particular morning Evelyn has woken up feeling angry with Casey. Evelyn wants to get married, but Casey insists she is not willing to do that until their communication problems are solved. They often argue without resolution.

Evelyn says in a demanding voice, "Casey, I've had it! You're either going to marry me or I'm moving out and this relationship is over."

Casey feels she is honoring her own boundaries, so she says, "Evelyn, do whatever you like. I will not be spoken to in that tone of voice. *I* am leaving."

Now, at first glance, it could look as if they have reached an impasse that was created by healthy boundaries. But let's look deeper.

When you have boundaries, you don't need to draw inflexible lines in the sand, expecting others to comply. Those are not boundaries, they are barriers to communication and to connecting deeply. They are walls that shut out each other and each other's feelings.

You create these walls because the process has triggered some fear or denial about an issue that you have not dealt with and may not even be conscious of. Nevertheless, your response is about *you*. Some of the ways you may put up walls when you encounter your issues may not be quite so obvious:

- Do you pick up a cigarette to keep from feeling painful feelings?
- Do you take phone calls in the middle of intense conversations?
- Do you let your mind wander when your partner is talking?
- Do you make demands of your partner, give ultimatums or give in to your partner?
- Do you answer your partner's question with a question?
- Do you point out your partner's errors in response to being told that he or she feels you have done something wrong?
- Do you use money, sex, material things, or emotional closeness as a weapon when you're angry?
- Do you withhold any of those things as a hostage when you're angry?
- Do you pretend you didn't hear or don't care when you really do?

I'm sure by now you have also thought of a million ways you each put up walls. When you have a boundary, you won't need to change others by controlling them. You don't need tactics such as those listed above. You don't need to use demands for instant gratification, disapproval, or projected guilt or shame. When you have a strong boundary, you don't need to threaten or control situations or your partner. When you have a strong, healthy boundary, you can work on the issues that prevent you from being present to your own feeling or those of your partner. You can simply state from an "I" space what it is you're feeling and then ask for what you need.

*If you are pushing to make things happen,*
*you are not in harmony with the universe's timing.*

Some people act like they are not in control, and yet they control situations by simply giving up or giving in. They use compliance to get control. Usually there is not a great deal said about this tactic and its use. When you give yourself up or give away what you really need to be happy out of fear or resistance, eventually you'll resent the other person and hate yourself for having done so. Becoming noncompliant by withdrawing or acting indifferent is a strong demonstration of *your* lack of boundaries. If you have strong boundaries, you do not have to respond with the passive-aggressive behavior of giving in, giving up, or withdrawing.

Let's go back to Casey and Evelyn and replay their discussion after they've read this book and have done some boundary work. Notice the "I" messages. Also notice that neither woman in this conversation tries to make the other feel wrong (or blame the other) for what is going on.

Evelyn says: "Casey, I've been feeling like I've abandoned myself lately. I really love you and moved into your place feeling like we were clearly moving toward a goal of commitment. Since I've been here quite some time and don't see any commitment plans happening, I'm beginning to think about the possibility of moving out so I won't feel as if I betrayed myself."

Casey responds: "I guess we haven't talked about commitment in a while. I want you to know, however, I've also been thinking about this issue. Lately I've become aware of some intimacy issues that have come up for me that really have nothing to do with you. I guess I figured I should try to work those out before we set a date. I intend to see my therapist about them next week. Is there some way we could negotiate an agreement that would feel OK to both of us?"

Evelyn replies: "Just talking about it helps me understand we haven't just dropped the issue. I can wait a while longer while you work in therapy without feeling as if I've abandoned myself, providing we're still moving in the same direction. Is there anything I can do to help in your process?"

Feel the difference? Strong boundaries allow for flexibility and change. They allow for openness, receptivity, and a willingness to be affected by each other's feelings and needs. With boundaries you feel your own limits and set them safely for your partner.

When you *don't* have boundaries, you become fearful of knowing or feeling what the other person needs or wants from you. You put up protective barriers that keep you from being connected because you fear being engulfed or taken over. You fear you won't have the ability to know how you want to respond and then set limits for yourself.

**Remember, knowing what someone wants from you does not necessarily mean you must give it.** If you have a strong boundary, you can hear what he or she wants, then make a decision about what is right for you to give or do.

**The minute you start to feel defensive or unsafe in any situation, stop the process and check to see if you have lost a sense of your boundary.** Chances are you have become defensive because your boundary is down. Usually some personal issue from your past has been triggered.

Having boundaries provides a means for being conscious and self-aware. With a boundary you'll be able to tell when you're not feeling safe and when you are.

## Boundaries and Anger

Speaking about safety, let's talk about what to do when hard feelings surface that might *seem* uncontrollable.

People who experience intense anger or rage and who do not have boundaries may be concerned that they will hurt either themselves or others with some form of abuse, either emotional or physical. **When the intensity of angry feelings becomes too great, we have a choice to either take positive control and vent those feelings safely or emulate our perpetrators and deny the feelings or vent them in destructive ways.** As children, we had no control. But as adults, we must each take responsibility for our own abusive behavior and denial. So while you are attempting to create strong boundaries on the inside, let's create some safe tools to help on the outside.

It's a good idea to designate a place in your home, preferably not the bedroom, that will be considered a "safe room." This space is to provide emotional safety. It doesn't matter how large or small your home is; the safe space might even be a bathroom. Once you've chosen the room, you both must agree that you will honor the contracts you make about this room. Contracts are the sets of agreements or boundaries that you both agree to about your process. You must agree that if either of you becomes so enraged that you feel emotional or physical damage could occur, you will allow the person feeling the rage to go to the safe room and you will not follow. This agreement is critical.

This safe room can also be used if someone is feeling too vulnerable and needs to take a break. This sacred space should act as a refuge to be used when you need to leave the communication process but do not wish to not leave the premises or abandon each other emotionally. You can return to the your discussion after feelings have had a chance to cool down.

Your safe room is for processing feelings of rage, anger, sadness, despair, or any other intense feeling that may surface. This room should contain:

- Pillows that can be thrown, screamed into or hit
- Paper and markers for writing or drawing about the feelings
- Telephone books that can be torn up
- A punching bag, if you feel you will be working with issues of rage
- Dolls or stuffed animals that may be used for comfort
- Blankets or soft covers

Providing safe rooms so you can honor and process your feelings is part of creating internal boundaries that are positive. There is *no* emotion that is bad or negative. Every emotion is natural and acceptable. **It is what you do with your emotion that becomes either positive or negative.** Spirit will not judge you for any feeling or emotion that you have or you express. Remember, Spirit gave you the ability to feel everything. The only thing that matters to Spirit, or should matter to you, is what you do with those feelings. That you are releasing and healing your feelings is in divine right order. You are creating a space inside yourself for more love and compassion. What could be better?

One of the biggest misconceptions you live with today is that safety is about what happens outside you in the world. Thanks to that untruth, you continue to expect that others can or should make you safe and should make life OK for you. You believe if the right person comes along to take care of you, you can finally be safe in your world. Unfortunately, believing this may create isolation for you, because people may not wish to be around you very often. Your unrealistic expectation that they should care for you is draining. Even if someone were foolish enough to promise she would care for you, you would still not be safe.

When you put your eggs—in this case, your safety—in someone else's basket, there's always the possibility he will get tired of carrying your issues around in his basket. Worse yet, he may even take his basket and leave. When that happens, you feel as if some part of you has left, and you are devastated.

*You never get abandoned without first*
*having abandoned yourself with some form of denial.*

**Safety is created from the inside.** If you have strong boundaries, you can trust yourself to see clearly, understand what your responses should be, and take care of any problem life might give you. No one else can or should do that for you.

I once counseled a woman who felt aghast at the idea of telling her partner "no" about anything. Her partner decided everything for her. If she expressed a single independent feeling, her partner would shame her into doing what she wanted. In front of the family, she treated her as if she was not valuable or worthy of her respect. Then, she later yelled at her because their children treated her the same way. She tolerated this behavior because of her own feelings of not being worthy. When we talked about setting boundaries, she was terrified. "She may leave me, and I'll have nothing!" she exclaimed. "She's already left you emotionally, and if you do nothing, what will you end up having?" I asked. "At least if you set some boundaries, you'll begin to have good feelings about yourself!"

She agreed reluctantly, and slowly but surely she did set boundaries. For a while everything was upside down in their world. But instead of leaving her, her partner slowly began to respect her. Eventually her partner also came into therapy. I'll never forget the look on her face when she said, "She didn't treat herself like it mattered. How was I to know the way I treated her mattered?"

The world around you responds to you in the same way you respond to yourself. **If you set boundaries for yourself and treat yourself with respect and honor, the majority of people in your life will do the same in return.** Those who don't will leave your life because it is too uncomfortable for them to stay, or you will leave them because you can no longer compromise being who you are. Either way, you will not feel a loss, because you have found yourself.

Now, some of you who are a bit codependent just decided not to go any further because you don't want to take the chance that someone will leave you. You don't want to be alone or be abandoned. Right? The truth is there are risks as well as benefits involved in taking responsibility for yourself. But here's the bottom line: **The risk that those you love will leave you is even greater when you don't respect yourself and when you don't have boundaries than it is when you do have them.** Look at this statement again and accept the truth of it:

*No one has ever been abandoned without first having abandoned himself or herself through some form of denial.*

Selling out and allowing people to break your boundaries and treat you without honor is no guarantee that they will stay with you. In fact, it may mean they have no choice but to leave you, because deep inside they don't like themselves for what they are doing or what is going on in your relationship. You've abandoned yourself by not asking for what you need, and ultimately you will get abandoned in your relationship. It's a no-win situation.

The best gift you can give yourself and those you love is to begin creating positive change and movement toward a healthy relationship, in small, consistent steps. Practice! Practice! Practice! Since we're talking about respect for ourselves, let's talk about more ways to take responsibility for ourselves, which in turn creates more self-respect. Remember *self*-respect, *self*-esteem, and *self*-love begin with *self*.

But first, take some time to complete the following exercise so you can see for yourself how you create walls instead of healthy boundaries.

1. What kinds of walls do you create when your boundaries are down and you begin experiencing fear?

2. How do your walls replicate the same kinds of unhealthy boundaries or walls that you encountered as a child?

3. What are the risks to taking your walls down?

4. How would having healthy boundaries reduce those risks?

Great, now you have even more insight. Now, take a breath and/or a break, and let's move on.

## Whose Job Is It Now?

When you were a child, your parents' job was to make sure your boundaries were respected. Some parents did a great job, others not so great. Either way, you may now have internalized their beliefs about your boundaries and your worth. Unless you've done a tremendous amount of work on yourself, you may be still functioning today as an adult from those old destructive internal ideas.

In today's society we've grown very comfortable with the idea of blaming our parents for everything that went wrong with us. They in turn have every right to blame their parents, and we all sit around on self-pity pots complaining about everything *our parents did wrong*. Putting the blame and shame where it belongs is one small but important step. But if that's the only step you take, you're still stuck. Unfortunately, no matter how true these accusations may be, blaming does not fix the problem. Besides, the bottom line is that your parents probably didn't have the right tools for doing a better job with you.

**Being spiritually evolved means it's your job to do better with yourself and your children than your parents did with you.** No need for resentment. This is how the process works. It's a gift you get to give yourselves. As your children grow up they will take the tools you incorporated with them, add some of their own, and do a better job with their kids than you did with them. We are all supposed to be growing from our circumstances in life. That's exactly why we're here dealing with the circumstances in our lives.

Having the courage to look at your feelings about the pain and abuse in your past is only the first step toward healing. You cannot be sure what you wish to fix unless you have stopped being in denial and are willing to see clearly all that happened, or didn't happen, to you as a child. Until you are willing to see clearly, you will continue to act unconsciously out of your denial.

The second step is to give back the blame and shame that we have internalized and use to abuse ourselves. That means we must be willing to put the responsibility for our abuse and shame back where it belongs—on the abuser. Until you are willing to do that, you will carry inside the shame and guilt of your abuser and end up abusing either yourself or others. Once you have given the responsibility back by becoming aware (or in some cases, confronting, prosecuting, processing, or whatever is right for you and your personal circumstances), then it's time to move on to the next step. **Confronting your parent may not always be possible, productive, or even necessary. However, confronting the issues of how it is you were not respected or cared for is always a necessary part of the healing process.** Until you see clearly and admit that you were not given the necessary tools or perhaps were given negative tools with which to create relationships, you will continue to berate yourself and feel unworthy.

It's not a betrayal to realistically see your parents and what they had to offer you. You can still love them, appreciate the good things they did for you, and maintain caring relationships with them. You can do all this while you're giving yourself better tools for living as an adult. That is, in fact, our job. We are here to evolve further in our emotional and spiritual development than our parents did. It's a gift we each get to give them and ourselves. We are supposed to create new ways of doing life, new ways of finding happiness and creating intimacy.

The third step is to get up off the pot and begin to change what's going on in your life so the wheel of pain and abuse gets stopped. A major step toward stopping the cycle of abuse is your willingness to resolve your denial and pain and then through understanding to create strong boundaries.

What happened to you may have been horrible. It may be inconceivable to even try to comprehend how such terrible things can happen. Even if you spend the rest of your life trying to figure out *why* things happened to you, you will probably not get an answer. And even if you did find the answer to why it happened, you will not be a single step further along on your healing path.

*There is no reasonable excuse or explanation for an unreasonable act.*

Please understand that I am not intending to diminish in any way the pain or injustice you may have endured. I am personally outraged that abuse in this country is the fastest rising crime and the best-kept secret. As an activist on behalf of children, I consider the issue one of my major concerns. There's absolutely no excuse for what happened to you; what happened to you was, without question, wrong. However, once you see the issues clearly, have confronted your truths, and, in some cases where possible and appropriate, have exercised your rights within the law to bring your perpetrator/s into accountability, there is only one remaining priority.

*From the perspective of your personal path and who you want to become, both as a human being and a Spirit on this planet, **what happened** to you is not nearly as important as **how you deal with** what happened to you.*

The fastest way out of pain is right through it. The longer you sit in it, ruminating, the more you prolong it. Notice, I am not saying skip over it, diminish it, or pretend it's not as bad as it was. That kind of thinking is what creates denial. I am saying:

- Identify your pain.
- Confront it.
- Explore, understand, and resolve it.
- Do what you can to resolve blame and shame.
- Get on with your life and your healing.

*You are not your past, your pain, or your abuse. You are a radiant Spirit that surpasses and is not touched by any human experience.*

There's a quote by Charles Swindle that I give my clients that reads:

"The longer I live, the more I realize the impact of attitude on life. Attitude to me is more important than facts. It is more important than the past, than education, than money, than circumstances, than failures, than successes, than what other people think or say and do. It is more important than appearance, giftedness or skill. It will make or break a company, a church, and a home. The remarkable thing is we have a choice every day regarding the attitude we will embrace for that day. We cannot change our past. We cannot change the inevitable. The only thing we can do is play on the one string we have, and that is our Attitude. I am convinced that life is 10% what happened to me and 90% how I react to it. And so it is with you. We are each in charge of our own attitudes."

In the past few years, we have experienced a necessary period of what I call the "me" attitude. We had to become focused on ourselves to understand the issues and challenges we were experiencing. Gay rights, minority rights, women's rights, and children's rights have all been the focus of our attention, and the result is that exciting new laws and protections have been created that provide for greater humanity and equality. However, we have focused on these issues from the perspective of the victim. Now we must look at how these issues and our feelings about them can be the catalyst toward profound healing in our lives. In other words, we must understand how these issues can be used to make us healthier, more whole, spiritual human beings.

A grave misconception that we have adopted in this time of focusing on abuse is that we believe others should still provide for us. As adults, we have not yet learned to provide for ourselves. This is an insult to your spirit. No matter how skilled the therapist, how loving the spouse or friend, or how kind the family member, at some point each of us must become willing to heal and take responsibility for our own selves and our own spiritual path. Who cares if society won't accept us? How long are we willing to use that as an excuse for not accepting and being honorable with ourselves?

I have a dear friend named Hugh Benson who is a movie producer. This very successful, loving man began his life in an orphanage. One day, while I was the motion picture coordinator for the city of Phoenix, we were sitting on the set of a movie he was making. I noticed the sun was glistening off bright gold buttons on a beautiful navy blue double-breasted jacket that had been haphazardly thrown over his producer's chair. I commented about how stunningly bright the buttons looked. With a wink and a bit of a hushed tone he informed me they were real gold. Astonished, I examined them closer, and, sure enough, real they were! When I asked him why on earth he brought a jacket to the set that had real gold buttons on it, he told me this story. Hugh said he had been raised in an orphanage. At a very early age he had been able to talk his way onto a movie location set on the streets in New York City. Day after day he showed up on set making a pest of himself until one of the directors took pity on this industrious teen and offered him a job. That was the beginning of a long and successful career. Slowly he worked his way up the ladder from grunt to major motion picture and TV producer. He told me at the height of his career he had bought that jacket and those gold buttons just to remind himself that no matter how hard things got, he had the strength of spirit to get wherever he needed to go. He had done it once. He could do it again.

In that moment he became one of my heroes, just as close to my heart as he already was to the hearts of many others. He is a loving, gentle, and wise role model for all who know him. His attitude was always to see the very best in himself, in others, and in everyone with whom he works. He never made anyone feel less or diminished no matter what their job or status in life. Instead, he always found a way to encourage each person to do and be his or her very best. Too many people are expecting someone else to take charge of their lives for them. Unless you are a child, I have news for you. Take a look out the window. **No one is coming! You are responsible for the quality of your own life, your own safety, and your own healing.**

Some years after Hugh and I had that conversation, I had begun working for a major motion picture association in Los Angeles. I was there more than five years, during which time the association was pleased with my work and I loved my job. At the same time I was doing community work with people who had AIDS and often visited them in the hospital on my lunch hours. This was an arrangement I had made years prior with the board that was then elected and an issue had never come up about it. When my naive young secretary found out about this, she became convinced by her father that she could catch AIDS from me and went to the current board behind my back. Within a week I was asked to resign. Shaken and still in shock, I thought about Hugh Benson. After taking some time to get my bearings again, I decided—middle-aged or not—it was time for a new career. So I went back to school to get my Ph.D. and enter a whole new vocation. Taking responsibility for yourself is a boundary issue and a spiritual gift that you alone can give yourself. Hugh Benson and millions of others like him have done it, and so can you.

I'm a human being. You are a human being. We are both living with red wagons that contain all our family issues. **If I allow myself to be in an abusive situation it is my fault, not yours.** My job is to get myself out of any situation that is not in my best interest and begin again. Your job, if you are abusing me, is to deal with the consequences of being an abuser. I need to take care of myself, set my own boundaries and stop being abused. If you allow yourself to be in an abusive situation with someone, your responsibility is to stop the abuse or get out. No matter how bad it may be or how long you may have endured the abuse, there will always be one small step you can take in your own behalf toward recovery. Then, after that first step, the next step will seem easier, and the next, and the next, until you have finally resolved the problem.

The only exception to this is when dealing with children. Whenever a child is involved, each of us is responsible to see that children are not abused and get them out of abusive situations, no matter whose child it is.

The next era must be one of personal accountability and personal integrity. The next era must be one of dealing with our personal and collective denial. We can't keep blaming, suing, fighting, and shaming each other. We are the ones killing our own spirits. As you develop stronger boundaries as an adult, you'll be able to see clearly that **the only times you ever get abandoned or betrayed are those same times when you have abandoned and betrayed yourself by not respecting your own boundaries. That self-abandonment comes from your denial.**

I have no hesitation saying to a client who is whining week after week about the raw deal life has given her, "I'm not willing to work harder than you're working. What single thing have you done this week to help yourself?" If the client is not willing to begin taking steps toward healing, I suggest that perhaps she is not yet ready to change her circumstance in life. Perhaps she should either find another therapist who is more willing to help her keep the status quo or come back when she is ready to do the work.

Now some of you who are into blaming will say, "But how was I to know he or she would hurt me, or how should I have known that would be a bad choice?" Well, if you are excruciatingly honest, I'll bet that somewhere along the way you saw, felt, or heard several different warning signs, great big billboards or bright red flags along your path, all of which said STOP or WARNING or TROUBLE AHEAD. You decided not to heed those signs. You might have even convinced yourself, despite those warning signs, that you could change the other person or that he would ultimately change for you. We have already talked about that illusion.

You probably discounted your concerns and told yourself you were being petty or silly when questions came up in your mind. You may also have wanted so badly to be with someone that you betrayed yourself by not listening to your inner voice. All of these are issues about respecting or not respecting your own boundaries, about abandoning yourself. By confronting your denial, you will learn to listen to yourself, identify your feelings, and act on them on your own behalf.

Create a boundary and take responsibility and credit for your good experiences and those that are not so good, from which you can learn. If you don't like what's going on, investigate how you can take one small step to change it and then follow through and take that step. You will be setting a boundary for yourself.

Before you do the following written exercise, take some time with your partner and do this experiential exercise to help you practice the process of setting solid boundaries. Bring lots of pillows into the room and put them near where you are working. Then sit across from each other and draw your boundaries.

This exercise involves role playing, so when it's your turn you will have to describe a current situation in which you are feeling victimized, guilt-ripped, manipulated, or controlled. Describe a situation that brings up these feelings. Tell your partner the kinds of statements, commands, or demands the person who is trying to control you makes. Once your partner has a good understanding of the circumstances involved, you can then begin to role-play the situation.

Each time your partner, now acting as the person trying to control you, makes a demand or guilt-trips you, she will toss a pillow into the space inside of your boundary. She will keep tossing pillows until you feel the same way that you do in real life when someone projects his or her needs onto you.

When you reach that point, say "Stop." Your partner must *immediately* stop tossing pillows and wait. One by one you take each pillow out of your space and give it back to your partner with an appropriate boundary-setting response.

For instance, if your friend Sally is role-playing your partner, Harry, she says, "My mother fixed dinner every night, and if you want to be a good lover, you are supposed to do the same thing."

You would reply as you give back the pillow, "That was your mother's decision to make dinner every night. My decision is that on one night a week I choose to eat out. You may join me if you wish."

Or here's another example. Your partner, who is now role-playing your mother, says, "I think you and your friend should get a room and not stay at our house this weekend."

You say, "But Mom, everyone else in the family is staying here for the holiday."

Your partner (acting as Mom) says, Why are you always trying to make things hard on me?"

You say, "I'm sorry you feel that way, Mom. That's not my intent. However, you raised us to believe you loved all of your children, including me, equally, and now I ask you to respect my life decisions and my partner in the same way you respect my sibling's partners. Let's talk about why that presents such a problem for you."

Keep going until all the pillows are out of your space. If you can't think of a positive boundary-setting response, ask your partner for assistance. If you're unable to think of any way to respond, act as if your perpetrator is hurting your inner child. There's a child inside you who needs protection and support. Often we are able to stand up to and deal with anyone who threatens our children, but we are speechless when it comes to defending ourselves. There's a good mother or father inside you, so you can access that parent by pretending you're standing up for someone that you love. Stay with the process, and do it several times until you feel comfortable with your responses. When you feel finished, change sides and provide the same process for your partner. You be present while he tells you about a current victimizing circumstance with which he is dealing.

This exercise is a wonderful tool you can use whenever you're unsure how to deal with a new circumstance, boundary issue, or pain that has been triggered and is troubling you. Just go back and role-play using this process and the new situation.

Now back to the written exercise. The process you just completed should help clarify these issues. Do the following exercise to see what steps you can take over the next few weeks to begin taking responsibility.

1. List a way in which you are currently feeling victimized in your life.

2. What feelings arise about this issue that you have previously held in denial?

3. How is not having a boundary affecting this issue?

4. Describe the positive changes that might occur if you had a healthy boundary about this issue.

5. Describe the risks of setting a healthy boundary about this issue.

6. Describe the risks of continuing without a healthy boundary for this issue.

7. Describe three realistic steps you will take during the next two weeks toward setting a healthy boundary in regard to this issue.

(1)

(2)

(3)

8. Describe how setting a healthy boundary will resolve some of the denial.

Wonderful! Now that you are clear, make a commitment to yourself to complete those steps. If you feel you have set yourself up for feeling like a victim or being a failure by listing steps that may be impossible for you at this time, simply go back and list three more steps that are more realistic.

If we lived in a world of people who were willing to confront their own denial, who understood and respected healthy boundaries, it wouldn't be necessary to work so hard to heal the pain of our past. By establishing healthy boundaries for ourselves and respecting those of others, we have, in effect, given the people in our lives permission to grow and work on their life lessons as we work on our own. Boundary-breaking—your own and other people's—is about the denial we hold inside. When we are not in denial, we are able to respect ourselves and those we love.

*It is a choice to greet growth joyfully, without fear.*

The people who come into our life reflect back to us how well we are doing. They present us with opportunities to act constructively or destructively in our process. We must each take full responsibility for our pain and denial and all of our personal decisions that result from not addressing that denial. This is what having healthy boundaries means. Although it may be painful, we must look at ourselves with excruciating honesty and examine how we may be deliberately or inadvertently breaking the boundaries of those around us. Take a minute to examine your life and the way you interact with those around you and see if there are positive ways in which you can change your approach to become more respectful of others' boundaries and their processes.

1. When you become angry, do you vent your anger in any way that is disrespectful of another person's emotions or physical well-being? (Do you shout, hit, shove, slam doors, throw things, scream obscenities, use name-calling, labeling, belittling, or shaming?)

2. Do you feel you have certain rights or entitlements that affect others? (Do you cheat insurance companies, receive unearned benefits, drive recklessly with others in the car, make decisions for other people, expect that you should be treated preferentially, or boss others around?)

3. Do you give others solutions or answers to problems without bring asked to do so?

4. Do you use hostile physical force to make younger or smaller people do as you wish?

5. Do you guilt-trip, project shame or blame, manipulate, interrogate, intimidate, or rationalize to get your needs met?

6. Do you use compliance, withdrawal, or emotional silence as a means for getting your way?

7. Do you feel you are somehow better than and, therefore, should be more privileged than others of different races, religious beliefs, sexual preferences, economic status, ages, genders, or career positions?

8. Do you feel you live in a country that has the right and obligation to tell other people in other countries how they should think and live?

9. Do you believe it is appropriate to create peace through violence?

If you work from any of these assumptions, you are, in conscious or unconscious ways, acting out of denial, and you are, no doubt, violating other people's boundaries. You are acting out of fear and not love. Once you become aware and conscious of the pain and denial that drive you to act this way, you will become more conscious of your own boundaries. You will then know when you are stepping over someone else's. This awareness can happen in one holy instant or be the work of a lifetime. The choice is up to you. Breathe.

*When you teach love by your actions, you become it.*

Don't get caught up feeling bad about your own boundary-breaking or a lack of respect for boundaries in the past. We are all working out of the denial and pain we carry inside. Some people have simply resolved more of that denial than others. Just confront the denial or the pain and begin with the process of having greater respect for your own boundaries. You do this by listening to yourself and acting accordingly. You will then more easily be able to make a correction in your behavior that is more respectful and honoring of everyone else's space, their physical and emotional well-being, and their spiritual right to their own process.

One of the most dramatic places to begin that kind of honoring process is with your partner during your healing sessions. When you respect your partner's boundaries, their right to have their own feelings and heal at their own pace, in their own way, without pressure or undue influence from you, you create safe boundaries for both of you. The more you respect your own and each other's boundaries, the more you will internalize these principles, and the more the process becomes natural.

Whenever you feel the need to change someone, you have moved into operating from fear. **Need and fear are not love.** Love allows the other person to be exactly who he or she is. Fear and control require the other to change so that you can feel safe. When you have moved into a space of needing to change others, you are in denial about your own sense of safety. That's called codependency, when you rely on someone else for your good or safe feelings about yourself. The only changes you are in charge of are those you make for/on yourself. In most cases, when you begin making positive changes by setting appropriate boundaries or acting in more self-loving ways, your partner will experience those changes and begin respecting you more as well.

*Those who need to be right are standing in their own ego and have left love.*

The denial or pain you hold directs your responses and causes you to act in ways that do not reflect respect for your own or other people's boundaries. Now you can see why it is so important for each of us to begin to deal with the pain and denial we hold inside. You can also understand the importance of boundaries in your process and in your life. If you need to, take some time to let these new concepts get integrated before you move to resolving issues. This issue of boundaries is critical, and having a good understanding of them will ensure your process of deeper healing.

When you are ready, we'll take a look how to deepen your connections to each other now that you have safe boundaries. First let's meditate together again.

■ ■ ■

Go back to your favorite safe place and envision yourself sitting in a comfortable area. Draw a solid visible boundary around yourself and your red wagon. Now ask someone important in your life to join you in your visualization and let your partner draw a boundary around him or herself and his or her red wagon. Make sure there's plenty of space between you. Take a moment to see clearly that you are two separate people, two separate individuals on different paths. Allow time for each of you to talk about the issues in your red wagon and how those issues have made is difficult for you to hear each other clearly and respond lovingly. Talk about what you could do to prevent yourselves from taking these issues personally. Talk about what you could do to support each other in healing them. Before you leave, thank your partner for having the courage and wisdom to participate in your unfolding.

After you've taken a break, you and your partner can do the next dyad.

1. When I was a child, communication in my house was:


2. This is how I felt about it then:


3. This is how it's affected my life:


4. When I listen to you, I listen through the pain of:


5. When I speak to you I speak through the fear of:


6. This is how you can help me feel safe to communicate my deep feelings:


7. This is how I am going to help myself feel safe:


Now take a real break. Put this book down. Take a shower or a walk and just reflect on all that you have learned. In the next chapter we are going to talk about what love is and what love is not.

# CHAPTER FIVE

# Don't Jump Ship—Go to Work Instead

*Careful.*
*I shall give you love so deep*
*it will take your breath away.*
*I shall bring you to my heart*
*and move profoundly to your soul.*
*I shall call forth your greatness*
*and sing unheard harmony with your Spirit.*
*For if I love you, you must deserve it all*
*and I shall give you nothing*
*but my very best.*

## Love Is...

I have never really believed that you fall in love instantly. You could conceivably fall into lust or trip mindlessly into passion—but love, real love, takes time—like cooking the perfect soufflé. Love creeps gently into your insides when you glance her way and see the sun gently reflecting off locks of red hair cascading haphazardly over her shoulder. Love wells up in your throat when you push *play* on the answering machine and hear his sultry voice telling you sweetly to "come straight home!"

Love smiles through lathered-up faces or legs and tucked-in towels. It hangs gently midair in tunes that get hummed against an early morning sun. Love remembers itself through Streisand's voice, passing shoulder touches, private notes, and anticipated needs before they are spoken. Love grabs you like gentle thunder in the middle of an orgasm, in the middle of laughter, in the middle of dinner. Love walks into the room, definitively beside you. Soul not searching. Eyes not roving.

Mind no longer seeking something fantasized but not yet found. Love is being present, profoundly here, solid and alive. Real love is the connection, the commitment, the ecstasy and the relief of right union. Love creates a direct path to Spirit parts, head parts, heart parts, girl parts and boy parts. True love touches every one of our parts.

When I was very young, I thought I'd fall into love repeatedly. Really, I was only practicing to be in love once, perhaps twice. When you are older, you stop trying to fall in love. Instead you become the love and then give that gift of yourself to each other. When you become love, there is no separation between who you are and what you feel, and no way to give less than your very best. If you still feel you are looking for the best, you have not yet found love. If you are wondering whether you are in love, you are not. When you are really in love, it is not an option and there is no question. The authenticity of real love speaks for itself, whether for a friend, a family member, or your beloved. Love just is.

Love is a surprise, because it's never what you thought it would be and it never comes when you wish it would. While we are waiting for the love, the universe provides us with family members, friends, and others with whom to evolve. When you are being love to these people in your life, you cannot feel lonely while waiting for your beloved. We have much to practice, and many with whom to do so. Love is never exclusive.

Love can appear to have taken a break, especially at times when the words seem hard to find. But love never goes very far away and always comes back to resolve any issue. Love believes there will always be resolution, and love chooses not to sleep until we find it. Love reaches across the distance when we have felt a need to protect ourselves and pulls us toward each other.

Real love demands integrity. It tests our ability to stay present, aware, and truthful. When we are both being love, we are able to cradle the child in each of us, respect the adult in each of us, and encourage the Spirit in each of us.

Love is always an inside job. It cannot be created by anyone or anything that happens outside us. When we are ready to experience love, we do so by removing the barriers to it on the inside. We release our need to be protected. We do so when the pain of being alone is greater than the fear of being loved.

Once love deepens, once it moves from fantasy to reality, it enters with great humility, humanity, and total honesty. Love is always a statement about who we are—the capacity to feel, give, and be. The quality of our love is never changed by anyone else's response. Love begins on the inside and gently moves outward like ripples in a pond. No matter who accepts it, how it is accepted, or even if it is accepted, it is a soul-deep mirror image of who we are. When we are able to realize that our love is precious and we are able to give it unbounded, without expectation, we are never disappointed by anyone's response to our love. Instead, we are grateful for our own ability to have known and given love to the fullest extent possible. This is the place we must come to, both in our relationships and in society. They get to be who they are, and our job is simply to honor ourselves and our relationships.

Never fear giving love. Once love deepens, it can never cease to be in some ever-changing form. Once it is real, authentic, it is never about the other, and it is never gone. When love is real, it is cherished as a gift one gives to the self. If I lie, cheat, or betray real love, I have committed an act of dishonesty to myself. I have pretended to not know what is most important in life. That is a lie. When love is real, it breaks open your heart, touches your soul, releases your pain, and gives you the gift of knowing that nothing in this world is of more importance. Nothing is of greater value. True love takes you directly to the divine— in yourself, in your partner, and everyone else in your world. It is undeniable, even in the midst of your choice to deny it.

Love is the finest healer, both for the giver and the receiver. Helen Keller once said, "The best and most beautiful things in the world cannot be seen, nor touched...but are felt in the heart." Love is the most intense energy in the universe, and therefore, it is also the most feared. In the instant that we give love, we have connected to the heart of the Divine. And no matter the outcome, it is always healing. Love removes isolation, allows difference, and unites us in the reality that separation is now and always has been an illusion.

Those of us who have never felt love must teach our bodies to hold it. We must breathe deeply and stay open to love for long periods of time. Our bodies are as starved for love as our hearts. It takes time to fill up. Slowly love will move into the closed spaces that hold pain and open them again. When we are afraid of love, we catch our breath and stop taking anything in.

Love is not an "instantly falling into" thing. Love is a "feeling fully, failing and forgiving, filling up and flowing over, finding you and finding me, slowly becoming forever" thing. We must learn to fall in love with our children, our parents, our friends, our teachers, our beloved, and our life.

## Stages of Love

Everyone who is in a relationship goes through stages, not once but many times as they and their commitment mature. Every relationship of every nature goes through similar stages as well. At first you go through emotional growth stages. Once you become conscious, you will also go through spiritual growth stages. Some people refuse to grow and, consequently, will not experience any of these passages. But this book is obviously not for them.

Let's talk about the emotional growth stages first. In the beginning of your relationship, you are caught up in the excitement, romance, and sexual connection, all of which is some of the most intense energy on the planet. You may even begin to ponder, with a silly grin on your face, whether it is possible to make a living from the bed.

Then, about three months, or three years, into your relationship, depending upon the amount of heat in the fire and your level of awareness, you will notice the fire is waning a bit. Once the sexual fire begins to dim, other issues may surface. For some reason, relationships seem to hit the wall in multiples of three: three months, six months, nine years. If your relationship is fairly new, you may feel this means you have made some error in choice. Perhaps you have chosen incorrectly and should get out quickly, before it's too late. Usually this is not true. If you have been together for some time, you might think you are just getting bored. Either way, it may be time to move your relationship to a new level, a deeper level.

It's quite common, at some point after you have found your mate, to awaken to the fact that you fell in love with your own fantasy, your own idea and projection of what you wanted your partner to be. Since you can't create a meaningful life with a fantasy, at some point you must awaken to the truth of who he or she is, with all his or her frailties and character flaws. It can take some time before this realization hits home. When it does, don't be surprised if you find yourself a bit taken back and saying, "Oh, this is who you really are!" This is a natural awakening that must take place if your relationship is real. Don't panic. It doesn't mean something is wrong, nor does it necessarily mean that you have chosen incorrectly.

Some people get angry, feel disappointed, and tenaciously hold on to their illusion with resentment or withdrawal. They feel outraged that this newfound beloved is not what he or she *promised* to be. I'll never forget the couple who came to me for help because one partner was furious with the other because he would no longer go to bars and get drunk with him. He was livid and eventually left, feeling it was his partner who had betrayed him. He felt his partner had changed the contract and tricked him. Fortunately, the partner did change the contract. He stayed clean and sober and met a lover who was more honorable and mature.

I often tell couples who come into therapy during this "wake-up" time in their relationship that before we begin to work, they must say to each other, "I forgive you for not being my fantasy." The truth is, you must get to this awakening so that you can begin to do the work of creating a sacred long-term relationship with depth and profound presence. Congratulate yourself, have a good chuckle over your need for this fantasy, and decide to just get on with it.

**The first stage of relationship is this bonded, fiery, connected state with tons of romantic and sexual energy.** There is unlimited sense of possibility, a shared vision, and a desire to be together every waking and sleeping minute. This stage is filled with excitement and anticipation.

Several illusions can accompany this stage, among them the belief that this person you have found will become your total happiness, comfort, and security. You may believe you finally have the attention, admiration, and concern you deserve and that you will never be alone again. You may hold on so tight to this illusion that you attempt to avoid any conflict out of fear that it may destroy this blissful vision. You may trick yourself into believing some display of jealousy means you really care or are cared for.

You could be so much in denial that you believe you will never have any problems because you are so perfect for each other. Depending upon how mature you are, you may unconsciously relate to your new love as an object, existing in your life for the purpose of filling your needs. It is as if you have found this wondrous new toy that you can gather into yourself to fill all those previously empty spaces. This stage is fun and exciting and should be enjoyed fully. But don't fool yourself—it will change.

**The second emotional relationship stage occurs when, God forbid, we begin to recognize that we might have different needs, feelings, and perspectives than our partner.** This awareness is a wake-up call, an abrupt realization that you are two separate individuals, not one. You know exactly the kind of wake-up I mean. It may come like a lightening bolt as you watch your partner put pickles on her peanut butter sandwich. OK, so it's my favorite, and I speak from experience. This jolt may be a bit disconcerting. Careful! If you are in denial, this is where you might start to feel betrayed, especially if he or she dares to have a different thought, desire, or feeling than you. Your ego may have tricked you into believing sameness means safety. After all, it is warm and fuzzy to have your partner feel exactly as you do about everything. When he or she does feel the same, doesn't that mean you must be right? No! It means you are addicted to sameness. You need it to feel safe.

At this point you may tell yourself that you can change your partner to fit your own needs and expectations. You just need to be patient and wait for her or him to get it. You may feel as if your mate belongs to you, and therefore, you have a right to expect certain things. You tell yourself that your partner will "learn to do things differently" if you give him or her time. Or, you could move into deep denial. With the back of your hand laid dramatically across your brow, in a slow Southern drawl you tell yourself that sacrifice and selflessness are the true measure of love. And since you can't face the idea of having to get out there and start over looking again, you will bite the bullet and stay.

Albeit for the wrong reasons, it's good that you don't jump ship. This is the stage in which the true work of relationship begins. In this stage you begin to see who you really are. That's right, it's not about your partner. You'll become aware of how addicted to sameness you are and how safe you are with allowing your partner to really be who he or she is. This is where you go to work on yourself.

**Great, you've made it to the third stage, during which you will, no doubt, begin to start really waking up and taking responsibility for having been in your own fantasy world.** At this point couples usually begin dialoguing and working through some issues, often out of sheer exasperation. This is a great time to improve your ability to negotiate, be flexible, and find out how invested you are in being in control. Is your ultimate goal to be secure in sameness, holding tight to the status quo? Or would you rather grow spiritually together? Do you want a numb, static state? Or are you willing to be in the joy of spontaneous growth in consciousness, individually and as a couple?

**The fourth stage will bring a greater sense of "we," because you have found ways to work through some of your disillusionment and false ideas.** You will probably find that the reasons you fell in love with this person are not altogether lost just because he or she is different from you. The same attractive qualities are still there, and you still want to be together. Relief at last. Maybe you are not such a *bad picker* (a term a psychic lovingly once called me) after all.

**In the final stage you have, no doubt, done some pretty fantastic work.** You may begin to feel so confident that you experience a desire to start connecting with the rest of the tribe—his family, your family, the extended family, the community. Now your relationship becomes an experience filled with excitement.

You may, at this point, become aware that something is still missing. Perhaps you are about to graduate into spiritual stages, doing spiritual work together. If you are not doing your work, you have probably moved back into denial and are telling yourself to be satisfied with what you have. Either you may think there's something wrong with you or you may tell yourself relationships just aren't what they are cracked up to be. Neither of these notions is true, but you can go numb if you aren't careful. If you do go numb, decide to settle, or become angry and disillusioned, you have hit a wall of fear. Pull yourself out of the denial and go to work to see what it is inside you that is blocking a full experience of love. What part of you has become afraid and is not willing to push forward?

Each of these emotional phases is natural. And you may go through them many times during your relationship as you take quantum leaps and deal with new challenges. If your relationship is alive and conscious, it's an endless process. You will never stop growing. These are spiritual stages as well. They bring you to your deeper soul work, together. The more your heart opens and the more enlightened you become, the less you need your partner to be anyone other than exactly who he or she is.

For your process to be as rich as possible, you must be willing to make a commitment to know and be known to each other at the deepest, most intimate levels. This is why your relationship must be a sacred trust, a place in which you can both let down and discover who you are at the core of your being. This is where most of our contracts get broken. We have not made the decision to treat our commitments as sacred contracts.

Your level of commitment is crucial. You can't offer anything less than total commitment. None of this *one foot in and one foot out* business, which is just more denial! No wondering whether you could find someone better. Of course you could. There's always greener grass somewhere, and there will always be someone who's just a bit better in some form or another. Do you want to spend your life going from one green patch of grass to the next? Or do you want to stay in your own yard and make it the place where your dreams get realized?

You see, it's not about finding a better partner. It's about you and your commitment to making your relationship the very best it can be. Real love does not just happen. You must create it. You must give yourself over to the process completely, without hesitation. Any resistance you have to doing so is your work on yourself. If this person you have chosen is worthy of your love, he or she deserves the best you can give. He or she deserves all of you. If you are not willing to give it all, that is about your fear and not about what your partner deserves. This is where you go to work and get the most out of this precious union. Don't let anything get in your way. Now the fun really begins.

## Going Deeper: Spiritual Phases

When you begin to get conscious or bring spiritual awareness to your relationships, they deepen and take on a new sense of sacredness.

Just as in every other part of your life, becoming spiritually aware in relationships is a growth process. It doesn't usually happen overnight, although you might get some new insight in a lightning-quick flash. The process also comes with varying levels, layers, and degrees of awareness. You will move back and forth along a continuum from beginning to end of each phase as new issues emerge. Your relationship becomes the tool in your growth, your catalyst for this school of higher learning. It becomes a love university in the most sacred and honoring sense.

Keep in mind, you can go through each phase many times over the years, as you encounter different issues and new levels of growth. There will be times just when you think you know everything and have it all worked out that you come across some new issue or a new form of an old issue and feel as if you are back at phase one of your process. Hopefully you will do this many times, because it means you are still growing. I am committed to growing until my last breath. How about you?

As in every system of learning, you may be starting at the beginning. Or you could be an evolved old soul who just gets all this spiritual relationship stuff at some core level. You might be well along your spiritual path but have never thought of relationships in these terms. No matter how far along you are on the path, when Spirit enters your relationships, wondrous new doors open to you that you may never have thought existed. New, truly profound levels of giving love and receiving love become available to you, along with a deeper understanding and appreciation about your connectedness to all of life. All of this emerges in grand array before you, almost in the same instant that you consciously make a firm commitment to yourself and your partner. Then invite Spirit in.

This is one reason why we need to celebrate our commitments. It is a rite of passage to the next level of awareness. Even without a ceremony, you celebrate in your heart the moment you decide to go through this process of becoming enlightened. When you opt to become conscious and choose to bring Spirit into your relationship, you have begun the most precious journey of all. Even without Spirit, if you choose to be in relationship, you will learn some things about your human self. Once Spirit has arrived, the process becomes illumined, and you have truly begun the journey home to the truth of your spiritual self. What you will discover is breathtaking.

As you do your spiritual work together, you will go through spiritual phases in your relationship. However, they are very different in depth and feeling than emotional phases of growth. It is as if you have graduated from high school to the college level of love. Your focus will be on new spiritual insights, awareness and coincidences and how they relate to you, your beloved, and your relationship. In other words, you and your relationship become living truth. Living love.

**In the first phase of conscious relationship, what you once experienced as a purely physical or sexual connection evolves into a union or orgasm of body, mind, and spirit.** When you connect solely at a human level, much of what you feel in the first phase of your relationship is "me" oriented: "How can this person fill my needs?" This phase is wonderful, healthy, and appropriate, but it's a more primal and basic motivation. Since your sexual and romantic centers are wide open, you receive tons of information about how this person looks, how he or she looks at you, whether he or she excites you. Most of the information you receive is about who this person is in reference to you or what you need as a human physically and sexually.

When your relationship becomes spiritual, your energetic connections become stronger. These connections come from energy centers in your body called chakras. Once your relationship reaches a state of spiritual awareness, this first phase feels different, expanded. The energy system for most of these feelings is located in the bottom chakra, at the base of your spine, which is your sexual/groundedness energy center. These energies have to do with establishing a firm connection to yourself, your commitment and your own level of integrity. This chakra is the center of manifesting a real, firmly defined, and yet unlimited relationship that you become willing to step into in a whole-souled way. Your focus has to do with establishing a sacred space between you and your partner in which to explore being fully sensual, sexual, and connected on every human level. It has to do with establishing a sacred space in your relationship and your home simply for *being fully who you are*. This bottom chakra energy, at the base of your spine, changes your set of values and judgments about physical/sexual issues, and you fall in love with the whole person—beyond the body and at the same time with every inch of the body. Instead of taking only a part of your partner into yourself, you take in the entire person and accept him or her as a sacred gift from Spirit. Your connection moves from being only sexual to being a union of soul and spirit.

Sexual issues become less "me" or need-oriented, and you may find you get great joy out of sexually giving to your partner, with or without orgasm. Lovemaking becomes like beautiful music, and you begin to *play* each other for the sheer joy of it, rather than to bolster your self-esteem or release your sexual tension.

The joy of sex deepens and becomes more expansive. You find you move from feelings of *need* to feelings of *cherish* about your partner and his or her body. Orgasm of mind and spirit may not always include physical orgasm, but still you feel totally fulfilled and cared for on every level. You find more acceptance for sexual play, without being attached to the end result.

Don't be surprised if you grow beyond the need to bring toys, sexual magazines, videos, movies, or pictures of other people into your process, because your beloved is more than enough. Not only is he or she more than enough, but also by focusing only on your partner, your sexual experience becomes heightened. Any outside energy or external stimulation may lessen the intensity and feel like an inappropriate detour from intimacy. If you insist on staying in your old patterns of using outside stimulation, it may diminish your excitement rather than increase it, as if you have brought Las Vegas to your sacred sexual space instead of Spirit.

I will never forget something I was told during in the '80s, at a weekend conference with Stephen and Andrea Levine, who are well-known partner and lover spiritual teachers and writers. They had made a decision early in their marriage never to bring any foreign energy into the sexual space between them. They wanted to create complete and total safety for each other without comparisons or outside stimulation. They created a space that was completely safe for unlimited exploration, sexual union, and deep honor. They wanted to sexually play with joy and excitement. They even committed to fantasize only about each other so that they could heighten the joy they took in just being together sexually. By providing this safe space, they were each able to explore their inhibitions, limitations, and hang-ups, and release them, becoming totally open, sexually and every other way. What a priceless gift they gave each other. Can you even imagine the joy two lovers could experience if they make a commitment to honor each other in that way? The sense of peace and safety would be ecstasy.

This process of creating a safe space for yourselves means you must be willing to look at all the ways in which you abandon yourself and each other out of fear. You must also be willing to stop leaving in any way.

**In the second stage of bringing spiritual awareness to your relationship, not only do you notice the differences in each other, but you begin to understand why those differences are exactly what you need.** They are exactly what you have created for yourself in order to push your soul forward. You did that, consciously or unconsciously, with your spiritual wisdom and choice of this particular partner.

There may be times when you wonder what you could have been thinking, because your differences seem glaring! Stay present and just take your time. At some point you will be able to see the lessons if you trust yourself. Yes, I said trust yourself. You can stop worrying, since you know that when you finally understand the lesson, you will be able to make the right choice for yourself about what to do. Very seldom does the lesson include leaving. The only time I have ever suggested that partners leave each other is in the case of abuse, or where one partner consciously refuses to grow emotionally or spiritually. Most of the time taking care of yourself will mean learning to set limits and boundaries, and honor yourself. It might also mean that you stop needing to change your partner, and you begin to see if there is any changing to take place, it is you who must do it. This is a period of profound coming together with empathy, acceptance, and understanding about your mutual paths.

You stop acting as if your lover belongs to you, and you start feeling the truth of the safety in your connection together. You stop feeling as if you have a right to expect certain things, and you become more grateful and honoring of what you share. It is as if two great spirits in their infinite wisdom have chosen each other so that they can do spiritual work. And that's exactly right. This spiritual work relates to the second chakra, or energy center, in your body, just below the navel. It empowers you to cherish your differences and use your own emotional responses to those differences as grist for your mill, the work on your own soul. You understand how it is that your partner mirrors back to you both the issues you need to work on as well as the beauty of your own soul. And you do the same for your partner. The result? A balanced relationship.

At the very same moment that you are able to fully embrace your union, you are also standing in the truth that in some sense you are totally alone. You alone are responsible for your growth and enlightenment. The existential truth is, you are alone. And yet it is impossible for you to ever be that. In the same instant you take full responsibility for your own growth and unfolding, you finally become safe enough to embrace your partner and your relationship, and in doing so, you also have a direct experience of your connectedness to all of life. You have reached beyond yourself to your beloved, and now you are able to reach beyond your beloved to the rest of the world. What great freedom. You understand there are two of you; in truth, there is also only one. At this point you begin to really understand that what you do to and for your partner, you also do to and for yourself, either positively or negatively. This awareness raises the personal integrity bar in a deeply fulfilling way. You are being who you came here to be. One divine relationship, with the one in each of you, and the one without.

**In the third phase, you may feel flooded with new spiritual awareness and you will begin to see how the puzzle pieces fit. The energy at this level of awareness, centered in the third chakra at your solar plexus, has to do with your intellectual understanding of yourself and the other as a spiritual person.** You begin to understand the ramifications of your actions on yourself, your partner, and the relationship. You may see how you alone have set yourself up for failure in the past or may have created exactly what you needed. You begin to step into your power as a soul mate, not only at times when you wish to impress your mate, but even when there is no one around to see. The motivation for being present and having integrity on every level comes from within you. *Your level of truth, honesty, and integrity becomes a personal issue about your own relationship to self.* You understand that your ability to keep your commitments to yourself directly affects your ability to keep commitments to your beloved and to Spirit. It is all one.

In this third phase, blame becomes boring. The only time you feel satisfied with your process is when you are able to get the spiritual truth about your actions or behavior for yourself. Being wrong becomes almost a delight, because you are able to see it as another step in your process of becoming more enlightened. Your relationships with your lover, friends, or family members become sacred workshops for your own soul. You and your partner begin to establish a space that is open, honoring of difference, and supportive of spiritual exploration. You are able to negotiate without blame or shame, because your shared ultimate goal is to dump your red wagon contents and get conscious with each other. Of course, one big payoff is that your love deepens, sex is more passionate and erotic, and you have a great deal more fun.

**In the fourth spiritual phase of relationship, you connect more deeply at a heart level than ever before.** This fourth level energy resides at the center of your chest in the area of your heart. For the first time, you may understand what true unconditional love is about, both given and received. Need becomes love. Human mate relationships become sacred spiritual connections, workshops for the soul. Once you have reached this level of love, you'll be less apt to consider leaving or betraying yourself, your partner, or the process. You have truly moved from "I" into the grace of being "we." In the most ecstatic way, you find that the deeper you are willing to go into yourself, the more you are able to take in your partner and his or her love, and the more you are able to experience the love of Spirit. It is all one.

Should you ever feel your work together is finished or you mutually decide to change the form of your relationship and become spiritual family rather than lovers, something wonderful happens. You are able to change the form without changing love. You are able to physically leave without abandonment. You are able to love with an open hand, with the highest and greatest good in mind for each other free of blame. It is my experience though, that most people fall in love so deeply with each other repeatedly in this process, that leaving is seldom an option. And, if the truth were known, given where we are spiritually at the moment, we all need at least one lifetime with each other to get our work done.

**In the fifth phase, you again focus on the importance of your integrity about ethical expression. You understand more than ever that words create your reality.** It becomes inconceivable to make jokes about your partner or discuss him or her in any diminishing way. The center for this energy is at the throat, your center of expression. No word is ever lost, just as no energy is ever lost. Your words become the tools for expressing the essence of your relationship and the way you honor it and your beloved. Now that the work of creating a spiritual union feels solid, you may begin to express your spiritual awareness to friends, family, and the world at large, as your way to make a spiritual contribution. Time to come out of the spiritual closet as an individual and as a couple.

You begin to unite yourselves in subtle ways in your expressing process, in the words you use and even in the times you do not need words at all. You speak a similar language in order to manifest what you desire both spiritually and materially in the world. You may find that often you don't even have to use words at all with each other, because the energy and intent in your expression is understood without a single utterance.

When you bring Spirit to your relationship, you have two additional phases that you and your partner will experience. **The sixth phase involving the sixth chakra, located in the middle of your forehead, has to do with deeper understanding of spiritual truths, psychic awareness, and divine inspiration.** You will begin to use this information from new states of consciousness in your relationship and your healing work together. You may feel guided to fulfill your spiritual purposes together. You may be directed to enter new states of consciousness together through meditation, trance work, or guided imagery. You will begin to understand at very deep levels why you were brought together, what you will or have taught each other, and where the future will lead.

Your work together will have brought great balance to both your relationships and your bodies. You will feel an equal balance of male and female energy inside each of you. Roles will have fallen away and given rise to great allowance for you to be all that you can be—two whole beings, loving each other. You become the divine trinity or triune—you, your beloved, and Spirit.

**Finally, the last phase, which involves your seventh chakra or your God connection, located at the top of your head, allows for an ecstatic awareness of your divine union.** You have reached you true self and the true self of your beloved, both of which have revealed themselves to be Spirit. You know, experientially, on a feeling and knowing level, that you are able to see Spirit in each other. Right there before you is some portion of Spirit in all Its glory. In the moment that you are able to see the truth of your being and the truth of your partner's being, you are also able to know the truth of the universe—that there is only one and that each of us is part of the one. In the most splendid sense, you will see how your relationship has brought you to the truth of yourself. The truth of your own divine heritage.

Once you have reached these spiritual stages, the direct experience of your love brings with it the joyful awareness that certain conflicts have become nonexistent. You have gone too deep for deception. You have come too far for infidelity of body, mind, or spirit. You become profoundly aware of that which you have been forever seeking—and have finally found—in the center of each other and in the space between you, called sacred relationship. This exquisite knowing is indescribable, inexpressible, and yet omnipresent in every thought, action, and decision you make. Once you have a direct experience of this presence, this level of love, it becomes the meaning and motivation in your life. It is, and nothing else matters. Finally, you have remembered you are it. You have found a mutual magnificence, a path so priceless that the only option left is to be and give your very best. To offer anything less would be to cheat on your own soul.

What an incredible journey you have in store for you the moment you commit to creating spiritual relationships. Ultimately, of course, this same awareness can be and should be in every encounter with every human being we meet.

## About Sex

Often lovemaking becomes void of passion because we use each other sexually to feel powerful, sexually skillful, or to experience our own prowess. We use sex and each other to release tension or feel in control. The moment you use sex to deal with your own issues of inadequacy, you have made your partner an object of filling that need. He or she is no longer your beloved. You have moved into denial. You are not being present, honest, or loving. For some, this is the greatest challenge. We have been taught to connect sexually without thinking about the deeper meaning and spiritual gifts of doing so with honor.

The underlying principle of lovemaking must be personal spiritual responsibility, both for the pleasure we give and receive. It's about the right use of power in our process. Much of our sexuality today is an unconscious attempt to deal with our childhood abuse and our issues of powerlessness about our world and our bodies. Tattooing, body piercing, sex clubs, pick-up bars, one-night stands, dominance, and submission are all attempts to take back control in a world that has taken too much negative control over us. It may have some value as an experience, but if you stay in it, you are reabusing the child inside yourself.

Lesbians have had the notion that establishing their equality with men meant expressing sexuality in exactly the same way gay men have done it. Unfortunately, we are now repeating the same mistakes of promiscuity, sex clubs, a lack of deep bonding, relationships void of intimacy, and a lack of love and commitment in bed. Monogamy to many of our young people is just another board game.

If we as a community are not making women victims who wait patiently in bed to be conquered, we are telling them through our advertising, Internet sites, and media that sexual liberation means doing it with the same lack of principles as men both straight and gay. Neither is correct. As gay men and lesbians, we have not yet begun to exercise our innate ability to harmoniously blend sexuality and consciousness. We have not yet ushered in a new era of conscious sexuality. True liberation, equality, and freedom will come only when we step into this opportunity to role model a new way, free from the past. The knowledge necessary for this task is already within us, waiting to be called forward. Our community must bring consciousness and spirituality into our sexuality, or we will never bring it into our hearts and souls.

Instead, the bedroom has become another metaphorical battlefield of dominance and submission, oppression and power, games, rules, and sexual politics. Just as in codependent relationships, we manipulate each other to get what we want sexually. Because we cannot own the beauty and potential of our sexuality, we act in covert ways. The guilt-ridden subtext of this dance is as damaging and out of harmony as a phone call from an abusive partner who tells his lover to take the day off because he longs to be with him after beating him up. We all act out of guilt. The result is that sex is still not fulfilling, and we are still at a loss about how to create the ecstasy we seek. That too remains patiently inside us, waiting to be discovered.

We distance ourselves from our feelings about sex and sexuality with games, roles, rules, and gender identification. Neither gay men and lesbians nor heterosexual men and women have given themselves permission to be fully and spiritually sexual. We have not yet embraced ourselves as spiritual and sexual individuals, uniquely different from each other, free of roles. We have not embraced our bodies or the beauty of our sensual nature. We distance from our true sexual selves with self-mutilation, multiple partners, and serial monogamy. We distance with affairs, shame, and taboos. The reason for this need to distance ourselves from sex is, overwhelmingly, guilt. It is a product of our internalized shame. The shame projected on to us by society.

We have incredible misplaced guilt about the fact that we are homosexual human beings. We have not given ourselves permission to explore our sexuality openly, lovingly, and without shame. Our bodies, no matter what age or color or gender, are beautiful and gifted with great capacity for passion and sexual joy, all of which is divinely inspired and created.

Lovemaking stops being *love making* when you are using your partner to fill your needs for security and self-esteem. Soon your partner will begin to experience the process as if something is being energetically taken away from him or her, rather than being given to him or her. It is. Your partner will feel the shift in your energy from having once been "the beloved," being given to and enjoyed in a loving way, to now being the object responsible for filling your needs. He or she will resent it, consciously or unconsciously. Instead of a shared tender experience, sex becomes an obligation, a service required to make someone else feel lovable or desirable. If you're using sex as a Band-Aid to avoid healing your issues, you're going to be disappointed, and so is your partner. He will become bored and tired of doing your work for you. Sex devoid of love is boring and soon unsatisfying, even though we tout the freedom in it.

The finest way to get back on track is to do your work. Deal with your inadequacy issues in your healing process, and bring your heart back to the bed. Act sexually out of love and not fear. Today we have so many misguided ideas about sex. Spirit created the body with the capacity to enjoy and be enjoyed. There's nothing wrong with any adult sexual activity that is motivated by principled spiritual love and preceded by honest, mutual communication and understanding between two people.

*Anything that allows for more love, aliveness, and presence is already approved by Spirit.*

Be careful, however. This is a place where we can easily fool or lie to ourselves, because the sexual drive is so intense. When you enter into a sexual activity with anyone, you are in the process of exchanging energy on every level. You are taking that person, along with every belief and fear that he or she has, into your being. Unless your partner is very conscious and has learned how to clear their own energy field, you're also taking the energy of every other person they have been with sexually into your essence. You must act with total presence, truth, and love. It is good to ask, "What is my intention here? Is this exchange going to enhance both of us, bring more aliveness and love into our lives and leave us feeling more whole? Am I being present to the needs and feelings of this person? Or am I just filling a temporary need without regard for the other person or the consequences of this act?" In other words, are you acting out of love or fear and need?

Another question you must ask is, *Am I acting with responsibility to the possibility that I may take another's life out of this exchange of energy?* If you are infected with any disease and have not been fully honest with your partner, whether you are male or female, you are not acting from integrity, and that is about you!

*We do not remember things or circumstances.*
*We only remember feeling cherished.*

Sexual activity of any kind that is loving is perfectly aligned with Spirit. When I say *loving*, I refer to principled spiritual love, not unprincipled sexual lust. This is another place in which to be careful. If you act out sexual fantasies or perform sexual activities that involve experiences of powerlessness, degradation, and objectification, you are not acting out of love. You are dealing with your own abuse issues through sex. There are better ways to do that which do not use each other or diminish your spirit. You know these things to be true. Sex for its own sake is never satisfying. It leaves you feeling empty and more isolated, it diminishes your self-esteem because does not enhance your spirit, it is of no ultimate value. **The fact that we have fallen into the trap of believing being gay is mostly about sex and not about spirit adds to our lack of self-esteem and the negative perception of society.**

*People become inspired by many things
but are fulfilled only by Spirit.*

If you use your spiritual principles of being fully present, totally truthful, and absolutely loving, your sexual experiences will deepen and become more exciting and ecstatic. There are hundreds of positions, circumstances, and joy-filled experiences that you can create sexually. All of them will enhance your spirit, if created out of love. Being spiritual does not preclude being fully sexual; it simply means that love, not need, motivates your sexual activity.

Sexuality motivated by love comes from the heart and spirit. It is not limited in its expression by gender identification or roles, lifestyle choice, marriage certificates or marriage, color, or the skill of one's sexual techniques. These are all individual choices and issues. Besides, we can see the value we currently hold for marriage certificates and commitments reflected in our divorce rates. The only commitments and marriages that are real are those of the spirit, with or without a certificate. Therefore, when made from a place of spirit, our commitments are just as valid as those of our heterosexual neighbors. Divine sexuality is motivated by one thing: principled love for yourself and each other. If you are aligned with your own spirit and present to yourself and each other, your lovemaking is already blessed and approved of by Spirit. If you are not, no amount of toys, sexual ambiance, techniques, or partners will satisfy you. If you are present with each other, you can only offer your beloved sexual activity that reflects the depth of your love. Anything less feels dishonest.

This gift of our sexuality is sacred. It is as a sacred a trust as our relationships. It can be profoundly erotic, abandoned, and spontaneous. It can be filled with passion, lust, fire, and fun. It can be fluid, free, romantic, and deeply sensual. It has the potential to be one of the most satisfying and fulfilling connections to each other, but can only be that if we are using spiritual principles. It can only be that if it is open, honest, direct, and free from shame. It can only be truly fulfilling in an environment of equality, truth, and love. This means we must be present—to our true intent, each other, and ourselves.

*Our whole and only purpose is to be and do that which is loving.*

## Creating the Connection by Being Present

As with any venture, especially relationships, if you are to have the deep, meaningful kinds of relationships you say you want, you need to be willing to commit the required time and energy. Without doing some work each day, you could not bring home a paycheck. Without sincerely committing yourself to the process of healing, the gifts you seek will not be forthcoming. The balance of this chapter and the remaining chapters provide the tools you need to be connected in the deepest and most meaningful ways. Take each step slowly, allowing all the time you need to make the process your own. If you do that when you are finished, you and your partner will have created a beautiful tapestry together that results in a bonded, spiritual, deeply connected relationship.

*Why are you waiting for something or someone outside yourself
to give you permission to live and love?*

Look at what's happening all around us. If each of us does not take responsibility soon and begin to heal our internal chaos and pain, we will never heal the external chaos and pain that threaten to destroy our spirits and our community. For this reason, this is the most important work for us on the planet at this time. It is less important for us to change the hatred projected onto us by society than it is to change the hatred we have internalized for ourselves. We need to spiritually come out as gay men and women who have deep abiding pride in who we are, individually and in our relationships. You have an incredible journey to look forward to when you begin this process. The wonderful thing about it is that the joy is cumulative. From the first moment you get a glimpse of how much healing you can do and how incredible it feels to do it, you are on your way to enlightenment. Once you understand a truth, you can never not know it. The truth you are about to find is that you have everything you need right now, right here, to begin a powerful, joyful spiritual process that will light up you life. Once you get that first glimmer, trust me, you will want more. This is one addiction I encourage.

Learning to be fully present is an art, and any art takes practice. Therefore, one of the greatest gifts you can give yourself is to choose someone with whom you wish to work and practice. At the same time that you are becoming more aware of your own level of presence in the world, you can do some focused work with a friend or mate. What you will get out of this process is astonishing. Not only does your level of safety and acceptance increase, but you will also find you have skills and abilities inside that you never knew existed. You will find you have an innate awareness about how to be honoring, how to listen intently, how to be compassionate and understanding. Wonderful gifts are in store for you once you decide to begin this process. Hopefully, you will find this so exciting that you consider doing it with friends and in groups. Naturally, all these tools apply, whether you're sitting across from each other in a quiet restaurant or in a focused session where you have agreed to do deeper healing work together. Let's look at some things you need to know before you begin.

### Step One: Choosing a Partner and Making a Contract for Deeper Work

Your partner may be your lover or a family member, friend, or anyone with whom you would like to have a deeper relationship. From this point on, I will simply refer to the person you are working with as your partner. Once you select a partner, take some time to discuss the idea with him or her. Have your partner read this book, so he or she can understand what it is you hope to accomplish. Take the time to explain what you want from the process and make sure the partner you have chosen is also committed to achieving deeper healing.

Remember to use good sense when making your selection. If you choose someone you already know is not dependable, chances are you will be disappointed. Select someone who is also on a sincere path of growth and discovery. Choose someone who wants to increase her own ability to love and who is willing to commit to you and the process. Every therapist has a process he or she uses to get communication on track. This is one I created, one that works best for my clients and incorporates the principles of Spirit. Once you have chosen your partner, then create a contract about the process that addresses some or all of the following questions:

• What day and time will you meet?

- What things might take priority over your appointment?
- How will you deal with rescheduling?
- Where will you meet?
- What will your agreements be about confidentiality and discussing the *content* of your sessions with others? Is it OK to discuss the *process*?
- What agreements will you make about discontinuing the process (i.e., 30 days notice, one-week notice, etc.)?
- What other personal priorities are important to you?

### Step Two: Scheduling

If you are unable to set consistent times each week, at the beginning of each week you will need to set aside at least 30 minutes for each of you. Don't schedule back-to-back on the same day. Lock that time into your calendar, as if it were the most important appointment you have. It soon will be! Since consistency and safety are priorities, it is important to honor the times you have selected unless an emergency arises that is absolutely unavoidable.

*There is nothing the world has to offer that is more important than being on your path to enlightenment.*

If you find that after you have chosen and agreed to specific times you are often changing them, someone is not committed to the process or is resisting in some way. The problem should be discussed immediately. Let's be realistic. Surely you have at least 30 minutes a week to devote to your own growth process. If you can't find that, you're dealing with unconscious fears about addressing your issues or are not really serious about getting conscious. Either way, some of your priorities need changing. In fact, this would be a great topic for your first session. Becoming a conscious, evolved human being who is responsible and aware of your own denial is the hardest work there is. It is also the most joyful and rewarding. But you must be willing to give this process at least as much attention as you would give that perfect person who just walked through your front door with whom you'd like to start a relationship. I'll bet you could find time for him!

Isn't it amazing how we can find time when we are in love, but we don't have enough love for ourselves to make spiritual growth a priority? By creating the time you need to explore and resolve issues of denial, *you are guaranteeing that your life and relationships will work*. Take your contract seriously. Have it in writing. You get to create your own guarantee and make sure you deliver the very best.

### Step Three: Creating the Right Setting and Space

It's important to select a place to work where you will not be disturbed. If you're working at home, unplug the phone or turn on the answering machine or select a time when you will not be disturbed. The people sitting inside you (your inner child or children) and that person sitting across from you deserve your full attention. Give it to them. The more you are willing to be present to the process, the richer the rewards that follow.

Do not eat, smoke or do other activities at the same time. You will find that you unconsciously pick up a cigarette or food to ease discomfort, or you will use them to avert your attention away from anxious feelings. If you can't be without a cigarette or food for 30 minutes, we know what your first topic of discussion can be, don't we? It can be about how you use food or cigarettes to distance.

*Behind all resistance is fear.*
*Behind all fear is a lack of faith in oneself.*

It's *not* a good idea to do the work while walking or driving. Remember, a critical aspect to your process is the feeling of being fully present. This is what you want to create with yourself and between you and your partner. If you're watching oncoming traffic or saying hello to neighbors, what kind of connection can you hope to have with each other? Your energy will be scattered, and therefore, your results will also be scattered and not very satisfying. Instead, make this a sacred time during which you and your partner have each other's undivided attention.

In addition, it is a good idea not to schedule your sessions back-to-back on the same day. Rather, consider scheduling each session on a different day. It is difficult to get into your own process if you have just attended to a painful, intense issue of your partner's. If you schedule back-to-back, human nature will make you want to use the second session to respond to your partner's content in the first. Not fair. Doing this will leave your partner feeling as if his space and feelings are being invalidated by your session. Just take the time to schedule a second 30 minutes on a different day. You are worth it.

## Step Four: Learning About Boundaries

Since boundaries are critical, we will work with this issue again because having a boundary is the first step to creating successful healing sessions and successful relationships. It's important to your process to understand boundaries right from the start. Hopefully, you worked with the previous boundary exercises. Even if you did that work, it's good to do the following exercises with your partner again, as a prelude to your first session together. It's easier to see where your boundaries are and how they affect you when you're working with each other. Once you have them set, you'll be able to hear each other without taking what is said personally.

Find a quiet place to work, then settle into comfortable positions, preferably on a carpeted floor or a bed. I suggest you use a flat surface for the first few times so that you can delineate definite boundaries. You do that, as you will remember, by literally drawing a circle around yourself in the carpet or on the bed. Make the imprint in the surface so that you both can really see where each of your boundaries is imprinted. Each of you should have enough distance from the other to make sure you have some space around you that allows you to feel your own energy more than that of your partner.

Again, let's go through the discovery process. Check to see if you have you drawn a circle around yourself right next to your body. Did you draw a wide, expansive circle? Adjust the space you have given yourself until it feels comfortable.

Check again to see where your boundary is in relation to your partner's. Did your circle/boundary go right over his or her space? Are you sitting close to your partner because you think that's what your partner needs? Are you sitting close because you begin to feel abandoned when your partner takes the space he or she needs? Check in with yourself to see if you are sitting where you really feel most comfortable. Then check to see if where you are sitting is comfortable for your partner.

You may feel like asking your partner to move back a bit or you may want to adjust your own position. If adjustments need to be made, check with each other to see what feelings arise as you adjust the amount of space and the boundaries between you. Those are childhood issues and/or feelings that will arise as you create healing together.

These critical pieces of information can make a world of difference in your process of creating successful relationships and successful healing sessions together. Once you understand the kinds of issues you each bring to your relationship from your respective families of origin, you can be more respectful of each other's needs without feeling resentful. You can stop taking everything so personally. You can stop acting out of your pain. You can begin to negotiate in a positive way what is best for each of you.

We all come into relationships carrying both the joy and the grief of our childhood with us. I will tell you exactly what I tell my clients. Try to imagine that you both have a huge Band-Aid on you for every time your boundaries were broken or you were hurt as a child. This is the pain with which we each come into relationships. Most of us would arrive looking like mummies, nearly covered with gauze from top to toe. **Unless you have attained a state of enlightenment, every response from either of you is based upon those childhood experiences. My responses come directly from all the feelings and denials I have about those experiences. Every response your partner has is about his or her childhood experiences and the pain and denial with regard to those experiences. We have no other reference point.**

Once you understand that your partner's responses are *not about you* but rather about his or her own childhood experiences and pain, you can afford to have greater compassion for your partner and yourself. And, naturally, all these great awareness can spill over into and enhance friendships, family relationships and all your relationships.

## Step Five: Creating Safe *Inside* Places

Most of you are not going to experience emotions that you need to be concerned about in any way during your process. If you have had a good cry at a movie, told a rude driver off a time or two, or yelled during your son or daughter's last home run, you are more than capable of doing this work. You probably experience this level of emotion in any given week. However, if you are as courageous and capable as I believe each of you is, you may want to go for deeper feelings. In that case, I want you to know what to do with those feelings so you can heal them and let them go as well. If you do get to those deep feelings, you have discovered the gold in your process. These deep feelings are the ones that rule your life. They are the ones that keep you terrified to be who you are. They are also all about the past. They have little to do with the truth of who you are.

Whether you are doing light or deep work, it's wise to establish safe places inside your mind to go to before you start working together. You do that by taking some time to visualize a safe and nurturing setting in which you feel completely safe. Perhaps it is a childhood place. It could be an imaginary place, a therapist's office, your grandmother's porch swing. Become very familiar with it. Use your imagination to bring the things or people to it you think would be comforting. This imaginary place you go to in your mind will become a wonderful meditation respite when you have finished doing deep work or feel like a quick getaway.

## Step Six: Creating Safe *Outside* Places

Every emotion you experience, including anger, is natural and appropriate. None of your emotions is negative or wrong. But what you do with them can become negative, if you do not know how to constructively process your emotions. Most people fear emotions. I often tell my clients I have yet to encounter anyone who has ever died from expressing his or her emotions. I have, however, encountered many people who have created disease, in either their mind or body, from not having expressed intense emotions.

When you were a child, many of the emotions that you felt, especially if you were abused, may have felt overwhelming. That's why you denied them and stored them in the first place. You may have felt as if those emotions could have killed you. When we are children, our bodies and minds are not physically or cognitively equipped to deal with the overstimulation of some situations. Therefore, when you reflect back as an adult, in order to begin healing those traumas, you may experience the *overwhelming* feelings, or a sense of being *out of control*, that you once experienced as a child. **This does not mean that you are now out of control or now overwhelmed as an adult.**

These feelings, when felt fully, will flow out of you and resolve naturally as you become aware of them once again. When you are in the middle of feeling them, however, you may feel as if these feelings could kill you or you will die. This is only because this is exactly how you felt as a child. Gives you an amazing insight to your past, doesn't it? You felt your fear and pain then, as a child, were so big they could kill you. **Those scared feelings are not about *now*.**

*Everything you think and feel is from the past*
*until you are standing in Spirit.*

It is critical that once you have selected the location for your work, you also select a room in which to express your intense feelings. That's what your safe room is. This real physical place should be considered safe territory. If either of you needs to take time out in this safe room to experience your feelings of rage or sadness, **it must be understood that the other person will not follow you into the safe room. You will simply wait for your partner to vent her or his feelings, and then you can both return to the process when ready.**

One of your most important emotions is anger, and believe me, if you were abused in any way, you have anger. You also have guilt and rage. Those of you who claim to never get angry are repressing your anger, and at the same time you are repressing your power. You, no doubt, take the anger you are feeling out on yourself or others in some self-abusive way. While anger is appropriate, it is critical for you to express it constructively. Often we can't access our own power until we are willing to embrace our anger. And all too often power and anger are tied up together. Until you have honored your anger, you may continue to feel powerless or vent it inappropriately on your partner.

If you have a tennis racket, use it while in the safe room to beat on pillows or the mattress on your bed. I encourage clients who know they have rage to keep an old overstuffed chair in their garage so they can hit them with baseball bats or clubs. A punching bag is also an excellent idea. Have a pillow nearby as well, in case you want to scream into it or at it. Hitting pillows with your fist works too.

## Step Seven: Creating Safety for Your Partner

It's important to have a way to express your anger safely so that your partner does not feel as if he or she is the target. Even if the issue is about your partner, don't direct your anger at him or her. Instead, vent these emotions in a safe way that does not escalate into further confrontation between you. Then go back to discussing the issue safely. Even if you're angry with your partner and you want to process your feelings while you're together, put pillows in a chair and imagine your partner is sitting in the chair while you yell at the pillows. This lets your partner hear your anger without feeling directly attacked.

Frequently we are afraid to express our anger for fear of what others might think. Many of us also believe our anger will get out of control. This is usually not true. We unconsciously disown our anger because we're afraid it's too similar to the destructive anger we experienced as a child. Usually, however, constructively expressing your anger will simply bring you to a place of resolution or exhaustion. If you get exhausted, simply return to your process of letting your anger go, on your own time, and vent it in a number of sessions in the safe room, instead of all at once. That's right, you get to choose to do it in bits and pieces. After several sessions, you'll probably get to the sadness that usually lies under the anger, and the issue will resolve naturally. It is never OK to take your anger out in a destructive way on yourself or someone else.

*Anger inappropriately directed at another is nothing more than a statement about how unsure we are of ourselves.*

Now that we have the physical setup and some agreements about how to process feelings, let's talk about each of your roles in the process.

### Step Eight: Your Role in the Process

In each session, one of you will be *sharing*, and the other will be the *creating the safe space*.

**If you are the partner creating the safe space:**

• **Your role is to provide a safe, fully present, holding space in which your partner can work.** It is as if you have created an imaginary circle around your partner. That is his or her sacred space, and your job is to be a compassionate presence while your partner does his work in the circle. That's all, nothing more.

• **You are *not* there to do your partner's work for her, and you are not there to do your own work.** That is, other than taking a mental note about the responses you have about your partner's feelings. However, this is not the time to share your awareness. You can do that in your own session.

• **You are there to ask questions that assist your partner's process and help her focus on her own feelings.**

• **You are *not* there to give your partner answers to her questions.** If you think you have the answers to her questions, your responses are probably not coming from you in a clean way (free from your personal agenda, judgments, or issues).

• **You are there to give your partner the experience of not being alone.**

• **You are *not* there to take away your partner's pain, joy, fear, guilt, or any other feeling.** You are there to be a compassionate presence as she experiences these feelings and creates resolution and healing for herself.

• **You are *not* there to physically hold your partner and make it better for him.** You are there to *energetically* hold your partner as he makes it better for himself.

**You are there to monitor your own feelings and maintain your own boundaries.** When you begin to feel you just have to reach out and hold your partner because she is hurting so much, don't! Just make a mental note about your feelings. Chances are, her pain has triggered some pain in you that is unresolved. Reaching out and holding her would cut off or inhibit her process of feeling and releasing her own pain.

• **You are there to fine-tune your listening skills and to learn to listen to your own inner guide and intuition.** You are there to learn to trust yourself and the reactions you have to certain questions. Most of all, hold a space of silence.

As the partner who creates a safe space, it is your job is simply to be present. **Be, don't do. Doing is very often a way not being.** There's nothing that you must do other than be fully present with your partner. Your partner's own inner healer knows what to do. If your partner is stuck, you can ask an open-ended question or provide responses to facilitate her process. For instance, you might say:

- What are you aware of?
- Say more about that.
- Talk about that feeling.
- Talk about not feeling.

Or, if you see that your partner has energetically disconnected from the process, you might ask,

- "Are you aware of anything that made you want to leave?"

In most cases, your finest healing tool is always silence.

*The path of spirituality is remembering what you already know.*

Just allow the space between you to be filled with silence until something naturally comes to the surface. That space is rich with feeling and energy. Take the time to check in with yourself and see what you are feeling from the space. Do you detect sadness, anxiety, anger? If so, and only if your partner remains silent, you may wish to say, "What are you feeling?"

If there's nothing but silence, ask if your partner is simply experiencing the connection or if some blockage or fear has come up to stop the process. Trust your partner's own inner guide to ask for exactly what he or she needs.

*The finest gift you can give someone is a safe space*
*in which to become who they are.*

## Step Nine: Listen to Your Body

The level of presence you create in this process is an energetic one that enables you to use your body as a tuning fork. When you feel tension in any part of your body, request that you each breathe into that part. You will often discover that is exactly where your partner is also feeling tension. The connection created by this work is so intense and real that you will eventually be able to feel what your partner is feeling.

**If you are the sharing partner, your role is:**

- To be aware of what you are feeling in your body.
- To be aware of when you feel you need to protect yourself or deflect your attention away from the process.
- To speak about your fears or feelings, the good ones as well as the hard ones.
- To speak about yourself from an "I" space.
- Not to talk about your partner or other people, not to label, invalidate, attempt to control or discuss any one else's behavior. When talking about someone else, you can say, "When this happened, I felt this way."

**The idea is to talk about your own feelings from an "I" space.** This means you and your own feelings are the *focus of attention.* This is not a grievance session or a time to talk about generalities like the weather. If you find you are talking about others rather than yourself, bring the conversation back to yourself. Most of the time, we talk about others because we are hold painful feelings that we do not want to face. Stay in the process by using phrases such as, "I feel angry when that happens" or "I feel abandoned when this happens because when I was a child…"

As the sharing partner, your job is simply to work on whatever comes up for you. Begin by noticing what your body feels. Or, if a feeling comes to the surface, talk about it. Take your time, check in to see what is going on in your body and simply be with the feelings as you discuss them. If you don't have any feeling at all, discuss with your partner what you notice about *not* feeling or *not* being present in this space.

## Step Ten: Right From the Start, Check Your Level of Presence

Make sure there's no issue so pressing on your mind that it would prevent you from being fully present during the process. You might say, "Gee, I forgot to call Mary back. Let me take a minute to do that so I won't feel distracted." The deep kind of work you will be doing will not take place if your partner feels some part of you isn't in the process.

Now take a moment to check in with your own body. Are you feeling fully present? Is anything else on your mind taking away your attention from the process? Do you need to do something to aid your physical comfort, such as putting a pillow behind your back? Do you feel ready to begin? Check in with each other and see.

Next, try to become aware of each other's rhythm. Take a few minutes after you have settled into your boundaries to just notice each other's breathing. The person who is creating the safe space will especially want to be aware of his or her partner's rhythm and breath. If you move too quickly, your partner may feel rushed and unable to complete the inner work. Simply relax and let your breathing move into sync with your partner's. Just stay present and follow, don't lead.

### Step Eleven: Be Conscious of the Space Between You and Your Partner

Now relax even more and let your awareness expand to the space where your partner is sitting, and notice what you begin to feel. Is there a feeling of connection? Is there a need to look away or break connection? If so, take a moment to talk about any discomfort that arises. Discuss any feelings of concern or need for additional safety. It may take several sessions just to reach a place of safety with each other. That's fine. **Take whatever amount of time is necessary to create safety.** What a great gift it is to give each other a safe place to explore. Most of us don't feel we have that for ourselves.

*Learn to become empty to know the truth.*
*It is found between the words, between the breaths, and between actions.*

When you feel safe, begin breathing a bit more deeply. Allow the space in the center of your chest begin to experience opening. Use the breath to create the connected space between you. It is as if you are breathing into the space between you and establishing a connection of energy that allows for a feeling of oneness. Take your time. As you increase the sense of unity, discuss how it makes each of you feel and the emotions that arise because of it. You may be surprised to find that partners who have been together for years still have difficulty establishing this kind of profound presence. They stay away from connecting at this level because of all the fear, pain, and denial inside.

Trust and safety get established in this first stage because you are creating attachment or bonding. Your main job is to be fully present, aware of each other's rhythms. Explore how it feels to be energetically present. If you need a reference point for how this energetic presence should feel, think about the last time you just "knew" something was going on with your best friend without having spoken to her. Or remember that connection you felt to a teacher, therapist, or family member that was distinctly different from your normal sense of being present. You were "energetically" present. It's as simple as that.

### Use Your Eyes to Intensify the Sense of Presence

Looking directly into each other's eyes will intensify your process. At first, this may feel too threatening to sustain. For some of you, any connection might feel threatening because the last time you experienced someone being deeply present, you may have been hurt and all of those feelings are still inside. Some of you may look into each other's eyes and yet not be there. If you find that "not there" expression, stop and talk about it. Take it slowly, and little by little you will become more comfortable as you experience safety.

Check your level of presence frequently as you work to establish a connection. Take it slow, look into each other's eyes, feel the connection and then look away as necessary. The most important task during this beginning stage is to feel present and safe with each other. **Don't attempt to process any feelings until you attain a level of safety. If you get to a place of feeling fully connected and able to stay in that connection, you have done fantastic work already!**

As you slow the process and settle into this space, a definite feeling of presence will occur. Talk about how you each experience that sense of presence. If this feeling is new to you, it may be important to agree to devote several sessions, weeks, or even months to simply experience this present state. Use the breath, the eyes, and a slow process of adjusting the boundaries and talking about the feelings that arise as you work toward this connected bonding. You are actually doing the work as soon as you begin to talk about the feelings that arise. You may say,

"I just had to take myself out of the connection because of a fear that came up. What I became afraid of was…"

## Using the Breath

In this first stage, it's important to pay a great deal of attention to your breath. Use your breath to slow things down. Breathing allows for greater relaxation into the space and heightens the awareness and sensitivity to the changes that take place in the surrounding energy. If you find yourself *holding* your breath or *catching* your breath, you have probably encountered an issue that needs to be explored. Slow down and take a minute to explore the thought or feeling that surfaced just before you caught your breath.

This beginning work, about how it feels to be present, is priceless. All the feelings that arise when you are just being present are incredibly important to you. They are rich with information. In fact, **your responses to this state will probably mirror many of the feelings and responses you have repeatedly experienced about connecting to life and other people.** You can learn a great deal about yourself from taking a lot of time in this beginning process. This exploration will enhance your work later, in that every time you remove a layer of resistance, you can move more deeply into the process.

Take as much time as you desire to talk about the experience of feeling this presence and all the time you need to deepen it. Several weeks could be spent really getting comfortable with how it feels to be present. Take time to learn about how you can help the connection go deeper. Try experiments with the rhythm of your breath such as breathing in unison or creating circles from you to your partner with the breath. As you breathe out your partner breathes in, and vice versa until you feel the circle of breath between you. (See "Connecting Exercises" on page 343.)

Try to establish presence through your eyes by looking beyond what you see physically. Determine when the feeling of being present deepens or when it leaves as you adjust your boundaries. All of this is excellent work that results in a deeper bonding and a better sense of oneself and your partner. A simple awareness, such as your partner worrying about being abandoned when you're physically too far away from her, can change everything about your dynamic together. From the moment you have this information, you can reduce the anxiety in your process by simply staying in the room as you talk, close enough physically to avoid feelings of abandonment.

This is the time when you also learn to become an objective observer and begin to awaken the different levels of awareness and consciousness between you. You can:

- Move your awareness back and forth between your partner and the space between you.
- Let your awareness take in the whole room and then only your partner.
- Shift into an awareness of your partner's emotional feelings rather than his or her physical self.

Learn to shift your awareness at will, and become aware of the feelings in your body (physical presence), the emotional responses (emotional presence), your mental activity (mental presence), and the spiritual responses and presence. Play with the level of presence between you and your partner, and try to focus on different levels of awareness to see how each of you responds. Then talk about your responses.

## Watching for Ego's Resistance

Some resistance may arise in this process—silly things, such as the fear that you could go "too deep or get caught and not be able to get out." All of these fears are simply because this process is unfamiliar. Or you might feel you need to cling to this warm, present feeling because you won't be able to re-create it again. You might fear no one else will be able to work with you, or you might feel it is necessary to do this work every day because it feels so good. Ego is great at creating a lack mentality with "not enough, too much, and too good to last" dialogue. Just ignore it! It's not real.

First, about going too deep: **Your unconscious will allow you to go only as deeply into this present state as is safe.** There is no danger of going too deep. It's impossible. You may occasionally experience some discomfort if you come out of this state too quickly, however, so take your time in order to prevent a possible headache. You can change the pattern of your breathing. Look away from each other gradually to begin coming out. If you have been using the breath to deepen the process and you wish to come out of the process, simply go back to your normal breathing rate. There's nothing to be afraid of and everything to gain. If you're able to reach this deeply connected state, it may be the first time you have ever felt so loved. Simply hearing and allowing the rhythm of your breath and your partner's to move in sync gives you an intense experience of being at one with each other. It could be that this is not only the first time that you have ever felt anyone totally with you, but, also be the first time you experience your own divinity.

Once you learn to create this state with one person, you can create it with others who are willing, so don't worry about scarcity. In fact, I urge you not to create this space every day. You need to allow time to integrate and assimilate the work you do in each session. Don't get addicted to this state; just make it a natural part of your life to enter into this fully present state and deal with issues regularly. At least once a week. Make this process your together time. If you are doing this work with a friend, you will surely begin to experience that person as true spiritual family.

## Seduction Versus Presence and Depth

If you're working with a mate, you may encounter certain feelings of seduction in this state, since most of us are so deprived of feeling deeply present to each other. When you find yourself beginning to eroticize this state, remind yourself that this is actually the natural state of being with another person. This deeply present state is how we can and should be connecting with each other most of the time. It is new for some, but don't confuse it with something sexual. This state need not become sexually seductive. **Spending time in this state fulfills our need to be in union, but this state is not about sex or sexual fulfillment.** You may find yourself confusing the feelings that arise, simply because most people do not allow themselves to feel these deep feelings outside of the bedroom. Isn't that a statement about how bereft we are of deeply present relationships?

*Being profoundly present, for even so much as a moment,
opens the doors to a rich eternity.*

If you're doing the exercises with your mate, you'll find that your process enhances your sexual intimacy. When you're being sexual, you'll find you can connect more deeply in emotional and spiritual ways as well. For those of you who have never felt yourself truly become one physically, emotionally, and spiritually, you're in store for a great surprise. The experience is priceless. All the times you felt you had deeply connected in the past pale by comparison. An orgasm, soul to soul, is without a doubt a precious gift from Spirit. The time you set aside for this exercise, however, should be for connecting energetically, not physically.

If you're doing these exercises with a friend and the process becomes sexual, you will find that you have missed the point of the process and the end goal of healing. Unless you process those feelings and take the heat out of them, you may be left feeling disconnected and unfinished, because the emotional and spiritual work was derailed and set aside. Very often we use sexuality to deflect from connecting emotionally and spiritually. We lead with the body and stop there, feeling empty and unfulfilled.

Unfortunately, many in our society lead with their bodies in the dating process, often before knowing whether an emotional and spiritual connection is possible. That's fine if you both agree that you only want physical pleasure and you are doing so consciously. Be careful here. Don't tell yourself you're only connecting physically because that's all you want if you're really *afraid* of going deeper emotionally and spiritually. If you're looking for a mate relationship, you might have a better chance of finding the right person if you give yourself some time to know who it is you are giving yourself to physically. For most of us, emotional and spiritual connections are the most profound, and therefore, they are the most feared. If you find you are sexualizing this connection, ask yourself if that's how you usually connect—physically or sexually first. Then let yourself explore why you may be blocking emotional and spiritual connections.

The energy of presence in healing sessions is a sensuous energy similar to the sensuality of the life force or the energy of the ocean. It's moving, alive, and earthy. Feel it fully, but do not sexualize it.

## Body Sensations Are Natural

In this present space, you may experience body sensations that are new to you. Your hands or feet may feel warm, or you may lose the awareness of certain parts of your body because you feel expanded. You may feel the boundaries around your whole body soften or diffuse, or you may experience tingling sensations. Since energy works in codes and patterns, you may feel a pulsing sensation. These are all normal responses your body is having due to accelerated amounts of energy moving through it. All of these sensations will return to normal as you leave the process.

If you do not feel any new sensations in your body, don't be concerned. As you move deeper into these present states, your body will begin to respond. You will notice different sensations depending upon the kinds of emotional energy you are holding in your body. Physical feelings are affected by the intensity of your work.

Some slight discomfort may arise as you recall certain events in your life that contain traumatic energy still held in your mind or body. For instance, you may feel a tightness in your gut or across your shoulders as you express some anger from the past. Normally, these feelings will release as you breathe deeply and bring your focus into that part of the body. Just exhale deeply and imagine the discomfort moving outward, away from your body. Imagine these intense feelings leaving on the out breath or exhale. These feelings do *not* arise because of your deeply present state, but rather, they come from previous trauma that you are still holding. They will usually come up only after you feel safe in your work.

This discomfort is temporary and very worthwhile. When you are in denial or your feelings are buried, you will unconsciously seek a way to vent these feelings. They usually come out in the form of physical or emotional illness, much in the same way a splinter festers and seeks to heal by becoming infected. When you take charge of your feelings and allow them to release naturally, they may cause temporary discomfort. The good news is that you stop manifesting them in your body or in frightening ways in your mind. The more you are able to vent, the less scary your feelings become. As these feelings are processed you will experience less anxiety or fear in your life. You will experience an expanded sense of well-being. And since you are healing and no longer repressing your feelings with denial, you can rest assured these feelings will end. Try to relax, use your breath to help release your emotions and allow the process to work for you.

Don't be surprised if once you have reached a present state, you feel like crying or laughing or find some tears well up. This present state is not one with which we are familiar. In fact, we feel bereft of it. We long for it. It is such a sweet experience that it literally brings us to tears. You may also experience various feelings that surface once the connection is made. Although you may have been holding back hard feelings you've been in denial about or weren't conscious of, these feelings arise because they are close to the surface. When we are relaxed and let our defenses down, feelings come bubbling up. This is exactly what you want to happen. There's no need to be afraid of your feelings.

*Releasing anything that does not support your greatness*
*is a gift you give yourself out of trust.*

There's nothing negative about having feelings. Remember, **it's what we do with the feeling that becomes either negative or positive.** Push them into denial and they create "dis-ease" either emotionally, spiritually, or physically. Focus on them, understand them, and release them on the breath and you create healing on every level. The highest healing state occurs when you allow your feelings to flow through you in order to reach a natural state of resolution. There is nothing healthier than a good long cry or the constructive release of anger.

If anxious feelings surface or you feel a need to take yourself out of the process, take time to talk about the fears that are coming up, and then move back into the present state. Let these unfamiliar feelings release slowly, a little at a time.

As you can see, a great deal of material will arise as you are getting started. Don't hurry the process. This is a valuable and critical time, and so much can be learned about yourself and your partner. You can discover all the feelings and denial you both hold deep inside just by being aware of what comes up between you. Take it slowly, and take the time to be aware so that you don't miss all the wonderful information that will come up between you.

During your first attempts at becoming present, you might encourage each other to play with the process. This play becomes a reference point you can use in the future that will tell you that you have all the control in the process. It will help you identify the differences when you are not present, as opposed to when you are. When you go into, and come out of, this present state, you begin to create a reference point for what this fully present state feels like. As you do this, also take time to notice any energetic changes in the energy between you and your partner. This altered awareness makes you feel very expanded and is great fun.

## Watching For Subtle Changes

Allow some time in the first few sessions to talk about the change in energy between you. Undoubtedly, you will both feel some of the same things and yet experience some of the more subtle changes differently. The descriptions I hear often include "a softening of the space between us and the surrounding walls, a present energy between us, a sense of oneness and safety."

Although these changes may be perceived differently by each person, I will describe how they appear to me and how my clients often describe them. Keep in mind, however, there are as many different experiences as there are individuals. And although there are necessary components to deep healing, there is no one right way. Your personal experience may be very different and exactly right.

There may be a softening in the awareness of the surroundings that occurs, which can result in the feeling that a tunnel of energy has been established between you and your partner. There can be such an intense focus that you lose awareness of the walls, the wall hangings, or other furnishings in the room. Depending upon how present you are and how deep you go into that connection, or this shared space may feels as though even the air between you has become focused and present. There is a heightened quality of authenticity and presence for both partners that contains a sense of closeness and richness. This space can be similar to that created by the drug known as Ecstasy (MDMA), that at one time was used by therapists to resolve childhood trauma until it became illegal. The space between you can also feel like the profound sense of presence felt in a very deep or shared meditation. An unconditional heart-space connection can literally be felt physically, emotionally, and spiritually. Remaining in that present state of awareness intensifies your focus. The space is contained by your focus and presence, and is filled with awareness and deep connection. You are doing it by being fully present.

You will set the pace and depth into which you go each session. As you get more comfortable with this kind of deeper healing, your sessions may contain depth, intimacy, a return to some point of injury, or the awareness of your past. You may experience immediacy, richness of experience as your work deepens, even an altered state. There can be an oceanic feeling of connectedness. The ability to stay in a fully present state is a result of integration rather than disassociation. With disassociation, there's a feeling of moving "away from" rather than "moving into." When you feel you need to move *out of* or *away from* this connection, you have encountered an internal fear. Great. That's where your work is. Just breathe.

### Let It Flow

Don't try to control anything, including each other. It's imperative that you each act with openness, freedom, allowing, and softness in the process. Just follow the energy and process and don't attempt to lead. Don't plan how it should work or invest in a specific outcome. Allow for surprise and new experiences. The degree to which these new feelings are experienced may vary. The length of your sessions varies as well.

*When there is trust, patience becomes effortless.*

Open your heart and allow what your partner brings naturally to the surface to be processed. Don't *lead* the process; rather, in a Zen fashion, *follow.* I follow the pacing of my clients' breathing during their sessions. Often I bring my breathing into sync with my client's so I can feel the rhythm established by them and move into their reality and rhythm.

### Take Your Time

Allow as much time as necessary in the beginning. Even if nothing from your past comes up or if issue-related process work does not take place, this present state is incredibly healing. I have spent many hours in this state, especially with sexual abuse clients, before one word of issue-oriented process began. Remember, for many of us, this may well be the first experience of deep bonding we have had, aside from orgasm. This connected state is a great gift you can give to each other, and one you will not want to hurry through. Many books talk about feeling connected, but I'm telling you how to create your own direct experience of this connection. Once you have this direct experience, you will know for certain that you have begun a journey of incredible possibility and discovery.

### Step Twelve: Relax—It's Easy

*There is no need to make demands when we are*
*filled with love and already whole.*

There are lots of little nuances mentioned here that come up during your process. Don't be in a hurry or be overwhelmed. Just enjoy the process. You have this book to read with your partner. You can highlight the points in it you want to remember. **If you just relax, most of your responses will come from a place of common sense and awareness about what your partner is feeling.** You will be amazed at how well you already know how to do this work. Remember the last time you sat with a friend as he worked through tough issues? You were probably gentle and kind and soft-spoken and knew exactly how to be present during the process. You already have many of these tools inside; you just haven't noticed them or used them to do focused work. Your inner healer and you partner's inner healer will take the lead, and you will both know what to do. Once the contracts regarding the process have been made and agreed upon, your roles will be clear and you can begin the work.

*Most answers are received long before they are heard.*

## Anticipating Resistance

Before we begin to discuss how to deal with resistance, let's take some time to explore what kinds of feelings might be arising from your past. These same issues will, no doubt, come up in your process, so it may be helpful to identify some of them before you begin.

### Personal Inventory: Identifying My Red Wagon Contents

1. When I listen to you and talk to you, I do so through the pain of my childhood experiences of:

2. Because of those experiences, I usually anticipate that you will:

3. Some of the things that actually happen between us that remind me of my childhood are:

4. I move into negative negotiations when I fear:

5. A safe and loving way for you to remind me that I am operating from fear is:

6. The personal childhood pain I am going to begin to resolve for myself is:

7. The positive ways in which my work will affect our relationship is:

8. The things you could do to support me in the best possible way are:

Now that you have identified some of your personal issues and know what you need in order to become more vulnerable and open, you can share your awareness with your partner in your sessions. Remember, **everyone has resistance, and everyone has a red wagon.** Just notice your resistance, and try not to judge or hide it. In the next chapter we'll discuss how you can deal with these issues.

■ ■ ■

In this meditation, create an imaginary session in your mind. You can go to your safe place and bring your friend or mate into your visualization, if you like. Make sure that your boundaries are in place. Imagine that you are starting a healing session and it is your turn to share. See how you feel about becoming fully present. See what part of you is afraid to do that. Is it the child inside? Is it the adult? Ask yourself what these fears are about and what you need to do to address them. Next, imagine yourself as the listening partner. How do you feel about being fully present in this role? What part of you is afraid to do that? What does that part need to feel safe? Now let the session just unfold, and see what it feels like to be in this shared healing process.

# Be Honest

# CHAPTER SIX
# Resistance: The Door to Growth

*Anger, hostility, pain, fear, confusion, and not knowing
are all the substitutes I use when I lack faith in myself.*

Consider the possibility that this planet is a school. Perhaps we come here to remember some important principles about ourselves—time and space, physical bodies, power and powerlessness, manifesting, walking in balance, opting for growth, dealing with fear and pain. I say *remember* because these are truths inherent in each of us, but we have forgotten. This planet is where we can remember what we already know. If we're going to benefit from this opportunity, we must become truthful about how we kid and lie to ourselves. Instead of pretending we have it all together, we have to admit we all have red wagons filled to the brim!

Are you convinced yet that everything you feel and believe is based upon your past? That very powerful statement has huge ramifications. It means that majority of your responses to life and those you love are also from the past. That's good news, because once you know that, you need not be so fearful. You may have developed an aversion to dealing with fear and pain because you believe you're not capable of dealing with them. Many people believe that. The pain or fear still feels as though it could kill you. That's what your inner child felt and you're still functioning from this belief. We all see and respond to life through the eyes of our childhood. The idea that these feelings are bigger than we are, uncontrollable, is a lie. There's no fear or pain from your past that you cannot deal with. In fact, you have already dealt with the worst of it and lived to tell the tale.

*Being safe is knowing that fear is an illusion
borne from doubt about who you are.*

Because we lie to ourselves about our divinity and our strength of spirit, we have come to believe pain and fear are always negative and should be avoided at all cost, even the cost of our own aliveness. To avoid pain and fear, we go dead inside, close in on life and ourselves, stay in the closet, refuse to spiritually connect, and force those hard feelings inside into denial, the same way we had to do as children.

Emotional pain and fear are a common part of our lives as adults, so we must learn to deal with them effectively or watch ourselves become increasingly diminished in aliveness, increasingly shut down. Our relationship to fear and pain, and to what we have been calling our red wagon, must change because they are all, in fact, great teachers. It is our response to them that immobilizes and terrifies us.

*It is no tragedy to die young. It is only a tragedy if*
*you wait until it is too late to begin to live.*

Surely being in angst or pain for a few moments at a time while you are doing your work is infinitely better than having that pain control your whole life and every decision you make.

## Some Fear Is Healthy

I fear walking across a busy freeway. No doubt you do too. That's a healthy and realistic fear for both of us. Nothing needs to be resolved about that fear because there's a very real danger of being hit by a car. **The fear you will want to resolve for yourself is not based upon a real or current danger; it's based upon the past.** It's the unfounded fear that is not about a current issue or in your best interest as an adult.

An example might be that a redheaded woman shouted at you as a child, and now you continue to fear redheaded women. These kinds of fears are crippling; they keep you distanced from life and from people who might have a positive impact on you. Because fears from the past are no longer needed, they are the ones you will want to resolve.

## Some Pain Is Also Healthy

When you were a young adult leaving home, you probably felt the very real pain of separation and also a sense of exhilaration and excitement. We often feel some sense of pain as we leave an old way of being that we have outgrown in order to seek a new way of being. I tell my clients they must always expect to feel "buyer's remorse" or the sadness of leaving pain even when they are leaving a bad relationship. It's natural. Letting go of anything familiar requires adjustment, even if the familiar is also painful. I tell participants in my seminars that **the fastest way out of fear and emotional pain is right through the middle of it.**

That's absolutely true for adults, but not for children. Children need support until they have the cognitive and emotional ability to resolve pain for themselves. As adults, we can determine where the fear and pain is and get support or the tools for ourselves to deal with both and let them go. The most powerful awareness I've experienced was in the middle of my worst fear and pain. In fact, if it had not been for those hard times, I would still be carrying that old pain.

*Fear tells us where we are covering up emotional pain and forcing it into denial. Pain tells us where trauma has occurred that is still unresolved or where we are refusing to accept change.*

To become fully empowered as an adult, you need to know about and be able to deal effectively with both fear and pain. That's why your healing is so important. You no longer have to shut down and hold on to pain and trauma. When you do that and move into denial, these emotions control your life. You unconsciously or consciously avoid certain situations or choose others based upon your need to avoid feeling your repressed emotions.

*Character is developed by learning to tolerate frustration in the process of seeking self.*

You can now make different choices. You can heal past pain and trauma. **If you choose to be alive, you will experience pain; there's**

**no choice about that.** There are, however, some choices you can make about how you will respond to pain and deal with it.

## Causing Pain Is Unavoidable

The first choice is that you can decide whether you will deliberately cause unnecessary or unhealthy pain. Notice that I did *not* say you could choose not to cause pain. I said you could choose not to deliberately cause *unnecessary* pain. There is a difference.

Simply by being yourself and honoring your own needs, you will at times cause another to experience pain with your presence. If you need to rest or give yourself alone time at the same time a friend needs you to be there in a crisis, saying no will be painful for you both. If you are attempting to go through life with your sole purpose being not to cause pain to anyone else, please go to the nearest codependency meeting. If that is your *sole* purpose, you are living your life distanced from joy and are dependent upon others for your good feelings. If you are solely concerned about not hurting others, you have no doubt forgotten to take care of yourself and your own needs.

*If you are trying to be perfect, you will never be profound.*

Even though there's a vast difference between selflessness and selfishness, they are both dysfunctional, and neither is spiritual. Selflessness implies that your self is not equally as important as the self of another person in your life. Do not lie to yourself about this and tell yourself that this is a correct spiritual attitude.

*There is no way to love another more than you love yourself.*
*It is not in your reality, and you have no point of reference for it.*

Selfishness and selflessness are both attempts at control. Too much love and too little love are both out of balance, and neither is unconditional love. Both are generated out of need. When one is willing to give himself or herself up, it is usually with the unconscious hope that if he or she just gives enough, some of what is given will finally be returned to the giver. In other words, selflessness is codependence. Selfishness also comes from need, belief in lack. The answer is when you are self-loving or loving of self first, you will find you have more than enough love for others.

*Beginning with self, true love is neither selective nor conditional.*

As an adult, you can now make choices about the degree to which you are willing to add to the pain in the world. But you will add to it. For instance, let's say you discover you have fallen in love with someone else after you are committed. You have many choices; among them, you can choose to leave your lover without lies, without breaking your commitment to monogamy, without deception, anger, or other dishonoring acts. But if you make the decision to leave your lover because it's the right thing for you to do, you will cause pain. Now, some may take offense at that statement. However, which is more evil, honoring oneself and your partner in truth or living in a loveless relationship filled with resentment? You both have the right to love and be loved fully. Sometimes letting go of what does not work makes room for something more loving to take its place—for both of you. It is never right to give yourself up for another. It is a lie to try, because you can never be fully present. Ultimately, your relationship will fail and you will both feel cheated. In less drastic circumstances, you may cause pain to a friend who calls for your support when you are too tired to give it because you have been working all night. Or, because you have been working under stressful deadlines at your job, you forget an anniversary or a birthday.

Pain can also arise from other kinds of inaction. We add to the pain of another person by simply refusing to deal with issues that arise. Unfortunately, this is true for many relationships. Pain is unavoidable in life, and in all my years of counseling clients, I have never known anyone to die from it. At times it just *feels* as if you might.

The second choice you can make as an adult is about how you choose to respond to pain in your adult life. You can lie about it, withdraw from it, numb out, pretend it does not exist, project it onto others, avoid it, postpone it, or bury it with denial. On the other hand, you can accept it, inhale it, exhale it, own it, fully release it, and understand that it's the downside of upward growth. We can trust the spirit within!

*Most pain is created by the desire for things to be different, and it is resolved at the moment of acceptance.*

Most of us create defense mechanisms and resistance to pain starting from the moment of birth. Because resistance was necessary, it needs to be honored as an excellent survival tool. Now your resistance is either a great red flag that can tell you where your healing needs to be focused or it masks your authentic self. As we grow up, new layers of resistance are added to the old ones, until ultimately we find our authentic selves literally buried under years of built-up resistance and defense mechanisms. The same walls we had to create as children to survive now prevent us from fully feeling life. They prevent us as adults from feeling love and experiencing aliveness.

*There are only two emotions: love and fear.*
*Everything else falls under one or the other. You choose.*

Entering a healing process will no doubt bring up resistance, which will rise whether you are doing focused healing sessions or just trying to be real with a friend over dinner. It's a natural part of the process. Most of us have resisted this process of dealing with our own issues for most of our lives because we didn't trust ourselves. It's an illusion that has had a tenacious hold on us, creating even greater distance from life and the love we desire. We don't need that illusion any longer. At the same time, we can respect the resistance we created that kept us safe while we grew and became more able to deal with life. **Resistance is not a bad thing. The fact that you have resistance does not make you a bad person.**

*To become who you can be, simply let go of who you are not.*

At first, present-day issues will arise, and as you go deeper, childhood issues will emerge. Most of the time our adult responses are based upon these same childhood issues.

Many forms of resistance may arise as defense mechanisms for avoiding the intimacy and vulnerability in your first healing sessions. You can expect this to happen—it is a natural part of the process. The fact that they arise means you are doing the work successfully.

Among the fears that may come up are:

- Fear about being fully present, because it requires some openness and vulnerability. "I may lose control or lose myself."

*You won't lose yourself, but you may momentarily lose some control. If you don't give up some control, deep healing may not happen.*

- Fear about not being able to survive the intense feelings that may arise.

*You already have survived them! Besides, it takes more energy to keep them in denial than it does to heal them and be done with them.*

- Fear about losing this quality of connectedness once attained. "I'll never be able to do this again."

*If you do it once, you can do it again.*

- Fear that you will not be able to be fully present with others, and therefore you will become dependent upon your partner. "I'll need you too much."

*So spread out. Re-create this connection with friends and family.*

- Fear that the new feelings of oceanic ecstasy will be lost. "It's too good."

*Indulge yourself! It's a legal, nondrug high that won't hurt your body or your mind.*

- Fear of physical effects.

*Yes, your body may feel temporarily numb, cold, light, expanded, or limitless. Or you may have no physical effect from the process. Either way, it's a small price to pay! It's also incredibly healing.*

• Fear that extended periods of being fully present will result in major life changes: "I can't go back to living the old way!"

*How wonderful for you. That's the whole idea. You're healing.*

Being fully present with another relates to the sense of oneness we once felt with our mother while in the womb and to a cosmic energy before birth. It's no surprise that it's a little scary. Just notice the fear as it comes up, talk about it as it surfaces, and keep going.

## Here Comes Resistance

Resistance appears in many forms. The first kind may arise after reading this book. You just won't be able to find the time or energy to be present. Stop lying to yourself! The only times you have felt fully alive and energized when you were being fully present. It's amazing that in my practice, the couples and friends who dedicate a minimal amount of time (20-30 minutes each per week) to this process make it together; those who just can't seem to find time to do the exercise stay stuck in their resistance. And eventually those are the relationships that fall apart. If life is so filled that you cannot take the time to connect deeply and do your own healing work, you are into resisting intimacy. You're using your busy life as a defense mechanism against deep bonding. If you're committed to the process, the first resistance to deal with is that of not making time for yourself.

*You cannot be fully spiritual occasionally.*

Once you have begun the process, the next resistance that may come up is a need to protect yourself from not becoming vulnerable. When this issue arises, it's time to talk about trust. How much do you trust yourself? Have you provided for the kinds of support you need? Is there a friend with whom you can process, and have you contracted with that person to do so? Have you looked back at the times when you were vulnerable in order to know that you can survive being open and honest? Have you examined your fears of vulnerability? Do you think your partner will abandon you, make fun of you, or hurt you later with the information you disclose? Who actually did that to you, and from where does that fear come? Chances are you would feel the same with any partner, and these issues are really about your own past and feelings.

> *No gift can be given to us until we are ready to receive it.*
> *Give yourself healing.*

Look at the issues, and if necessary, you can provide yourself with some safety about these fears by asking for what you need in your contract. For instance, if your mother yelled at you each morning for how long it took you to figure out what you wanted to wear or eat, you could ask your partner to allow you as much time as you need in the process. Also, make a contract that any feedback or statement about your way of presenting information may only be giving with your consent and must be made at a time separate from your healing session. It is critical to establish contracts that result in the utmost safety during the process. If you cannot negotiate for safety about this or any difficult emotion, do not go forward with this particular partner or with the process until this trust issue is resolved.

## Trust Issues: A Form of Resistance

Next, you may consider how much you trust your partner. Remember those contracts you can make with each other to ensure that you have created a safe and loving space. Did you do so? If not, go back and reestablish your individual contracts.

The most important step is to honor you. Listen to what's going on inside, and don't begin the process until you have established a safe environment for the exercise. If something inside is still saying, *Don't do this*; simply wait until you have greater clarity about your hesitation. Is it about some issue that needs to be resolved with your partner? It's important to learn to trust your intuition in the beginning rather than abandon the process after a few attempts because your fears were legitimate.

*Wisdom is the only protection you need. Listen to your own voice.*

Just wait. The answers will come if you are open to them.

Once in the session, other kinds of surprising resistance may come to the surface:

- boredom
- a lack of presence or full attention
- denial
- avoidance
- projection
- disapproval or self-judgment
- compliance
- shutting down (as painful feelings come to the surface)
- indifference
- desire to withdraw from the process
- anger

I'll bet you didn't realize all those responses were forms of resistance, did you? Just be gentle with yourself or your partner as you notice these defenses. These forms of resistance are the same tools that you both used to survive. Once you have noticed and dealt with the resistance, move gently to take yourself back into the process without judgment.

## Great News:
## You Do Not Have to Heal Every Old Injury

In order to heal, you do *not* have to heal each hurtful occurrence in your life. This is not even possible and certainly not necessary, and is true for most pain. Just trust the process and let issues arise naturally. You don't even have to go digging for them. Your Spirit knows exactly what you need and when you need it, so as you are ready, the right issues will arise for healing. It's a process. A lifelong process. Just enjoy the ride. As you release core feelings, very often other, similar, feelings will be released as well. You may, however, depending upon the extent of the injury, have to return to some experiences several times to heal the whole issue or different aspects of it. That doesn't mean you're doing it wrong.

While in the process or out, **it's critical that you do not pressure each other to deal with issues before you are ready.** Take as much time as necessary just to stay in the process, providing safety until the issues come to the surface and resolve naturally. **Do not attempt to get your partner to deal with issues he or she may not be ready to process.**

*If you are pushing to make things happen,*
*you are not in harmony with the universe's timing.*

Each time you choose to move through the resistance into understanding and release, you have created a healing that can now contain more joy and aliveness. That's how things change for the better. Whether you're doing this work in a focused session or in the car alone or in a moment of enlightenment or awareness at work, it's all healing. Let go of needing any specific form or technique. Just embrace the process and the insights no matter how they choose to arise. Although I am giving you some tools, I want you to use them to get started and then forget them as the process becomes more natural. This process can and will be a normal part of your life. It's called becoming conscious.

Take a minute now to complete this inventory of the resistance you might encounter during your work.

## Personal Inventory: Identifying My Resistance

1. Take some time to write down the resistance or defense mechanisms you had to create in order to survive. Did you numb out, stop feeling, deny, avoid, become compliant?


2. If you don't know, ask someone close to you what she thinks you do when painful things arise. Now take a minute to write down your fears about what would happen if you didn't use these resistances. As a child, were you criticized, belittled, punished?

3. Now write down the ways in which life is different for you as an adult than it was as a child. What bad things are not happening to you now, and what are the reasons you can now become more open and vulnerable and deal with the denials?

4. I move into my resistance when I fear:

5. A safe and loving way for you to remind me that I am operating from my fear is:

Try to remember that we are all still in the process of remembering who we really are. Everyone has some resistance or childhood defense mechanism to work on and resolve. You just took a major step in that direction by identifying yours and becoming willing to work with them. In the next chapter, we will look at the power of your words and ways you can, together, resolve the issues and problems that arise. Before you start the next chapter, take a minute to let yourself feel how exciting it is to begin understanding yourself and giving yourself opportunities for greater authenticity and awareness. Pretty incredible, isn't it?

In this meditation, imagine you have created a personal spiritual lab for yourself. It can be on a mountaintop, on a cloud, in a forest, or wherever you wish it to be. Bring to your lab any equipment you wish. You can add more anytime you return to this lab. You might want computers to see past lives with, sacred writings that you can use for reference, stuffed animals or power objects. Take all the time you need to create your personal lab and feel safe in it. Then, on a great big writing board in your lab list, on one side all your resistances to being present and being truthful. List every one you have discovered in your work in this book. Don't be afraid to write them all down; no one will see them but you. When you have finished, next to each resistance write a truth about yourself that deals with this resistance. For instance, perhaps you tell yourself you don't have the answers, when in truth you know you do. When you have finished dealing with every resistance, erase them and leave only the truth about yourself on the board. Take all the time you need to accept this truth and agree to become it.

# CHAPTER SEVEN
## Be Honest

*While in the center of healing moments*
*in your progression toward wholeness,*
*you are balanced*
*between the ecstasy of awareness*
*and the excitement of change.*

## Be Honest: Language, Words, and Flow

We are not very honest about honesty! I would venture to say there are as many interpretations of this concept as there are people who have them. According to Allison Kornet in an article in *Psychology Today* (6/97), most people lie as often as they brush their teeth. The average person lies at least once or twice a day, and dating couples lie in about one third of all of their interactions! The figures are even higher than that when people are talking on the phone instead of in person. In one survey, nearly 75% of those polled said they would lie if necessary. In our community, there's a pipeline that functions faster than the speed of light. We all know who has slept with whom, and in many cases we know every detail of the encounter. Then we lie about it.

For me, honesty has the most to do with intent. Since words and actions are an outer manifestation of our inner essence and spirit, honesty takes place on many levels. For instance, it's not honest, in my opinion, to tell ourselves that we don't have the answers, do not know what to do, and don't understand how to be real. It's more honest to say, "I know these things but am choosing not to act on them." That's a conscious decision that can be respected because it's honest.

It's not honest to say you love someone if you don't, because that's crazy-making. The result is that the person who hears this feels the truth between you, which does not contain love, and then begins to question his or her own sense of reality and truth—which is cruel.

*What you want most for others, you shall also receive,*
*both good and bad.*

It's not honest to answer a question with a question when you don't wish to 'fess up to a situation or own your own feelings. It's not honest to tell other people about your lover's shortcomings without speaking to him or her directly. It's not honest to create a diversionary tactic to avoid telling the truth. Situations in which honesty is lacking are all about fear. They are about making decisions that lack integrity, due to fear. Simply put, honesty means acting in alignment with your spirit. When you abandon yourself, your spirit, you are not acting with honesty.

Words can destroy a relationship or empower it. They can provide safety or erode it. Words can create a healing or a hostile environment. Words can define our relationships as sacred, holy, ordinary, or debased. Words are the bridge between thought, manifestation, and reality. Therefore, they are of great importance. Everything was first thought of—and then defined by—words and then made manifest. Miracles, life changes, and enlightenment evolve from words. Words have great power in relationships because they speak of the heart's intent. Spirit created everything that is, through the power of words.

No word is ever lost. Words are energy. Have you ever heard anyone say, "Forget I ever said that?" Impossible to do, isn't it? In metaphysics, we have learned that words carry great energy and always manifest on some level at some time. Words can protect the sanctity and boundaries in a relationship and allow for deeper, more intimate healing. Or words can break boundaries, reveal secrets, and leave lovers feeling betrayed and unsafe. Words have great power to unite or separate, create love or isolation.

*Small people attempt to make you feel small.*
*Great people call forth your greatness. Choose to be the latter.*

Words define our relationships to ourselves and to one another.

They tell us whether we have integrity, emotional courage, compassion, and understanding. When we abandon or betray our partners, we have in fact abandoned and betrayed ourselves, because our personal level of integrity is reflected in our words and actions. Any betrayal or abandonment reflects a lack of integrity in us, not our partner. If you have chosen to make love with someone, at the very least they deserve your respect. Even if they later disappoint you, move on and deal with your own lack of ethical choice by healing yourself rather than destroying the reputation of the person with whom you have been.

With words we can create information that is derogatory or harmful to another. With words we can treat one another with awe and respect as precious human beings courageous enough to walk this path together. Do you not think it is astounding that we have the courage to make commitments to each other to peel away the barriers to intimacy and sit together, willing to show the truth of who we are? When one makes this incredible commitment, he or she deserves the best we have to offer on every level. It is our individual job to see that the best is what we offer in our actions and our words. Society has enough derogatory words to define us. Must we do that to each other?

*The quality of love you offer is never diminished*
*by another's response to it.*

Being in a relationship is truly the only opportunity we have to finely hone our skills of honesty and loving. We demonstrate that skill through the words and actions we choose. Take a minute to go over this checklist to see if your words and actions are aligned with your spirit.

1. Do you share information with others that is derogatory or harmful about your partner other than in a therapeutic setting in which these issues are being addressed?
2. Do you create a nonsafe environment by bringing up issues from the past for which you have said he or she was forgiven?
3. Do you use your partner's shortcomings as a weapon to diminish him or her?
4. Do you invite energy into the relationship that is not supportive to your mate or your relationship bond?

5. Do you share private or intimate information without your partner's permission?

6. Do you share his or her shortcomings or character flaws with others?

7. Do you talk about the ways in which he or she is remiss as a partner to others?

8. Are there ways in which you are deliberately inaccurate to win your point?

9. Do you call in the troops or relate how "others" feel similar to you when addressing an issue with your partner?

10. Do you discuss issues with others that concern your partner before speaking to him or her?

11. Do you bring up information about your partner's past, family, career, or other issues that could be painful to your partner in order to get a winning advantage?

12. Do you use shaming or blaming language to reinforce your point (name-calling, labels, foul language, derogatory sexual terms, etc.)?

13. Do you become verbally abusive, use threats, fear, guilt, control, physical threats?

14. Do you use passive, noncommittal, compliant, indifferent language to manipulate your partner?

15. Do you use "payback" or vengeful language and techniques?

16. Do you answer questions with questions?

17. Do you avoid taking responsibility by pointing out your partner's failings?

18. Do you deliberately verbally inflict pain to stop the process?

19. Do you avoid the issues by talking about unrelated topics or withdrawing and not talking at all?

20. Do you often think things you never say or withhold information?

21. Do you ever tell your partner what he or she should do?

22. Do you ever make "innocent" or critical remarks that hurt your partner?

23. Do you feel it is unnecessary to apologize?

24. Do you express cynical, doubting responses to attempts at growth?

25. Do you make commitments you do not keep? Do you promise to honor requests and then fail to do so?
26. Do you express yourself with ambiguity and uncertainty?
27. Do you withhold praise and encouragement?
28. Do you solicit information that your partner has told you he or she is not ready to share?
29. Do you exaggerate or embellish information?
30. Do you shift the blame to others for your own actions and behavior?

Now perhaps you are beginning to understand the power of your words. If you answered any of these questions affirmatively, you are consciously or unconsciously creating a lack of safety in your relationship. You may want to ask yourself why you are creating this unsafe environment. Is it because you lack emotional courage? Is it because you are unwilling to deal with your issues and your healing? If this is true, you are hurting your own spirit with the lie that you are incapable of doing it differently, better. Instead of telling your truth and addressing your issues directly, you choose to place the responsibility and burden on your partner for cleaning up the mess that results from this self-deception. You don't have to do that. Don't lie to yourself by saying you don't have the courage to do it differently. I know you do, and so do you!

You deserve to experience the strength of your own spirit. This is your task on the planet at this time. Your partner deserves absolute truth and integrity. Your relationship deserves a chance to be a sacred healing space for both of you. This is one of the most important gifts you give to each other.

Imagine you and your partner have created a third being or entity out of your love, much as you would create a child. This child, called relationship, deserves every ounce of integrity and love you can bring to it if you are both to succeed. Together you have given birth to an incredible opportunity and process. A sacred trust. It should be inviolate. You must protect it and your partner if it is to flourish and grow. Your relationship is the one gift that offers you the finest opportunity you will ever have to evolve your own soul. It can give you the greatest gift of learning how to be truthful, courageous. and aligned with Spirit. It can be the finest tool you will ever have for becoming a master at love, and there is nothing more important. If you turn your back on this opportunity to grow, experience integrity, tell your truth, and experience the fullness of your capacity for love, it is not about your partner. That decision is about you and your own lack of courage.

*When your will and Spirit's will are the same,*
*everything simply works.*

On the other hand, if you create a trustworthy environment that supports truth-telling and honesty, you will find you are both able to grow without fear of betrayal. Your intimacy will deepen and your sexuality will get better because you are connecting on all levels during lovemaking instead of only connecting physically. You and your partner will feel safe enough to give yourselves completely to each other, without holding any part of your selves back, because you have created a safe space. Your opportunities for ecstasy will become endless. In the center of every interaction with your mate, you have the potential for great growth. That is where you will find yourself. That's why relationships are about you!

*A moment's hesitation before any decision or act*
*gives one time to opt for the greatest good.*

When you're not emotionally or spiritually present to yourself, it's impossible to be present with your partner, which results in relationships growing tedious and mundane. **If you're bored in your relationship, you are disconnected from yourself and your partner.** Your intent must be to truly *find and know the truths* of each other in your process of connecting. Do you stay on the surface or do you go deeper? Couples, friends, and families who truly love each other don't really care, other than in passing, what you bought at the grocery store, how your day went at the beauty parlor, or what you accomplished at the office. They want to know what you long for in your life. What would bring you great joy. What you dream of becoming. They want to know what your soul aches for, and how they can help you fulfill your dreams.

When people really love you, they don't care how old you are or whether you are wearing the latest craze in fashion. They want to know what your most recent life adventure was and if you are willing to risk being foolish, honest, or outrageous for the next one. They want to know if the next phase of your life feels frightening, freeing, fuller. They want to know what priceless lesson you have learned about yourself and the world each day. They want to share with you each pearl of wisdom they have gathered for themselves. They don't care who you know or how you got to know them. They care who you are, the truth of you, and which parts of yourself you still hide.

People who love you want to know if you have dealt with your deepest disappointments, satisfied your soul's spiritual aspirations, faced your fiercest fears. They don't care what astrological sign you are, what gender you are, who you have chosen to love or spend your life with. They want to know *if love has touched your soul* and *if you have touched back* in return.

They want to know if you have fallen apart, so that, should it ever become necessary, they can do the same with you. They want to know if you have made mistakes and if you'll forgive them when they do. They want to know if, like them, you are seeking ecstasy, so when you find it they can be sure you will share it.

They want to know if you have sat in the center of your sorrow and if you have become safe enough to sit with them in theirs. They want to know if you are courageous enough to want life as it is, rather than fixed up, covered over, less offensive, and less honest. They want to know if you allow, respect, and even ask for the truth, real feelings from yourself and others. They want to know if you are capable of loving them enough to bear red wagon issues, out-of-context accusations, misplaced anger, unconscious betrayal, and love occasionally diminished by fear. They want to know if you are capable of loving yourself enough to tolerate accusations, healthy anger, a lack of betrayal, and love mostly undiminished by fear. They want to know if you have reached that place of exquisite knowing that you both teachers in each others' life, on a wondrous journey home, and that you chose each other for the trip. And let's raise the bar a bit more—we should want to know these things about each other, whether we are women or men. We need to cross the gender gap in our own community.

When you are finally present, doing life and your relationships superficially is simply not an option—it's tantamount to returning to kindergarten after graduating from college. It's an insult to your own spirit and your partner's. Since you are in spiritual college—or you wouldn't be reading this book—let's give you the tools you need to go to these deep places with the right use of language.

## More About Language When Working On Issues

We have discussed becoming fully present and establishing a contract to make sure safety is in place, and now you can begin to deal with issues and problems that come up. Some may come up in your everyday process with people. You can choose to deal with those in the moment, with the other person or alone. Any of these options is fine. The only important thing is that you choose to heal. Now, with these tools, you're going to have the wondrous experience of really doing the work to heal yourself. Obviously the deepest, most meaningful work will be accomplished when you set aside time to be more focused. That's why I'm giving you this format of contracts, settings, and tools so that you'll know how to get started. After a while, this whole idea and process will become second nature, and you'll see so much benefit that you'll probably do as most of my patients do and make these sessions a weekly gift to yourselves. After a while, when you are comfortable, you will drop all these tools and just become the process of being real, trustworthy, and present.

When you choose to do more focused work with your partner, it's critical that during your healing sessions the partner creating the safe space be very aware of her own boundaries and become an objective observer. Your job is to stay present and understand that anything being said is not about you.

For instance, Janice says, "I feel so scared I could die!"

Her partner making a safe space would not say, "I don't know why, I've been home with you, right here, every night this week!"

Instead, she might say, "Tell me what it feels like when you're so scared you could die." Remember, the content coming from your partner is not about you. It really isn't! It's about her and every life experience she has had in her life. You are simply someone who is trying to better understand why she feels as she does.

Being curious and receptive to whatever your partner feels will allow you to understand her better, and promote feelings of being heard and understood instead of being embarrassed or shamed.

## Learning to Mirror Each Other

The partner creating the safe space provides supportive mirroring for the feelings that are being shared by the partner who is working. The concept of mirroring is simple. Imagine you are a mirror simply reflecting back to your partner what she's feeling without including any of your influence or feelings about it. Mirroring means there's no need to change the feelings being shared or correct your partner's perception.

*The only thing required to make your relationship work*
*is unconditional love.*

No doubt, in the process, you will discover that your partner's feelings really are *not* about you anyway but rather have to do with issues from his childhood. If you interject your opinions or needs, the flow will stop and your partner may feel ashamed or guilty. Or if he becomes concerned about your response, he may then feel a need to take care of you instead of experiencing his own feelings fully.

## Do Not "Fix It" For Each Other

Be careful that you do not try to "fix it" for your partner. In fact, the best response may be to encourage your partner to amplify his or her feelings rather than get out of them, in order to get a better understanding of them. The need to "fix it" arises when someone else's pain triggers the pain inside you. In order not to feel your own pain, you may unconsciously try to get other people out of theirs as quickly as possible.

As you support your partner by not doing her work, but instead being with her as she does the work, she will relax more into the process, feeling safe and assured. She can rest assured that you will not have judgments or expectations.

If you want to comment during the process, use open-ended questions to help your partner focus on her own feelings or awareness. Questions such as:

- What are you aware of?
- Did something just take you out of the process?
- Could you say more about that?
- What did you just experience?
- Could you make that bigger?
- What's happening inside right now?
- Where did you just go?
- Was there something that made you want to leave?

*When you have begun to think you know the answers for your beloved, you are working from ego and not heart or Spirit.*

## Using the Breath

You can continue to use the breath to focus on issues or feelings that you experience in the body. You can remind yourself or have your partner remind you to, "Breathe into there (in the body) and let yourself become aware of what's there."

Breath is a wonderful tool that can also help *release the issue* once it has surfaced. Allow the fear to come up and out on the breath as you exhale. Breath also *deepens the process.* Breathe deeply and let yourself get to where it is that you would like to be.

You may often experience long silences, and deep breathing will allow your partner to take herself deeply into a relaxed state of awareness. You may both agree without words simply to enjoy this state of being fully present. If so, that's fine. However, if a process issue—meaning a fear or problem arises, in order to deepen your session, there must be a feeling of sequential rightness to the questions you use to guide the process. In other words, if your partner was experiencing a feeling of sadness, you would not want to remind him about how happy he was this morning. Instead, you would want him to go deeper into the sadness in order to resolve it naturally. So you might say, "Talk about your sadness."

Language and tone become very important. Your tone of voice must match the affect of your partner. For instance, if she is very "little" and into the child state, your tone must be quiet and nonthreatening. You would speak to his or her child in a soft, comforting manner.

My friend Carolyn described it this way: "Your voice was important as I tried to move myself into this place it created for me. It was much a part of the safety, the love. Most of the time my only way to understand what was going on was to say you were like a tuning fork. When we were in this space, you rang out the true pitch, and parts of me tried to harmonize with it. Your repeating the words I said, your voice, was a large part of trying to harmonize with the tone you set for me.

"Maybe it was a look, maybe a few simple words, a question of something I said, which hit inside of me. Each time I would leave, repeating whatever it was that had struck me. Over and over I would say it, think it, and go through a rash of responses. It seemed to me that the vibration of your tune had to shake out some dirt, some old baggage, or old thoughts. As I rehearsed what you said I would think of what was not consonant with this tone, and I would slowly work to finish those parts."

## The Gift of Vertical Language

This process needs to be paced very slowly so that each resistance can be dealt with as it arises. Language and words become very important. I'm going to introduce you to a new kind of language called **vertical language.** Don't be overly concerned about it, but be aware of how your language affects your partner. Your goal is to take your partner vertically *down* into his or her feelings. If you just keep that in mind, you'll understand what I mean by vertical language in the discussion that follows. Try, as I have said before, to use or mirror your partner's words and inflections.

The questions presented to your partner should be in what I call vertical language. Vertical language takes your partner down deeper into emotions or feelings rather than out and away from them. Most of the time, you can determine which word or phrase will take you deeper by becoming aware of which contains the most energy or impact. Remember the bouncing ball above the lyrics at your neighborhood karaoke bar? Just listen for the most important words. An obvious example would be, "I felt like killing myself." Obviously, the words "killing myself" contain the energy. Or if your partner says, "I feel completely alone," the word "alone" contains the energy. You would prompt, "Talk about 'alone.'"

**Refrain from using words or asking questions that take each other's awareness away from the feelings.** Instead, use language that takes your partner deeper into her emotions. If your partner says, "I'm scared about too many feelings coming up," you could respond by saying, "Talk about feeling scared," as opposed to saying, "Don't worry, I've felt that way too." Feel the difference? Encourage your partner to go *down and into* his or her feelings.

Refrain from using language that moves attention to yourself or anything other than your partner's immediate feeling. Remember, it's as though you have an imaginary circle drawn around your partner that creates a "holding environment." You do not want your language to take your partner's attention out of that circle, nor do you want to impose your feelings or agenda into his or her circle.

When problem solving takes place, new resolutions to existing issues are automatically discovered. Resolutions, answers, may come in the form of greater awareness about the issue. It may be as simple as finding out your aversion to blue comes from your Aunt Judy, who used to pinch the heck out of your cheeks. Every time she visited she wore her blue blouse to the house. Knowing that, you can now make a new decision about whether you ever want to wear blue again, which happens to look great on you. It's good to keep in mind that as you uncover issues, you can also remind yourself of all the ways in which they are now different for you. You are older. You are physically bigger. You have more cognitive skills. You have more support. For instance, you may have lived with an abusing parent, whom you feared. You can remind yourself that the parent is no longer with you and you have an adult (you) inside now to protect you.

Some people don't feel they have an adult inside who knows what to do. In fact, they don't think they can take care of themselves. It's fun when this issue arises, and I ask, "Well, OK, what would you do if your child or best friend was being assaulted?"

"I'd go right over and stop it," they reply.

"That's the same person who can take care of you," I remind them.

We all have an inner parent; however, it can feel difficult while healing to connect with that energy when we are immersed in the inner child's feelings of helplessness.

Problems about intimacy, vulnerability, taking charge of your life, commitment, joy, fears about abandonment, engulfment, success, self-esteem, success, creative expression, and many other issues arise from your own childhood, long after you have become an adult.

Questions and comments from partners who are creating safe spaces might be:

- How does that affect you?
- Talk about that experience.
- Let the feelings of that experience come out on the exhale.
- Is that in your body?
- Is there a name for that feeling?
- Who inside is feeling that? (An inner child? How old?)
- What would you like to do with that experience?

## Important Tools for Dealing With Intense Feelings

If intense, seemingly uncontrollable fear or pain floods to the surface, remind your partner that he or she can choose to deal with small pieces of the issue at a time. Don't panic! This could happen but usually does not, because inherently your inner healer or Spirit knows when you need specifically trained support to deal with these kinds of feelings. When your partner feels he needs to stop or some portion of the work is sufficiently done, take him into his safe place—the one you each created before starting the work. Just ask him to close his eyes and visualize that safe place.

Once he is in his safe place, help him create a box or drawer in which to put the rest of his feelings until he feels able to return to the process. He might prefer to wait until your next appointment time or until he can meet with a professional. That's fine. Simply have him make sure his feelings are secure in the container and he feels safe that they will remain there until you meet again.

When your partner is feeling safe again, you know you have completed the process of helping to regulate or titrate (allow to surface in manageable portions) the feelings that came up. You had to develop great coping skills as children, such as repression of bad memories. You can now use those same skills as the adult, in a positive way as you heal. It's fine to use your ability to store memories in order to work with them at a safer pace or in order not to be overwhelmed by them as you begin to heal. Simply locate your safe container and begin to store the fragments of the memory that are available. If all parts of the memory are not be available to you, then store whatever portion is accessible.

The facilitating partner can assist by saying:

- OK, now store all the feelings about this incident with dad.
- Store all the things you see.
- Store all the things you were told.
- Store all the pain or discomfort.
- Now make sure all the kids inside have stored their feelings and pain.

The late Dr. Steve Ray and Dr. Pamela Reagor, who treated survivors of ritual abuse with dissociative identity disorder, created the concept of storing memory. This idea is also extremely effective for any kind of abuse and traumatic memory resolution.

If the intense feelings your partner has just experienced trigger some vulnerability that might prevent you from being fully present for her process, don't work on this issue together. Explain that you are having difficulty staying present, and ask your partner how you can support her in dealing with this issue with someone else or a professional. Find someone else to work on the issue with you both, preferably a qualified therapist specifically trained in your issue.

It is a real disservice to the person attempting to heal issues to go forward when you can't be present with each other. Not much can occur beyond a lot of frustration and possibly a feeling of overwhelm and abandonment.

Most of the time, the only resolve that may be needed is to understand your feelings and responses about an event in your life and their effects on you now. That alone will have a huge impact on changing the degree to which you remain in denial, thus allowing an issue from your past to control you. That's also why a great deal of healing work on issues can and should be done outside the therapy office. Although I may be talking myself out of a job, the truth is that much of the work done in therapy offices could be done together at home if we trusted ourselves.

So to recap, when hard or difficult feelings come to the surface you can:

- Process them through your work with your partner.
- Process them alone in your safe room.
- Process them with a qualified professional.

Probably as much as 85% of the time you'll be able to simply deal on your own with whatever comes up. Trust yourself, your inner healer, and your partner's inner healer or Spirit to decide what's best for you. Talk openly about your concerns and go forward *only* when you are feeling safe. The most important aspect of healing is listening to your own intuition. Some of the time healing is not necessarily comfortable. But genuine healing always has an element to it that feels right, good.

*You know everything you need to know to end emotional suffering.*
*Trust yourself and the Spirit within.*

You may find some uncomfortable feelings and yet feel confident that you can talk them through and handle them on your own. If your intuition tells you something is off or wrong about discussing this particular issue at this particular time, simply stop. Wait until you can figure out what is off and address it in another session. That process of asking for what you need to feel safe and giving it to yourself can play an important part in your healing.

## Some Illusions

Be careful at this point. You may begin to think you know what your partner needs or how he or she should approach certain issues in order to resolve them. Remember, the deepest and most effective healing always comes from your own inner healer. Your ego may also trick you into believing you don't have the same kind of resistance your partner does and therefore you are more evolved or superior. Perhaps your issues are not the same, but, trust me, you will discover that you have some comparable ones of your own. We all do.

Think for a minute about those people in your life who have taught you or helped you along your path. Rather than pretending to be flawless and more advanced than you, didn't they honestly examine their own issues with honesty and compassion?

*The person needing to be right is standing in ego, not Spirit.*

We are all able to learn from others who offer support in a non-judgmental way. Little is learned from people who perceive themselves to be somehow better than we are. The finest lessons learned in life are always offered from a place of compassion and humility.

Remember that your answers are *your* answers, and they may not apply to your partner. The fastest route into deep healing is into a space that contains no preconceived ideas and is guided solely by the working partner's inner healer.

Another illusion that may arise is that now that you have talked about the issue, it is finished and you won't have to deal with it anymore. But more than likely you have responded to certain circumstances in the same way for most of your life. The new understandings you gain will serve to change your awareness of the problem, but **you may have to continue to work to change your old responses and habits.**

Yet another illusion is that other parts of the same issue will not arise and you are finished with the issue in just one sitting. Sorry, but another piece of that issue might come bubbling up again, so that's not always true. There are often many facets to an issue, so be patient with yourself and don't become discouraged if the same issue comes up repeatedly. You will simply be dealing with different aspects of the problem. When all aspects have been dealt with, the problem will feel and be resolved. The issue goes from a full-blown living-color photo to a tiny negative without much impact. Be patient. Growth is a lifetime process.

## Integrity

At this point you may be tempted to talk about the process with people other than your partner. Because this work is very deep, most people get excited when they see progress toward health, especially regarding long-held issues. Keep in mind that you have entered a sacred passage with someone who trusts you. Therefore, keep your word about not breaking confidentiality about your sessions. If you feel you can't contain your excitement, write about it in a journal. It's a great idea to keep a journal about your process anyway. You'll be surprised when you later read your journal and see how far you have come along on your path.

Authentic healing is distinguished by not needing to embellish or edit. You experience realness in the exchange. When it's real, you don't need to add anything. Feelings, thoughts, and responses will flow freely, uncoerced and without exaggeration. Important expression flows naturally and without self-judgment. If you find yourself editing, go back to the initial stages and deal with your resistance or fears about telling your truth or disclosing. Examine what's going on, and explore again why you may not be feeling safe.

## Leave Room for Exploration

The support person's words should provide encouragement and space for many options. Get creative and explore more kinds of open-ended questions for your tool bag. **It's important to avoid leading the process.** I use statements such as

- You could explore that feeling or not.
- You could wonder about what could happen differently.
- Talk about your dad.
- Say more about feeling angry.

The intent here is to use language that is open-ended and designed to encourage internal exploration with, and curiosity in, your partner.

## Keeping the Space Separate

Try to keep your responses untainted by your personal assumptions or agenda. If I am holding the space but not in it, I can be very present with you, and yet my reality is kept out of your space. In other words, my focus is totally on and about you. It is not filled with any of my feelings, perceptions, or needs. Examples of questions that diffuse the focus and split the space are: "How can **I** help?" (moves focus to partner), "What do you want to happen?" (moves focus to thoughts, not feelings), or "I want you to tell **me**" (moves your agenda into the space).

Try to avoid intruding upon your partner's space with your questions or drawing your partner's attention out of her space and to you. In your sessions, the most meaningful interpretations are those arrived at with the help of questions free from anyone else's point of view. Your partner's inner healer will direct the process and provide the answers. Remember that your mirroring process must be uncontaminated by your agenda or need-to-know information.

*The moment you expect something, you have gone from love to need.*

## Take the Time to Go Slowly

The more accustomed you become to the process, the quicker you will be willing to go deeper. We need time to "grow into" experiencing deep healing in the same way we needed time to grow into each stage of childhood. Your sessions and process can span from 20 minutes to an hour or longer. If you get ahead of yourself, you'll miss the depth and quality of feeling that can be found by staying with and perfecting each stage.

## Session Progression

In the time span of one hour or more you'll go from energetic connection to resistance/support to issues that surface to resolution/integration to energetic release and completion/healing.

You can move freely back and forth along the continuum, depending upon the issues that surface. In the beginning, stay present as long as you like. Once you feel comfortable with the process and are doing the deeper work, make sure you go through each stage completely. In other words, you don't want to invite your partner to bring up deep issues and then leave him or her hanging with them and all the accompanying feelings and emotions. Make sure he or she feels some resolution and is ready to come out of the process.

## Mirror Your Partner's Words

We all use different kinds of language to describe our feelings, even if we are all speaking English. One person might use **metaphorical** references such as "I feel like a black cloud is hanging over me" or "I'm locked up inside." Some use **physiological** language such as "There's a knot in my stomach" or "a fist in my gut" or "My heart is broken." Sometimes people use language that comes **from the past**, using phrases such as "I remember…" or "It all started when…" or "I keep going back to…." Some people avoid speaking in the "I" space and use **collective** language. Your partner may do this by making over generalizations like "All people feel this way…." or "When people get scared…"

Do not ask what any of this language means, because answering requires your partner to move immediately into an intellectual process. Instead, work with the metaphor, using a question such as, "And when you're locked up inside, where are you locked up inside?" That question will usually take your partner to a physical place within her body, and she can begin to work with her feelings.

Whatever your partner's language, you follow its use. It takes a little practice, but you'll find your listening skills improving. And your partner will feel both seen and heard by you more than ever. Your new listening skills also create big payoffs in other aspects of your life, such as at work or with your family.

At first you may have to slow things down and take a minute to respond appropriately, but after a while this kind of listening and responding will become second nature. You can know you are successfully using the appropriate language when the questions make sense to your partner even though those same questions might not be in your own frame of reference. Your partner's response will reflect a flow without hesitation or obvious effort to comprehend.

If you're not sure you asked a question that was helpful, simply ask your partner. She will be able to tell you, "No, that took me into my head," or "Yes, that took me into my feelings." The point is to learn to take each other vertically down deeper into the feeling states.

## Relax—It's Easier Than It Looks

I have given you many things to think about. Don't be overwhelmed. Remember the first week of your last new job? Remember how confused you felt until suddenly right in the midst of doing some task, everything fell into place and you got the big picture and understood what was happening? The same holds true for this process. All these little details may seem like a lot, but they fit into a big picture that makes sense as soon as you start the work. Once you start to practice, you won't have to even think about any of these techniques. The energetic process will become simple to follow and easy to feel. Remember to have fun! You can do this. It's just a matter of becoming a better listener and using these new tools.

Now that you have the idea, take a minute to write down your own list of open-ended questions so that you will be ready to begin. Remember, open-ended questions are those that encourage exploration and don't give your partner any particular direction. Such as, "Say more about that."

1.

2.

3.

4.

When you feel stuck, the finest tool you have is simply silence. Take your time, breathe often, and simply allow the healing to occur naturally. There's really nothing more important than being a compassionate presence for each other. Something incredible will happen between you merely because you have created a focused space for each other in which to do your work.

*Spirit is in the silence between your thoughts.*

Take time now to write down some of the issues you feel might arise as you begin to communicate with your partner.

## Personal Inventory: Identifying My Issues About Communication

1. What are the resistance or defense mechanisms that prevent you from communicating your feelings easily?

2. If you don't know, ask someone close to you what she thinks you do when you resist sharing emotional issues.

3. What is the resistance or defense mechanism that prevents you from listening well?

4. If you don't know, ask someone close to you what he thinks you do when others are attempt to share emotional issues with you.

5. When you stop being present during meaningful discussions, what can you do to become more fully present?

6. Write down the ways in which learning to be a better communicator and listener will enrich your relationships.

Good! Now sit back and relax with this meditation.

■　■　■

Close your eyes and envision a time in the not-too-distant future when you and your partner have completed some of the work that allows you to become more fully present. Imagine how it will feel to be fully connected, honest, and truthful. Experience the freedom of this state of consciousness. Take a minute to see which new endeavors and experiences you and your partner might look forward to creating together. You and your partner can do this meditation together and then compare notes about what you hope to create for yourselves on this journey.

All right, this next dyad is a bit deeper. If you find you're not ready to share at this level, that's fine. However, make a commitment to your partner that you will come back to this one and do it together when you feel safe enough.

1. The judgments I have about you are:

2. The ways those judgments reflect judgments I have about myself are:

3. The good qualities I see in you are:

4. The ways those good qualities reflect good qualities in me are:

5. The thing I have been most afraid to tell you is:

6. The thing I have been most afraid to tell myself is:

7. The thing I am able to teach you in this relationship is:

8. The thing I am going to learn for myself in this relationship is:

# CHAPTER EIGHT
## You Get Immediate Gifts

*Greatness may be sought*
*through the doorway*
*of the mind.*

*Greatness arrives*
*only through the doorway*
*of the heart.*

## You've Started Healing!

When you become willing to confront and resolve your issues, you give yourself an exquisite gift of more life and love. You will also be delighted to find that the process becomes easier each time you do it. Almost from the beginning, your listening skills and level of presence will improve. These improvements come from allowing yourself to focus in a positive way on your own issues and those of your partner, using your new tools. Soon you will feel safer about exploring places that may have in the past seemed scary. The issues inside you that once felt so dark and foreboding now prove to be filled with potential and possibility. The same issues that were once frightening are now wonderful, limitless opportunities for healing.

It becomes easier to be honest—primarily because you have so much less to hide. Second, because you discover your issues are no worse than those of your friends and loved ones. So you feel less desire to hide. You experience less shame. You can get honest, knowing we all have our own individual red wagons. You stop feeling as if you're the only one in the world with issues. You're not. In fact, everyone has something in their past that needs healing.

Whenever you choose to consciously be in relationship, you're living on the edge of the unknown. This is a place of discovery, a place where you both meet that soon becomes a sacred ground for doing deep experiential work together. Being genuinely present with another forces us to dance on that edge. Getting to those places with your partner brings so many gifts, the first and most important of which is autonomy, a sense of self-empowerment. Committing to your own healing puts you in direct experience with your own strength, courage, and integrity. Your sense of personal power returns. Personal empowerment means a return of Spirit to us individually and to us as a community. As long as we walk around without a strong sense of self inside, we will keep trying to siphon feelings of fulfillment from everyone else. In some ways, we have all been relationship vampires. We seek safety, control, feelings of being loved, adoration, and trust from everyone else, but we have refused to create these feelings for ourselves. We suck the energy out of each other because we have not dealt with our own levels of need. We leave one relationship after another, feeling exhausted and drained ourselves or having exhausted and drained our partner. And still we are without the peace and security we seek. Quietly it waits inside us.

It's thrilling to know you have the answers inside yourself to most of the problems that arise in daily life. This is spiritual awareness and truth. Unlike what society teaches, we don't always need to seek someone we perceive to be more knowledgeable than ourselves to do deeper healing. You can do most of this work with someone you love and trust. The moment you make a decision to stop running from yourself and become still enough to hear the wisdom inside, a great weight is lifted from your shoulders. You have found that elusive something you always knew life had to offer, but which you couldn't name. Your personal road to enlightenment leads directly within. It is you that you must find—and when you do, you become the light of your own experience.

*There is nothing the world has to offer that is more important than enlightenment.*

Another benefit of being present and doing your own work is a sense of greater aliveness and real movement in your life. All of life is energy. Energy that is stagnant, dense, and unmoving soon becomes lifeless and dies. You cannot hold onto the old. The old is leaving every second of every day. Energy that is changing, alive, and filled with momentum adds vitality to your life and sense of well-being. If you're not growing spiritually, you're dying.

There are no better workshops, more precious or perfect for your work, than your own relationships. Every encounter you have is your personal opportunity for greatness, grace, and increased understanding. Even if you never read another book your entire life, the universe and all it offers would open to you the moment you became fully present to those you love. This world of opportunity is waiting right in the space between you and those you love. Every feeling, thought, idea, fear, insight, and gem of wisdom is right in front of you. But you must be willing to become aware of it and conscious to its potential.

Knowing you are on a sincere spiritual path to understanding builds self-esteem and greater tolerance for others. We each hold so many feelings in denial, once you have discovered your own issues and begin to have compassion for yourself, you naturally have compassion for others. It's easier to act out of love. This satisfying process helps us fill the emptiness inside and replace it with deep, meaningful connections to those we love. Our connection to those we don't even know also becomes apparent. You will find you have greater compassion and appreciation for people in general. None of us is fully enlightened. As Ram Dass says, "We are all still works in progress."

*Whenever you sacrifice anything for spiritual harmony,*
*something greater will always take its place.*

After years of focusing on our individuality, piling denial upon denial, many couples and friends are finally getting it. They are now satisfying the craving for deep connection by learning to be present, get honest, and act out of love for each other. They are finally connected in the deepest sense. These three simple tools have an amazing capacity to give you exactly what you want: profound love.

I have learned that the universe, in its infinite wisdom, has created an important trick when it comes to allowing us to be profoundly connected to each other. One of my teachers, Gangaji, brought this to my awareness when she was discussing the issue of guru-devotee relationships. I have always resisted this type of connection and perceived it to be a one-up dynamic that was not very healthy. In her discussion she pointed out that the student-teacher or guru-devotee relationship is a very delicate one. It is one that has much to teach us, in the same way mate relationships teach us about ourselves. Our resistance to it may be a lack of faith in ourselves and our own ability to trust what is loving. Gangaji asked a student who had inquired about this issue to explore her resistance as a means of understanding herself. She pointed out that if the teacher or guru were corrupt, one would know that and, therefore, leave. On the other hand, if the relationship were real, one would also know that. And, in the moment of true acceptance, we would have the direct experience that there is no difference between the teacher and the student or the guru and the devotee. In other words, she was saying that it is all one. In that instant of true connection, there is no longer any separation; there is only one truth. And that truth is love. That insight is also what you will discover in your relationships. There are many of us, and yet, only one.

Your mate relationships are no less delicate. The principle is the same. Whenever you resist allowing total union with your beloved, there is work to be done on yourself. Your resistance is never about the other person. In exactly the same way, when we are able to experience and embrace the spirit of our partner, we are facing a direct reflection of ourselves and the divine. It is all one. All of your resistance to falling into this state is your work. Tell the truth. If you were not afraid in some way, why would you need to resist? Would you not just allow yourself to feel love and give love with great abandon and openness? Of course you would. But we are afraid. We are afraid of being loved and giving love. We do not trust ourselves to be who we already are. We do not trust ourselves to have enough, to be able to hold onto love, to be worthy of love. It is as if we are saying, "I will not eat today because tomorrow there may be no food." Address these fears in your process with your partner. Take a deep breath and allow each other to come spiritually, emotionally closer.

If you want more love, you must release the pain and the barriers you now hold to receiving it. The good news is that you have control over the pace and depth of your own work. That alone instills greater courage and willingness to face past issues. You will become so good at dealing directly with your own issues that, in many cases, the simple awareness of what has caused the pain and how it has affected your life will instantly resolve it. The courage and commitment of your own Spirit are heightened and reflected back to you, repeatedly, as you explore issues and feelings you previously feared. Those same issues, which may have negatively controlled your decisions in the past, are now easily resolved. You experience greater freedom, more aliveness. The moment you are able to fully accept yourself you have taken a quantum leap personally and for our community. You will finally begin to make decisions free from your past or your pain. **You will make decisions based upon your path rather than your pathology—out of love and not fear.** In other words, you will get back to Spirit.

Many of you have been seeking your soul mates. In some sense, we are all soul mates to each other. Soul mates are those people with whom we choose to do soul-deep work. There is an element of divine grace, spiritual insight, and wisdom in committed relationships that comes from our intent to heal at deeper levels with each other. You might find that with a friend, a family member, or anyone. But if you think of soul mate as the life partner with whom you experience so intense a connection that you feel as if you are both from the same bolt of Spirit, you can have that as well. Soul mates can be two spirits who are destined to be together or they can be two spirits who create a destiny together because of their intense commitment. If you want a soul mate relationship, find your partner and commit, soul to soul, to see and honor the spirit in each of you.

## How to Know if You Are *Really* Healing

There will be no doubt that you have authentically created healing, because you will reach a very different level of consciousness about the issue you are working on. It is as if someone has drawn back the blinds and let in the sunlight. Old injuries once had the impact of big full-blown, living-color, drive-in theater–size screens will now feel like small photo-strip negatives. You will be aware of the facts about what happened to you, but the experience will no longer control or trigger you. Old pain will no longer prevent you from embracing life fully.

Your process will give you greater understanding about every issue you choose to heal, which, in turn, gives you a greater sense of power. You start to feel in control of life, rather than having life control you. You will feel more connected to others than ever. You will catch yourself sitting back in awe and amazement at the newfound level of love you feel for those in your life. You will definitely become more vulnerable and open than ever in a good, safe way that moves you to wanting more. Naturally, the more you are consistent in doing this work the more you stay aware, the deeper the work will become. Can you imagine what life could be like if you were able to greet it with open arms and little, if any, fear?

*The ability to transcend limitation is yours*
*the moment you release your belief in it.*

As you continue in this work, you'll notice subtle changes in yourself. You'll feel more courageous. You'll be able to view issues from different perspectives, with less limitation or need for negative control. You'll feel a greater sense of aliveness, joy, and sensuality. You'll be able to express more compassion, understanding. You'll be more willing to express yourself in general—who you are, what you believe. You'll find you greet life with a new sense of adventure, a greater sense of self and a lot less fear. Because you are more open to all that life has to offer you, boredom, mundaneness, and tedium become responses of the past.

You'll no longer need to lose yourself in constant activity in order to deny an inner emptiness. You may even want slow down because you sense you could be missing life and all it has to offer when you are rushing. As the mystic Thomas Merton wrote, rushing becomes "another form of violence." Life is precious. Love is precious. Both are to be savored, safeguarded, and slowly embraced.

*You experience as much joy in life as you can conceive of*
*until you are open to receiving it all.*

Don't be surprised if you also find yourself becoming very excited and joyful at the prospect of each new encounter. There is equally as much learning from every new joy-filled experience as there is in those old ones with uncomfortable feelings. We are a country bereft of joy. It's time to experience a renewed sense of value for the times in your life when you are simply overflowing with joy and bliss. This work will bring many such opportunities. Hopefully you'll learn to laugh often at yourself and with those you love. In the past, spirituality has been seen as a serious and somber matter. In actuality, as we get lighter we should also be able to feel more happiness and take ourselves and life less seriously, because we trust the process. You will begin to greet every day and every person as a new opportunity to learn something fun about yourself. Don't miss even one. No matter where you are or who you are with, there's an opportunity for great healing and the return of great joy. You may even find you experience ecstasy for the very first time. You'll have resolved the self-loathing and shame that society continues to feed upon. When you are truly self-loving and treat yourself with respect and honor, there's very little society can do to hurt you ever again. You check out of needing their approval and check in to living life fully.

The delightful thing about this work is that although you may occasionally be processing experiences and feelings that are uncomfortable or even painful, there's great joy in the fact that you are healing. It is like doing the hard work of building your own house and then having the great satisfaction of moving into your creation and having everything in it reflect who you are. What a wonder. Hopefully, you will also spend a lot of time allowing yourself to be with that joy and each new awareness. Each step you take toward yourself brings greater aliveness and feelings of health, spirituality, and grace. Don't worry, you'll be able to know you are truly healing. Just becoming present is the first step. Here's a list of questions to ask yourself which will help you tell whether your work of becoming more present is truly being effective. I've provided a list of questions for those of you working with a partner and those of you who are working alone.

If you're working with a partner, after you have gone through a few sessions, ask each other these questions:

- Do you feel you are heard and understood?
- Which kinds of questions take you away from your feelings?
- Which kinds of questions take you deeper into your feelings?
- Do you feel your partner is fully present with you while you are in the process?

- Is there something you needed that you didn't receive?
- How is the pacing?
- What would you like to do differently in your next session?

If you're doing this work alone, you can ask some of the very same questions of yourself to check your personal progress.

- Are you expressing your truths and being heard and understood more fully by the people around you in your life?
- Are you more present to the truths of others?
- What fears still take you out of the process of being fully present and truthful?
- How can you get more present with yourself?
- Is there something you need that you can give to yourself to add safety?
- What can you do differently?
- What prevents you from starting that now? (Tell the truth here.)

■ ■ ■

Let's see what happens for you in this next meditation. Close your eyes and imagine yourself back on the road of life where you met your Spirit. This time look at the different roles that you play in your life, such as lover, mother, father, teacher, mate, employee, or boss. In your mind, create a road that depicts each of your roles. Imagine you are standing in the middle of an intersection, and before you are many roads, each road a role that you fulfill in your own life. Place yourself at some point on each road that depicts how far along you have come toward being fully present, honest, and loving in each of these life circumstances or roles. Are you halfway to your goal? Have you just stepped onto the road? Are you all the way there? Once you have determined how far along you are in each area of your life, come out of the meditation and draw what you saw. Date your drawing and put it away. Mark your calendar six months from today, and do this visualization again to see how far you have come.

# Act Out of Love, Not Fear

# CHAPTER NINE
# Acting Out of Love

*In the healing connection,*
*oneness is absolute.*
*It is the host reality.*
*The aliveness of that space*
*is a mandate for extraordinary change,*
*the first of which is*
*the experience of right union.*

## Let's Recap the Benefits of This Work

There are some very basic reasons for increasing your spiritual lovability, the biggest being that you finally move into harmony with how the universe works. There's a system to everything in life. Once you understand how the system works, you're no longer at odds with life. We have a place in society. We have a place in each other's lives. We have a place in the universe that is unique and precious to each of us, and none of these places is complete until we step into them. In addition, we are so rushed and preoccupied with survival that our usual state of awareness does not focus deeply on healing ourselves. In fact, just the opposite is true. Not only do many of our issues go unnoticed, but also we keep running madly around looking for new emotional Band-Aids to cover those we become aware of. We live busy lives in a busy world, and our inclination is to avoid any uncomfortable feelings, as if they were the plague.

In this process, you learn how to safely focus on deep feelings in order to embrace and incorporate the positive ones into your life or resolve and release those that bring you pain. This intense focus provides greater awareness and understanding about all the different aspects of any given issue. **Events do not change. Your understanding and your response**

**to them does.** If you're not accepted for who you are, you understand at a core level that it's not about you. It's about the person who has the prejudice or who does not have the capacity for unconditional love. With new understanding comes healing and greater aliveness. You also increase the amount of love in your relationships and in the world.

*When you use principled love to decide,*
*all decisions become perfectly clear.*

You will begin to see how your life path and all of your experiences have brought you greater awakening. This awakening may not mean you are finished with an issue, but understanding the issue does lead to resolution. Each time you revisit an issue and gain additional understanding, you're one step closer to alleviating the pain it has caused you.

You will start to be more alert to the *meaning* of circumstances, coincidences, and events in your life. Suddenly all those circumstances and events you didn't understand now have meaning, and you understand the contribution they have made to the quality of your life. You will feel greater compassion for yourself and for others. Everyone whose life touches yours becomes your teacher. All the people whose lives you touch are also blessed in the same way, whether they are conscious of it or not.

Events from your past that appeared to have been a *fait accompli* become instead grist for your spiritual mill. You will have a feeling of greater control over the events in your life, whether from your past or present issues. You will begin see every event with a larger meaning as a part of your path to yourself. Decisions are made more slowly because you now understand their impact on your spiritual journey. Every decision you make has an effect. Every decision you make is either for love and life—or for death: spiritually, emotionally, or physically.

*Every day you are alive and every decision you choose to make*
*is your opportunity to achieve greatness.*

In addition, because you are committed and have deliberately set your intention on healing, you will feel justified in taking the time and attention necessary to look at issues differently than you normally might. Most of us have difficulty feeling good about taking time for ourselves. The healing process gives you permission to focus on your issues and heal them. Becoming aware that you are already spiritually enlightened is a process. Each enlightened awareness leads to a more enlightened life. It is as if we are walking out of a long, dimly lit tunnel into the brightness of day. The sun is finally able to shine in us, through us. There is nothing left to hide.

You get to be the director of your own life movie in this process. You can focus on different parts of each issue. You can magnify the details of an issue. You can deal with certain portions of a problem at a time.

Sit down, take a piece of paper, and draw or write down the different issues or aspects of a problem. Let yourself have complete freedom in this process. Write down the words or truths you could never dare to say before. You will prove to yourself that you have more power than they do. When you are finished and there's nothing else to write about, you will have a picture of the issue, which you can begin to resolve by addressing any of the parts of the issue you have on the paper. This allows you to release major problems in your life in a regulated way without the risk of being overwhelmed. When you feel you have resolved the entire issue, take the paper into the backyard and burn it. Release it along with any misplaced guilt and shame you may have been carrying. If you really did do something you think was/is wrong, forgive yourself. Just say it out loud, and then let go.

If there's an aspect of the issue that feels particularly dangerous for you to look at, it's usually because you haven't had the support, time, or safety to deal with it. Now, if you are working with a partner in this process, all those support systems will be in place.

## The Safety to Look Within

Your process allows you to look within at matters that normally cause negative reactions in your life. For instance, you may perceive people who are really nice as threatening or fearful because they remind you of some past issue. Perhaps you were treated badly by a person with blond hair and have chosen solely for that reason never to make friends with blond people. In your sessions you can examine the reasons you feel this way and begin to change any distorted response to life or the people around you. Think of how your world could expand and how much more open you could become to new experiences.

## Presence Gives a Sense of Enough Time

The experience of being fully present also allows for a feeling of *enough time* to explore how things are different in the *now* than they were when you were a child. Have you noticed that when you are intently doing something you love, time is not an issue? Hours can pass by without your giving it a second thought. Somehow, in those moments when you are sharing with a friend or completing a project, time slows down and you have all the time you need. This process offers that feeling of unlimited time, which brings new options for changing your behavior and focusing on the positive aspects of your life.

In this connected, present state you can easily examine issues of the past. It's also easier to be aware of how things are different for you now, in the present. I can't count the number of times clients have come in feeling afraid to face what they perceive is some deep, dark issue from the past. Once I have reminded them that they have already survived this issue, have already felt most of the feelings about it and now have a great many new skills with which to deal with it, clients move right through issues without trepidation. In just a few moments of concentrated time, you can remind yourself how different things are now than they were when you were child and how many new cognitive, emotional, and physical skills you have now than you did then. This reminder will give you the confidence to look at almost every issue.

## Dealing With Abuse

The only exception to the ease with which people deal with their issues is in the case of abuse. Abuse issues are not easy to deal with, and often we need the support of a trained counselor or therapist to deal with these issues because of the intensity of feelings that may surface. If this is true for you, give yourself the gift of healing with someone who has been *specifically trained* in the area of abuse. Many clients have come to me who had been in therapy for years with therapists not qualified to deal with abuse issues. Surprisingly, many therapists have not had this kind of training. Consequently, these clients felt they had wasted great amounts of time and money, and experienced unnecessary pain. In the end, they felt abused and ripped off by their therapists.

If you're in a situation where you have feel you have not made positive gains for quite some time in healing your issues, find a new therapist. Here's what I mean by "quite some time": All of us experience periods of time, in therapy or any healing process, when things are just not moving inside, or resistance comes up that needs to be dealt with slowly and gently. However, even in these times there should be some awareness that you are doing good work and making some headway. But if you have been in therapy a couple of years, or even many months, and you are experiencing no change in your feeling states, no change in your fear levels, no sense that you are healing on any level, leave. Do not stay with your therapist because you are afraid to hurt his or her feelings by leaving. Do not stay because he or she *feels* like your friend. Find a new therapist who is skilled at helping you heal, and call the old one for lunch in six or eight months if what you want from her is friendship. You owe it to yourself to find a *qualified* support person. If your therapist has not taken the time to get good, specialized training in this area, it's not your fault. Start shopping for a new therapist. It's your life. Don't waste it.

By the way, we are a bit of an incestuous community. If you are seeing a therapist whom you also see socially and who knows all your friends, run, don't walk to a new therapist. Don't put yourself in a situation where your boundaries are violated. You have a right to a clean, honorable space, in which you can do your work without worrying about the ramifications of it later or how it might affect your social life. A therapist who sees you socially and treats or knows all of your friends is not a good choice and probably has poor boundaries.

## Creating a Connected Sense of Oneness

In your process, being fully present results in an energetic connection that allows for a shift in consciousness. This shift gives you an experience of other states of consciousness with their own particular benefits you can call on for problem solving. As an example, when you feel present and establish a connected feeling with your partner, you may be surprised to find that you suddenly have a more concentrated understanding on an intuitive and spiritual level of what he or she feels. You may notice that moving into an expanded awareness makes it possible for you to search for new answers on how you can respond to your partner's issues differently. To begin with, you can stop taking everything so personally. You may become more patient and empathic because of this awareness.

*It is impossible to overestimate the power of love.*

## Accessing Your Internal Healer

When you begin accessing new states of awareness and finding answers that are productive, you will begin to trust your own intuition and inner-*knowing* ability. Are you going to be surprised at what and how much you already know! You will begin to act out of love, because you have learned to trust your own Spirit and the truth of what it tells you. Once you understand that, you have access to other states of awareness and can tap into them for greater knowledge. You may choose to deal with certain problems in your life from that expanded state, instead of from limited past perspectives. For instance, your friend Janet comes over and is acting differently than usual. She's uptight, talking a mile a minute, interrupting you several times during her visit. In the past you might have gotten angry and decided to distance a bit. Instead, after she leaves, you take a quiet moment and become present to Janet's energy. You check in with yourself to see what you feel. Perhaps you'll suddenly have the feeling Janet is dealing with some crisis in her life that she has not yet talked about with you. So, knowing that, you pick up the phone and tell her you just wondered if she needed some support because she wasn't quite herself today. Janet immediately tells you her mother just got some frightening test results back from the doctor, and Janet is very worried. Just by using your expanded awareness, you have saved your friendship and acted out of love rather than fear.

These kinds of circumstances and events will soon become commonplace in your life. I have many clients, family members, and friends who often tell me what they used to consider *very far out* is now quite natural to them. These skills and tools become part of who you are and how you respond naturally.

Your willingness to become an objective observer teaches you that **very little of what goes on with those around you, even with your partner, is ever about you.** For example, if five people heard the same statement made by someone they loved, they would have five different interpretations of what was said and meant. Each interpretation would be colored or filtered through the life experiences of each different individual. **Therefore, most of what people feel about everything in life, including you, is mostly about them.** Once you have this awareness, you become more willing to listen and allow others to have their feelings and experiences, without needing them to change. You know their feelings and responses are not about you.

Becoming present, getting honest, and acting out of love instead of fear also helps you become more aware of what your basic qualities as a person are, as opposed to those you learned in order to survive. Reacting from the past, you might have written Janet and your friendship off. Acting from your center, which is *always* loving, gives both you and Janet a great gift. Changing yourself from being an angry person into your natural state of being a peaceful person is easier once you realize the angry person is not really who you are but rather who you learned to be out of necessity. Who you *really* are is waiting—and wanting—to step forward.

*Remember that we see ourselves and everyone else
through our past life experiences, until we see from Spirit.*

From these deeper states of awareness we realize we are, in some way, connected to all of life. This connecting, *present* energy results in a keen awareness that we are, in actuality, separate from nothing. Everything is connected and wondrously united on some level of awareness. That awareness alone results in greater passion and compassion for ourselves and others. When you start to literally feel the connected energy between you and a loved one, you also become more aware of it between you and the rest of the world. We're all one.

*Spirit is all there is. Everything else is an illusion.*

Accepting this interrelatedness shifts your perspective of the world and helps you realize you are an important part of the whole. What you do matters. In fact, everything you do matters! Not in a way that should make you anxious, but rather in a way that makes you a joyful, willing participant in life.

## Presence

Jon Kilmo, in his book *Channeling*, says it simply: "I will take the stance that perhaps everything that exists which is a subjective and mental nature—thoughts, feelings, knowing, and consciousness itself—might be composed entirely of the kind of substance that physicists recognize as real: energy in the form of wave systems."

We transcend the barrier between ourselves and another, or ourselves and healing, by accessing certain levels of energy or thought. This is exactly what takes place in your healing process. Simply put, we connect to the waves that connect us to each other. At times, that simple yet profound awareness is all that is needed to create healing. Very often, the holding energy between you and another person is such that a quality connection is created that requires no verbal exchange at all. The awareness that we are not isolated, not alone, not separated from the rest of life is, in and of itself, a precious gift of Spirit.

It is not at all unusual, once you are conscious, to experience a simultaneous unity with yourself, other people, an entire group of people such as your family or native country, or the entire planet and all of humanity. Imagine for a minute what the quality of our lives might be if we took the focus off trying to teach the world to love us and simply loved ourselves and each other. Imagine the power in releasing all that combative energy we expend trying to change others and instead used it to create peaceful families and relationships for ourselves. Imagine what could happen if we stopped begging to be accepted and simply accepted our own lifestyle and the inherent beauty in our partners and ourselves. Imagine feeling this connected to yourself, your lover, and life.

Some of my clients and friends become so acutely aware of this energetic connection that even with their eyes closed, in the silence, they can tell if my awareness has shifted away from them for even a minute. I am also able to detect when they have for any reason begun to close down or disconnect. I can even feel *why* they have done so before they tell me.

In the space where we do this work, when there is no form—no questions, no exploration of thought, no words, nothing other than emptiness and our presence—the *energy* is still doing the work and filling the space. The healing is contained in the energy between each thought, perception, feeling, or other nonverbal experience. That incredibly rich energetic connection is evident in the form of *presence*. Your presence. Divine presence. Alive and very real.

I have one client who was so abused as a child that she often began our work on sensory overload and could not tolerate *any* discussion or sound between us. Any movement or sound felt like attack. Her lover did not understand her need for space, and my client often left home feeling overamped and craving silence. Together we sat in the silence of our session while allowing her to experience the connection, the safety of our union. I simply focused on fusing my energy with hers in an empathic, caring way. It was not unusual for her to call a day or two after the session to tell me she felt much stronger and able to cope. Sometimes she called between sessions, when she felt particularly on edge, and asked me to just hold her in that space while on the phone or after hanging up. Soon she learned to do it for herself and then with her partner. Time or space does not limit energy. One of my clients, Belle, told me:

"I can immediately recognize what I call a 'good' session. I reach deep and touch large feelings. I'm not simply sad, I grieve; I am not merely happy, I am joyous. Although I am aware of your presence, I experience it as background. I concentrate on my own issues, not our bond, so somewhere beyond me I sense the energy of the holding space, while I dig into my own heart for its secrets.

"There are other sessions when I feel 'nothing' happened. I think. I dig. I may cry. But I don't feel the exhilaration that is part of what I call my 'good sessions.' After a 'nothing happened' session, the next day belies the calm. I sit at work, quiet in my chair, touching paperwork that doesn't touch me. But the subterranean plates have shifted. I can never identify what it is that has happened, changed, or been resolved in the preceding session with you, but something very valuable and profound moved. Bountiful energy pours forth from my heart for hours at a time. This shifting of buried layers and the freeing of that energy that flows so profusely are part of what is called my healing moments."

I have had many personal experiences of these expanded states of awareness, but perhaps one of the most memorable was one I had with my unborn grandchild. My daughter, who lived in Phoenix, was told by her doctor that she would deliver within a few days. I waited three days and then left my job in California, using vacation time to be with her for the birth. I arrived in Phoenix, and we waited and waited. A week had passed, and still no baby. I began to feel concerned about the possibility of using all of my vacation time waiting and then not being able to remain with her to help after the birth.

After discussing this possibility with my daughter, we both agreed that I should return to California until she began labor. Upon my return to Los Angeles, I went to my office and sat in the space in which I had become accustomed to doing deeper work, and I moved into the connected energy. I focused on my unborn granddaughter, Brittany, and, in essence, told her that if she wanted me to be there for her birth, she'd have to give me enough notice. She did exactly that in a dream I had shortly after.

*Wherever you are, you are in the right place at the right time.*
*Embrace the lesson and the opportunity.*

I have been told many times by my own healing partners that they experience an unexplainable difference in the attitudes of people on whom they have focused during their sessions, even though the people were not physically with them in the session. My clients had some difficulty, and were attempting to send loving energy to create some resolution with these people. Often the person is even in another state or country, and yet upon having literally contacted him or her later, clients find some shift in attitude has happened. Perhaps the person involved has suddenly become more open to communication or has made contact on his own with my client for the first time in many years. Very often the explanation for such action is simply that he felt my client's presence with him or in some way felt *moved* to acting without understanding why. Could society and the world be affected by the power of our love for ourselves and others? Indeed it could.

I have done long-distance healing work with clients just by being present to their energy although they may have been away from their homes on vacation or in crisis. Even clients who are initially unfamiliar with this process are usually soothed and reassured by the energetic connection. Continued opportunities to experience this connection and healing eventually moves my clients to teaching others as well.

Think what could happen as you sit across from each other in the intense energy of being fully present. We are able to see unquestionable evidence of the mind's contribution to physically healing in the body. Surely we are ready to explore the benefits of using the mind to enhance emotional and spiritual states.

During an experiential exercise with one of the women in my spiritual support group, I became unquestionably convinced of this power. Aron had to leave California and go on a business trip to the East Coast. We agreed that at a designated time, we would each move into an aware energetic space and see if we could connect with each other. When the time arrived, I went to my meditation space, centered myself, and concentrated on her whereabouts. It took a very long time before I was able to feel connected with her, but the instant her presence came to my awareness, all the details were vivid. It was as if she had *landed* prominently in my awareness.

I was able to visualize the room she was in, the color and style of decor, the location of the bed on which she sat, the lamp, the window, and even the fact that there were several papers and books on her bed. I was able to know the clothes she was wearing and the position in which she sat. I had looked at the clock the moment I *felt* her *with* me. Just as I was getting comfortable with the process, I felt the jolt of a sudden absence of her energy.

I phoned her, describing what I had become aware of. She verified every detail. She even explained that she had hesitated to do the exercise and didn't begin until the exact moment at which I had felt her energy connect with me. She also explained that she had become afraid and had suddenly withdrawn at the exact time I had experienced her absence. She too had a distinct awareness of me and my environment. We agreed to try the process again, but this time we would both attempt to allow our consciousness to leave our respective rooms and meet somewhere in the middle in space.

We hung up the phone and began. Again, as she took her time to connect, I viscerally felt her hesitation. Once the connection was made, however, it was again vivid. I felt I could outline her body. When I raised my hand in midair to do so, it felt as if the texture and density in the space was heavier where I pointed. Without having previously arranged to do so, we moved into new positions with each other. My hands were palm-to-palm touching hers. I reached out to touch her face when she abruptly again withdrew. I felt as if I had been suddenly dropped. She called me moments later to say the experience had been so real to her that she felt as if my presence was in her room, as if I had touched her. We were astounded when we were able to describe every move each of us had made during the process, down to the exact position of our hands. We were further amazed as we talked about the fact that I could feel the precise moment when she became frightened and needed to withdraw. She said she too had *felt* my hands.

The rich, sensual, soulful connection we had created together gave us the experience of each other, rather than only the knowing. She had come through and into me. I knew her as if she were me. We became *one* in that moment. We had opened to the feminine, receiving parts of our souls and allowed each other to come fully in. My spiritual sister and I had created soul-deep connection.

As you clear the denial and pain that keep you from them, these kinds of amazing experiences can be yours as well.

> *The journey to "I" is simply remembering*
> *all that you already know and are.*

Many kinds of new experiences will be yours as you heal. The simple reason the process works is that you become energetically present enough with each other to be open to and feel safe about having new awareness about yourselves and others. Simply, you get present to your life and those in it. You get honest, and you act out of love. You go into healing together. Feeling connected and safe with another person you care about is a great gift. It allows you to look more deeply into the issues that prevent you from enjoying life fully. You have searched so long for a way to experience this aliveness, and all the while it was here within you. It excites your heart, lifts and moves your body, frees your spirit and mind. It is your intrinsic right to dance, while you are here, free of your pain.

*You are never alone when being Spirit. There are always two of you.*

You seek enlightenment in every form and every country known to humankind. You have not yet recognized that it is in the same room with you, as close as your willingness to begin. Expanded consciousness and vision, greater understanding and compassion, a deeper sense of self, the experience of connection to others and the resolution of past pain—these are all enlightenment. This healing process provides the opportunity for all this and more. Your relationships become your temple, your sanctuary, your highest school of spiritual truths. Relationships return to the place of honor they deserve, as sacred. All of these gifts come simply from getting present, being truthful, and acting out of love. It's worth it to me. How about you?

Where do you want to be in the next week, year, five years? Do you still want to be the person *acting* as if you are lovable and worthy? Do you still want to be *looking* for the right lover who can make you feel all those things about yourself? Or do you want to *be* the right person, *know* that you are lovable, and *have your life together* to prove it? Do you want to *become* your highest spiritual Self? You are only a breath away from your own healing. The opportunity for personal growth exists with every breath you take. From the moment you open your eyes in the morning, you have an opportunity to take a minute to feel the wonder of life. You can feel the miraculous sensations in your body, the miracle of the person lying next to you. In every meeting with other people there is an opportunity for growth and learning—in the privacy of your mind or openly and in your communication with this process.

*Those we consider the most gifted in life
are simply the ones living life as it was designed.*

As you sit reading this book you can begin to practice expanding your awareness. What is your body feeling? What are you aware of outside yourself? If you are willing to push out the boundaries, you can be aware of all the space around you even as you focus on these words. Notice how time seems to slow down when you relax and expand your awareness. You may even find that when you push out the boundaries, you no longer feel limited or focused inside yourself, but rather you become an objective observer to what you are doing as well as to all that is taking place around you. You can step back and see safely, without feeling fearful. You can see all of it, including your current choices and your options for new choices.

This mindfulness or presence will provide you with the awareness of many new opportunities for healing that used to just pass you by. But it takes practice. Get curious about the space around you, the coincidences that come into your awareness. Relax into a more expansive space several times during your day, until it becomes second nature to just stay there for good. You may be surprised to find out all that you *didn't know*. Now close your eyes, and take this break.

■ ■ ■

Imagine you are walking along the beach. Feel the warmth of the sun on your face and the wind in your hair. Hear the birds overhead, and listen to the ocean softly ebb at the shore. You are finally safe, growing and sensing your aliveness. There is nothing to fear. Notice, up ahead there is a cave. Be curious and go inside. There are steps leading downward. You are not afraid. Every step you take makes you feel safer. Soft, warm light coming is off the walls to welcome you. Down you go, farther and farther, until you reach the floor of the cave. The energy inside is welcoming. Right in the middle of the cave is a lounge chair, wide and soft, with plenty of room to stretch out and lie back. You sit in it. Suddenly you have the sweetest feeling that your Spirit is speaking to you, telling you it is your turn to simply receive. Slowly you lie back and experience the warmest, most loving energy filling your body and mind. You experience this energy as if you are in the arms of Spirit or God. You are cradled like child. You become aware that the divine is thanking you for being so courageous and willing to step into who you really are. Stay as long as you like, and come up gently.

# CHAPTER TEN
# Special Relationships and Spirit

*The fear of intimacy with another*
*is really only our fear*
*that we will once again*
*have to experience*
*the excruciating pain of separation*
*which we originally experienced*
*with the Divine.*

There is a wonderful short story, "Appointment With Love," by S.I. Kishor, that one of my most important teachers, Dr. Ben Levine, shared, and which I'd like to paraphrase for you. It is about a young man and woman who became pen pals while he was a lieutenant stationed overseas. During the many months he was away they fell in love through their letters. Her words carried him through the trenches, and his gave her hope. The soldier asked the woman to send him a picture of herself, but she refused, telling him that if his feeling for her had any basis, what she looked like would not matter.

After 13 long months, they agreed to meet at Grand Central Station. He watched the large clock on the wall tick away the minutes until 6 P.M. His heart pounded as his eyes searched for his love amidst the people walking by. She was to wear a red rose on her lapel.

Suddenly he saw a young, beautiful woman in a vibrant green suit walk toward him. She was all he imagined, with delicate brown curls, blue eyes, and soft features. But she wore no rose. Then, directly behind her, he spotted a woman well past middle age, her graying hair neatly tucked under a worn cap. She was more than a little disheveled, her thick ankles thrust into low-heeled shoes. But she wore a red rose on the rumpled lapel of her brown coat.

The lieutenant felt torn in two. He wanted to follow the first girl he had seen, and yet so deep was his longing for the woman whose spirit had comforted and upheld him all those months…and there she stood. Her eyes were loving and warm.

He did not hesitate. In his mind he knew she would not be his true love, but he could have something so precious, something perhaps rarer than love—a friendship for which he must be forever grateful. He took a breath, and although the words were broken with disappointment, he asked her to join him for dinner.

The woman's face broadened with a tolerant smile. "I don't know what this is all about, honey," she answered. "That young woman in the green suit, the one who just walked by, begged me to wear this rose in my coat. And she said that if you asked me to go out with you, I should tell you she is waiting for you in that big restaurant across the street. She said it was some kind of test."

OK, tell the truth. What would you have done, had you been Lt. Blanford? Is our community any different? Would you have left without speaking? Would you have considered this meeting more precious than any other? Most of us walk through life missing the many opportunities we are given for deep and meaningful relationships. We limit ourselves by wearing prejudiced blinders of sexism, ageism, racism, weightism, genderism, and lifestylism, and we believe the only person who can give us anything meaningful will be our mate. Our mates are people whom we must learn to honor, with deep awe and gratitude. They have chosen to walk with us through life, and what a precious gift that is. However, *every* person we meet is someone to honor with awe, someone who can be just as great a teacher. Each one is a teacher who brings a message vital to our growth and unfolding.

*You have always found the right person when Spirit is what you see most, and that is always possible, always your choice.*

It makes absolutely no difference what someone's nationality is, what the color of their skin is, what their choice of lifestyle may be. These things are irrelevant. But your response to these things is not irrelevant. It is your work. You may decide certain things about a person are important to you, such as one's religious beliefs. That's perfectly valid for you. However, after that person is gone, it is not their religious beliefs you will cherish. The soul of a person is the only thing of importance. It is the part of the person that will touch you and the part you will remember long after he or she is gone. Every person is a part of and a reflection of the one. When you find the Spirit in each other, you have found the Spirit that is in all things. If you are throwing these opportunities for deep connection away, you are missing so much of life.

Overwhelming sadness rises in me each time I hear an older gay man or lesbian speak of his or her aloneness. I fear seeing myself in his or her place at some point in life. We discard our older gay men and lesbians in an even worse, more despicable way than straight society does. Once they have lost their physical attractiveness, they are no longer desirable. How is it possible for us to be more despicable? We know prejudice, what it feels like, how it hurts, and yet we are not more honorable. We do not cherish the company of our men and women of character, commitment, and honor anymore than the rest of society. We must heal this in ourselves.

*When you are gone, only what you have accomplished through love*
*will be remembered.*

In some way, my having grown up ostensibly alone has given me a gift. Out of a need for survival, I had to learn to reach out to a diverse group of people, only to find, in some way, that we are all connected. We eat, think, breathe, and believe similarly. We all want quality lives, people who love us, less pain, a sense of freedom, and a fulfillment of purpose.

*Whenever you meet anyone it is a spiritual event,*
*if you meet with love.*

If I were to ask, "Are you in a relationship?" most of you would automatically say "yes" if married and "no" if single. Actually, we are all in relationships with the people in our lives. But we don't think of these interactions as real relationships unless they are with our lovers. Nor do we put as much time, energy, and effort into keeping these relationships alive and energized. Instead, most single people feel empty and incomplete because they haven't yet found the love of their lives. If we do find that special someone, we neglect the other people in our lives, believing they are somehow less important.

Our society fosters the belief that the only people with whom we should become emotionally and spiritually intimate are our partners. That's not true, and in fact puts an inordinate burden on our significant relationships to expect them to provide all our emotional and spiritual intimacy. It's unfortunate that we become so single-minded. We can have as much deep and meaningful contact with someone who is not a partner as we can with our partner. We even have trouble expressing affection to those in our community, and to our family and friends. How many withhold or refuse affection because they feel it makes them too vulnerable? We are not talking about sex; we are talking about love. If we are unable to share our love with our families and straight friends, are we not doing exactly what we are asking society to stop doing?

I am talking about sharing affection and love openly, and there's nothing wrong with that. Women should be able to hold each other, gay and straight. Men should be able to hold and kiss each other affection-ately, gay and straight. However, we teach our children at a very early age to hold back. I remember when my son began third grade and I went to kiss him good-bye as I dropped him off for school. He pulled back and quietly suggested in the most adorable way that he was a bit too old for his friends to see him kissing mom. So we agreed that from that moment on, a private, less obvious *I love you*, in the form of an unobtrusive stick-ing-out of our tongues at each other, would have to do instead.

The relationships I have had with friends and family have been among the richest I have ever known. These relationships act as the fire in my growth and the sustenance for my soul. From my experiences with friends come new ideas and gifts that enhance my mate relationship. Without exception, every friend teaches me about myself and reflects back to me the progress my soul is making. They are all precious gifts. Healing with friends or family is an invaluable experience and a top priority.

## Healing With My Family and Friends

On the morning of my 50th birthday, a familiar tap on the window awakened me, indicating I had a visitor, my son J.D. With a long-stemmed rose in hand, he promised to pick me up later that night for dinner with my daughter Mia. Lauren, my daughter who lives in Phoenix, called to wish me happy birthday and to remind me to expect a package. I called her at about 5 o'clock to let her know it had not arrived. The person who answered her phone told me she was out of town. I thought, "Hmm, something's up."

My son came back to get me at 6. And as we waited for Mia, he began to fidget and act peculiar. Finally Mia arrived and we started for the restaurant. On the way, I noticed J.D. frequently glancing into the rearview mirror and making what seemed to be strange signals out the window. I looked away several times so he wouldn't see my knowing smile. We arrived at the restaurant, and very soon after, in walked Lauren. I was elated.

We ordered drinks. They presented me with cards and tiny packages, neatly stacked. My son put his arm around my shoulder, the way he does when he knows I'm about to cry and wants to assure me—as well as himself—that it will be all right. I paused before I opened the first card. I shared a thought I'd been having, that getting older was bittersweet because I could now recognize all the ways in which I had screwed up as a young mother. Guilt was still heavy in my heart about all our hard times together. As my process of getting my degrees in psychology and as my own therapy deepened, I had begun to see the many ways—because of adversity, inexperience, and youth—that I had missed so much with them. I nearly grew up with my children, having had my first child at 18. I thanked them for their resiliency and patience. We all laughed, and they assured me that some of their most prized possessions were their family stories of growing up.

I opened their cards, filled with words so wonderful that I could barely see through the tears. My heart was so full. Finally, one tiny card with an immense message read, "Mom, we have always known our four separate souls were united in a very special way. These gifts are to show you how special our love is for you. This is our way of uniting us, for always, in heart and mind and spirit. You are such a meaningful part of our lives."

A little package was pushed my way. Inside were three gold rings neatly placed in the bottom of the box, tied together with a tiny bow, one for each of them. I took a breath, understood their meaning, and closed my eyes as they lay cradled in my hand. Silently I blessed these little symbols and affirmed that the rings were so intensely filled with my love that my children would feel it throughout this life and beyond. I placed a ring on each of their fingers.

J.D. then pushed another little box toward me that contained another very special ring. Lauren, who has an uncanny ability for combining the earthly and the spiritual, had designed a ring with a beautiful diamond in it. I instantly flashed back to the family story I had told all too many times about having had to sell all my jewelry in order for us to eat. With a tinge of guilt, I said, "I hope you all know I would have sold my right arm to keep us together, and you are all gifts enough."

Silence filled the space around us. The rest of the room seemed to disappear as we basked in the connected feelings we had for each other.

*Oneness has arrived when there are no words left. There is only love.*

They had created a commitment ceremony in which we could renew our love and dedication to each other. I began to cry, and as I looked at each of them I wondered what I had done to deserve these special people.

In that experience, I breathed in the energy of these three mirrors of myself. My son possesses great tenderness and compassion, has unwavering conviction and intensity, and often pays the price for upholding his beliefs with a bit of an edge. Lauren is the determined part of me, the one who can accomplish anything and who must remind herself to breathe in order to experience her deepest emotions and let in the beauty in life occasionally. Mia, my youngest child, is the same-spirit part of me that is filled with wisdom yet still seeking peace. She knows somewhere inside that she is special. Her relationship with her father diminished that awareness, as mine did with me, and she is working hard to give herself full acceptance, just as I am. She is a kind and gentle spirit who feels deeply and wants to experience it all. All three of these people are teachers, my precious teachers, as well as reflections of my soul.

In that moment a flood of emotions from our years of struggle, laughter, pain, and possibility filled each of us. In that openness, we found the only issue of any importance: our love for each other. With every breath I took, I released more of my judgment and denial about my own loving ability and presence with my children. I released my guilt for all the things I hadn't known and didn't have to give them. Instead I gave myself permission to notice all that I had given: my love, commitment, and dedication to making sure they had more of everything, including love, than I had as a child. My children are my greatest gift of all. We each validated, though never before discussed, the reality that we had a profound spiritual commitment to one another. It was as if in that moment we realized that from some distant past we had agreed to come together in this life to discover love. This moment was the acknowledgment of that discovery and would serve us throughout life.

The gift we had in each other seemed monumental compared to the years of struggle and uncertainty. We could have stayed in that energy, in the silence, just loving each other, had the waitress not danced into our space and decided to serve. In that special slice of time, each of us was fully present, open to every truth of our being and acting out of the love we felt for each other. We did that with total abandon, right in the middle of a Pasadena restaurant. Open, honest, and in celebration. We often have these moments; they are the gold in my life.

I met Franci when her son Peter was dying of AIDS. Peter came to me for help, and as Franci and I walked him through his grueling death process, we discovered a spiritual bond with each other. It felt familiar and permanent. We stood together, facing our own mortality and the pain in Peter's face and body, and watched as he lost hope of recovery. After Peter died, Franci and I continued as family for a long time. Our healing came often in silence, as we sat together releasing the pain and laughter at a world whose values are topsy-turvy. Healing arrived as she sat playing wistfully with my grandchildren, in the same way she once had played with her Peter.

We met and shared "spiritual bread," as she called it, and then left feeling filled up with each other and our connection. Franci was a fine teacher for me. Her 74-year-old inordinate need for independence often flew in the face of my need to *know* and to keep her safe. She could disappear for days and I'd find myself wrestling with thoughts such as "Is she upset with me? What might I have done to make sure she was cared for?" Each time she returned happily, safely, having been scooped up by a friend and taken on a jaunt. My fears were never about her. They were always about me. Her continual disappearances reminded me that deep inside I still had misplaced, unresolved pain and guilt about not having been able to keep my mother alive, to save her. No one reminded me of the healing I still needed to do on that issue like Franci. The issue was always in my face, and she was an ever-present reminder of the principle that no matter what the circumstance, if I am upset, it is never about the other person.

I explore different spiritual truths with five special friends now, and many others throughout my life, and we exchange challenges in our effort to push toward greater presence, truth, and love. We find healing in our explicit understanding and commitments to each other to step beyond our everyday presence into our truths, fears, and joy. Healing arrives the moment we get present to ourselves and then to each other. Healing opportunities often appeared, even without words. They are discovered in the middle of your spiritual circles, in realness of the family dialogue, and yes, even across the table in a restaurant. Healing can be found in a grocery store line, on the path while you are walking your dog, or behind the eyes of your best friend. Sometimes healing waits in that call you've been meaning to make, in the note you've wanted to write, or across the table from you in the touch of your mother's hand. It can be found in your father's response when you slow down enough to ask what he is *really feeling*. Healing is not just found in your church, hospital, or even your living room. It is everywhere when you are open to finding it. With my own family and with each deeply loved, uncommon member of my extended family that has been adopted though the years, and, yes, with perfect strangers, I have cried and laughed and reached into greater depths of my soul than I knew existed. There is not a single one of these people who could be said to be remotely like me, and, yet, because we chose to risk with vulnerability and openness, many have become closer to me than my own parents. I have gone from living in the middle of a barren Yuma desert as a child, with no one present, to an adult whose world is filled with growth and immense love. Trust me. Spirit also wants this for you. And you have already *qualified* to receive all of it.

*Becoming fully spiritual means bringing heaven to earth,*
*or Spirit to humanness.*

## Learning to Accept All the Teachers in Your Life

There is no way I could ever know all there is to know about these important people in my life or about those clients who also demonstrate courageous spirits, absolute vulnerability, and deep connection with me. Because these people are in my life, there is no way for my existence to be boring. Life is filled with energy, excitement, robust pleasure, sensuality, and healing. Relationships that are deep and meaningful cannot and should not be limited to mate relationships. A miracle is about to occur every time you enter a relationship with anyone. Begin to expect it.

*Once Spirit is found within, we are able to find it everywhere.*

Deepak Chopra, MD, author of *Perfect Health*, once said, "We have 60,000 thoughts a day, and 96% of those are the same as the ones we had yesterday." You know what that means, don't you? You and I are in a rut!

Not only do you ruminate each day with the very same boring thoughts, you also base everything you believe on the past. You have to; the future isn't here yet. So day after day you walk around with all the past experience and denial from yesterday—and you bring it into the "now" and use it as the basis of your decisions. Chances are, because you have no new information, you make the same kinds of decisions day after day. In doing so, you unknowingly perpetuate the cycle of pain and limitation of the day before. And you learn very little.

*The future must be created through the newness of nothing.*

We live in a society addicted to comfort and sameness, so we box ourselves into little cubicles of safe thought, such as *I know everything there is to know about my lover,* or *I'm safe because there's nothing I don't know about my friends that could surprise me.* A greater truth might well be that you, your partners, and your friends have learned about each other only as much as you have been willing to risk sharing.

Each time you encounter people close to you, you are standing in front of multidimensional, multifaceted human beings, who bring with them all the experiences of their childhood, all the knowledge of their parents, and all their current and past life experiences. You are standing in front of a portion of God experiencing Itself as a human being. Our brains hold more information than the world's largest computer, and we have a capacity for feeling emotions that no man-made machine could ever replicate. The essence of our souls contain the wisdom of lifetimes, the divine knowledge of Spirit. Now add all of that information and array of possibilities to the vast variety of people we meet and work with in any single day—and dare to tell me that you are bored.

If you become fully present and willing to know any of these people, you'll have a million new thoughts and awarenesses as well as a million opportunities for growth. Until you reach a place in your life where you are willing to become more conscious and open to the diversity and value in the rest of humanity in this world, life can indeed seem dull. But once you become curious and conscious, life becomes alive, rich, filled with new beginnings and opportunities to learn more. I can honestly say everyone in my life has taught me something.

When you are conscious, how is it possible to be bored? The opportunity for relationships is everywhere, and therefore the opportunity for healing is everywhere. Relationships are critical to our growth. The process of having a relationship is indeed a tough yoga, and if we could peek into the spiritual curriculum for the planet, it's probably among the top requirements for passing. If you fail this one, you will no doubt want to come back and try again, so it's worth trying to get it right. Nothing else is more important. Nothing else has a greater impact on the quality of our lives and the evolution of our souls or our planet than our relationships—to ourselves and each other.

*We must widen the circle of our love*
*until it embraces the whole world.*

## Increasing the Quality of Your Relationships

You have relationships with everyone right now. Like it or not, there's no choice. Any decisions you and I make ultimately affect our community and the planet positively or negatively, even if we are apathetic and do nothing. Doing nothing is making a decision. What we do have a choice about is the quality of, or state of, our relationships. If you are open to receiving information about yourself, the feelings you notice inside from the first moment you encounter someone tell you a great deal about who you are. As you stand in line at the grocery store or attend a community dance, do you find yourself being critical, patient, understanding, nervous? Is your body holding tension or anger? Do you judge people by their physical attributes? Even your relationship to this task tells you a lot about yourself. Feel any resistance to doing it? Think checking in with your feelings is silly or too much trouble?

In any given second of the day, moving into a state of awareness or mindfulness can give you a world of information about yourself and your relationships to those around you, as well as to life itself. How you deal with life and your own inner growth is reflected back to you through relationships. Where are you in reference to the rest of life? Are you absent or fully present?

> *You will learn a great deal by being open to everything*
> *and holding onto only that which makes you more.*

When you begin to work from a more conscious level, you will understand that every time you have a reaction to anyone, that is an opportunity to learn something new about yourself that you won't want to miss. For instance, if someone makes you very angry because of being a certain way, here are some questions you can ask yourself:

- Why does that way of being bother me?
- Why am I invested in having him or her change?
- Who in my past made this type of behavior an issue?
- What does this behavior mean to me?
- From where does my need to control another's behavior come?
- Is there some insecurity within me?
- Why am I staying in a relationship with this person?
- What do I need to learn about myself so this won't be an issue?

Imagine what this simple little quiz could teach you about yourself. That is exactly the purpose of having relationships—to learn about *yourself*. All of life is here to teach you about yourself!

# Examples of Teaching by Presence

Years ago I was an administrator for the Director's Guild of America. Several members of the board and I became close friends, and they came to my metaphysical classes. I remember a story about one of the late board members, a unit production manager named Wally Worsley. He had begun working in the motion picture industry as a young man, following his father's example. He worked his way up, assuming greater responsibility, until he became a unit production manager who was revered and respected in the industry. Wally was unique. Gay, straight, purple, brown, short, tall—nothing mattered to Wally but your character. I remember when I interviewed with the Guild for my job as executive director. He was present, sitting silently at the end of what seemed to be the longest conference table known to humankind. After the other 12 board members had posed their questions to me, this ominous, bearded presence raised his bowed head for the first time since we began and asked, "What makes you think you could do this job better than the last guy?" Something in his tone told me it was a sincere question and the "guy" could have just as well been a female. I also instinctively knew that my answer to his question would make or break the interview. I answered. He grunted. Later I got the job and a good friend.

Wally was a spiritual man who never talked about his beliefs. But you knew he was a spiritual man because of how he dealt with people. He was on one particularly difficult movie shoot when the first assistant director came to him and said the crew was complaining furiously about the lunches. Wally listened and calmly replied, "I'll think of something."

Wally was known to have never eaten with the crew. Instead, he used his lunchtime to meet with his department managers. But for the next four days after his conversation with the first assistant director, Wally sat in the midst of the crew eating lunch. And after each meal, he could be heard loudly praising the quality of the food that had just been served. The first assistant never heard another complaining word. Wally was not interested in making the crew act differently; he just sat with them and his presence resolved the issue. Wally's ability to be fully present to those around him without taking an adversarial role often brought out the best in people. Before he died, his attitude resulted in relationships of deep respect and love by all who knew him and still miss him.

You and I can change how society feels about us without another single political fight. We can change the perception that we are people who are not worthy of respect simply by having respect for ourselves and our own relationships. We even bash the Ellen DeGflenereses and Anne Heches of our society ruthlessly in our own press for being human. We feed on the same self-hatred the straight community feeds on. As a friend of theirs, I can tell you it is devastating to know that these two people who had the spiritual courage to stand up and be counted for us over and over do not understand any more than I do why we have not moved beyond this limited level of consciousness. Ellen and Anne's journey was a spiritual one that took great courage—our response to them and many others of our own in high-profile positions in many cases did not. This lack of consciousness is a stunning revelation that grieves our spirits and our communities. We disable ourselves and sabotage our own power with this ingrained self-hatred and shame. Change begins inside us, not inside the rest of society.

## Don't Miss Your Opportunities

There are so many opportunities for healing, but sometimes we miss them because we are not awake to the possibilities. We have all been taught to look behind us as we change lanes in traffic because blind spots prevent full vision of other cars. There are also blind spots in life. These unconscious spaces provide opportunities for healing, but you won't catch them unless you look closely. There is always a great deal that you don't know in any given situation or in any relationship. If you ask yourself, *What don't I know about this person or this circumstance, and why do I resist knowing?* You will begin to find yourself working from a more open and consequently more present state.

It's so simple. To create healing in your relationships—no matter what kind or who they are with—you must **stay present, be honest, and act out of love.** Sounds simple, is simple, but until now has seldom happened. It's been the hardest thing in the world for most of us because we have been so distanced from these feelings inside that most of the time we don't even know what we are feeling. It is critical to your own safety to know and own your truths to the best of your ability. Every time you abandon yourself by not staying present, not telling your truth, not acting out of love, you have given your inner child or your own spirit the message that he or she is not important enough to be honored. One of the most profound truths in my life is: **No one abandons you without you having first abandoned yourself.**

Even in a situation where someone has left you, there was probably something going on in the relationship that you chose not to see or talk about before your partner left. In some way you abandoned yourself and what you needed—your truth, your feelings, your gut instincts—before the other person abandoned you. The truth of that statement should prove to be a wonderful welcomed awareness, even if it smarts a bit. It's wonderful, because it means that when you are listening to yourself, fully present to your needs and acting out of love, the chances of your being abandoned are greatly reduced.

Many clients come to me to begin their healing after their relationships have broken up. While in the midst of great grief and feelings of loss they tell me, "I don't understand. I did everything for my lover. I gave up everything and was there for him in every way. Even when something inside told me not to, when he asked me to, I gave up my career to support his. How could he not love me back?" Love does not require us to give our all or give ourselves up. It never has. There are two kinds of unhealthy love: not enough love and too much love. Both are controlling and both are codependent. They are circuitous, dishonest ways of trying to get our needs met without asking directly.

Balanced love begins with a healthy love for one's self. Whenever you give yourself up in a relationship, ultimately your partner will have to leave you. The burden of being someone else's reason for living is just too much. Now, you might ask, "How can there ever be too much love?" There cannot be too much healthy love. But when you have forgotten to love yourself at least as much as you profess to love others, the love you are offering is not healthy love.

Unfortunately, we have experienced two very dysfunctional para-digms for relationships. Remember these?

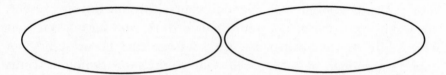

*Your way or my way!*
*No negotiation. If I am right you are wrong or vice versa.*

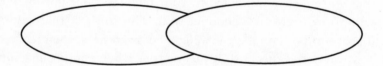

*I am nothing without you!*
*If you love me, I must be lovable. If you don't, I am not.*

Both of these paradigms are dysfunctional and codependent.

In the "I am nothing without you" paradigm, you may feel as if you are dying if your partner leaves, because you have given him or her responsibility for all your good feelings about yourself. It may feel like this without your partner:

You feel empty because your good feelings about yourself leave when your partner leaves.

Remember our healthy paradigm?

a whole and healthy you · loving, authentic relationship happens here · a whole and healthy me

I have discovered a great truth worth repeating here: You are only able to reach as far across to your loved ones, and out to divine energy, as you have been willing to reach down and inward into yourself. You can never give what you don't have or teach what you don't know.

*Love cures both the giver and the receiver.*

Every relationship is a 50-50 deal. Some of you won't like that, but its true nevertheless. Even when there is an identified bad guy, someone who needed the experience of being with a "bad guy" voted to be right there. That person is also working out of his or her own denial. Guess what? Those "bad folks" who start wars and pollute the planet— and this country—are *us*. We vote for them and continue to let them do these things out of our denial. That significant other or friend sitting across from you right now who hurts you—*you* entered into that relationship and are still there out of your denial. Whatever the relationship is like, you voted to be in it, or that person would not be in your life. You were probably very wise in doing so, because there was something important you needed to learn about yourself that could be learned only with this type of person. Some of the best teachers I have had in my life have also taught me the hardest lessons.

I have also been the bad guy in relationships. We all have. I have been the one who left out of fear, who made some unconscious mistake, or through some lack of awareness hurt someone without meaning to. I have been the one who didn't stand in integrity, who didn't know or tell the whole truth, or who wasn't as spiritually courageous as I would have like to have been. The most important thing I've learned is that we are all growing and no one is doing it perfectly. With each mistake, however, we do it better. There's no need for judgment or shame. We are all simply each other's teachers. Knowledge liberates you. It returns your power to you and provides the awareness that you can change your mind and vote again. Unfortunately, most of us have gotten so distracted from our true purpose that we need very tough teachers and very big lessons to get our attention. But we have to forgive ourselves and each other. As Einstein said, "The greatest spirits choose the greatest challenges."

*Whenever you are listening to the wisdom within,*
*you are hearing Spirit whisper in your ear.*

When you accept the concept that *everything* in your life is a reflection of you, the circumstances and people in your life begin to make sense. Take a look at what society reflects back to us about how we feel about ourselves! Remember, there are no closed systems of energy, so something has to be working in you to have been attracted to the people in your life. We are such great masters at our own evolvement that we can call to us the most painful and often the best lessons in order to give ourselves the growth we need.

*Everything we believed in yesterday, we are living today.*
*And everything we believe in today, we will be living tomorrow.*

We each come to this planet having opted to experience certain life lessons that we need for our own soul's evolvement. Once you understand those lessons, you can relinquish the unconscious need to repeat the same lessons with the same pain. In your sessions you can look at these experiences and begin to understand and heal that cycle. You'll stop repeating the same painful mistakes and patterns.

## You and Your Mate

Naturally, all of the principles in this book apply to mate relationships. There is no one who is in a mate relationship who has not voted to be there, who is not consciously or unconsciously learning something significant, and who is not contributing his or her 50% to the issues. No matter how hard we try to deny that, that fact is nevertheless true.

*Every experience in life is a teacher*
*attempting to teach you to be love.*

Working in mate relationships opens up a whole world of information about you and about your partner that may as yet be undiscovered, no matter how long you've been together. When people commit themselves to you, they perform the most courageous act on the planet. Sharing your innermost secrets and frailties is no small task. It deserves great respect. If a person in your life has given you that commitment, you have been given a miracle. This miracle is not just a name and age. This miracle is not just the color of skin, or hair, the height, weight, or shape of your mate. This miracle is so much more. This miracle has feelings, fears, doubts about herself. She has suffered on the way to you and often endured great challenges in life. This miracle has not been understood, not been heard, not been cherished for who she is. This miracle is filled with potential and has not yet even realized the most of who she is. This miracle is a spirit struggling to remember. A soul struggling to find honor and her own enlightenment.

Whether male or female, this miracle was created in the mind of the divine and has within him or herself the memories and experiences from every life he or she has touched. This person is a miracle and a mystery all at the same time. This miracle, who is courageous enough to offer him or herself to you, is sacred, and so is the relationship that you will create together. If you do not feel this way about your partner, you have not really seen who he or she is. You have not really allowed yourself to be fully present to the miracle of this gift who is your mate. He or she is precious. Your beloved. He or she is a refection of your own soul. He or she *is* your own soul. Wake up. Stop and see this miracle right now, perhaps for the very first time.

## Do the Work—Stay Together

This work is not a cure-all and certainly no guarantee that your relationships will magically change. However, I can tell you that the couples in my practice who practice this healing together stay together without exception. They experience greater intimacy, improved sexuality, and deep abiding love and devotion for each other. Their relationships become the central motivating force in their lives. From the center of their loving relationship, all else is accomplished.

*With spirituality, love, once simple, becomes profound.*

Couples who simply can't (won't) find the time usually end up more separated and isolated and ultimately break up.

## Identifying the Patterns in Your Relationships

One thing that will usually surface for both of you is the realization that you somehow re-create your family scenario in mate relationships. Family scenarios can become like a vise grip you don't understand and feel you can't escape. It may seem that no matter what you do, the same issues keep coming up repeatedly. That's a perfect reason for beginning the process of understanding these patterns.

In the exercise to follow, you will be asked to recall the most significant or traumatic experiences in your life. When you are finished with the exercise, step back and analyze it like an objective observer. Then take a look at what major theme or pattern repeats itself. Once you understand it, you can begin work to change your inner beliefs and feelings about yourself and stop re-creating the pain. Take some time to do this exercise alone so that you can really see beyond the pain of each event into the obvious patterns. You may need additional pieces of paper and some quality time to be able to stay with the process until the patterns emerge. If you feel safe and cannot see a pattern, ask a friend or loved one for his or her perspective.

This is an important exercise, so take all the time you need to complete it. Too many of us walk through life wondering why bad things happen to us when, in reality, we are the producers and directors of our own drama. We do repeat the same patterns unconsciously. The problem is that we refuse to take responsibility for healing the pain inside ourselves, so it continues to direct our life. We all received messages as children that work to either enhance our lives or limit them. Until you commit to changing those unconscious messages and replace them with new beliefs, you stay in the cycle of pain. Don't blame yourself or feel you are at fault. Simply be open to discovering what those messages are, then proceed to change them.

In your sessions you can focus on those negative messages and beliefs, feel the feelings and emotions attached to them, and then safely release them. You can then focus on the new beliefs you want to have, talk about why life is different in the present, and think about how it is possible to have positive beliefs guide your life. Once you understand why you choose certain situations and people in life, you can then go about making new choices. Think of the process as a new beginning. It is!

The following exercise will help you to see the patterns you are creating in your life. Take all the time you need to complete this exercise, and be honest with yourself. Once you identify the patterns, you can change them.

## Life Patterns Exercise

| List the most significant traumatic experiences in your life: | The underlying fear in each of these experiences is: | The opposite feeling or belief would be: |
| --- | --- | --- |
| | | |

Now take a moment to look for the recurring theme or pattern in each of these experiences. Is it abandonment, betrayal, abuse? List the recurring themes:

Take a minute to reflect on your childhood experiences and define how they affect your life and relationships currently. (For instance, if you were left as a child, you may now believe everyone will leave you, so you may unconsciously choose people who are not trustworthy in order to re-create and heal the pattern.)

The issues I have in my red wagon are:

When I begin to act out of fear, the things I can do to change my process are:

After you finish, take a minute to look the patterns and themes that keep repeating in your life from your issues and denials. Some of the themes that come up with my clients are:

- I'm responsible for everyone else's good feelings.
- Other people are responsible for my good feelings.
- People always leave me.
- I am never enough.
- No one listens to me.
- No one understands me.
- Others make me feel bad.
- I am doomed to failure.
- I don't have what it takes to be loved.

There are as many different themes as there are people. And for each theme in your life there is a corresponding injury you had as a child that resulted in your believing as you do. Every belief you have came from somewhere.

## Seeing the Truth in Your Current Relationships

Not only does that belief become a recurring pattern in your life, but you also call in the exact people you need to make your personal drama happen. Most of you will deny that. But before you do, think for a minute about that last bad relationship you had, whether it was friend or lover. You knew at the beginning something was off, and you probably chose to ignore it. In fact, you may have even told yourself you could change the other person or that the person would change as he or she grew to love you. Then, not having listened to your own truth in the first place, you cleaned up the mess for months or years after they had left. And maybe you even blamed them.

> *When there is an intense feeling about another,*
> *he or she is mirroring something inside yourself.*

The following exercise will help you see that your partner is a reflection of some part of yourself. Doing this exercise will free you from having to stay in the shaming or blaming process that comes from your denial. It will move you into seeing more clearly and helping you make changes inside yourself.

When you're ready and you feel strong enough to be vulnerable and open, you can do this next exercise with your partner or mate. Be careful, though, because this one requires you to tell the truth and take the responsibility for your choices.

Sit across from each other, draw your boundaries, and decide who will go first. Then respond to the following questions from your heart. After one of you has completed the whole list of questions, then the other partner can do the same. Remember to keep breathing!

1. The negative beliefs I have about you are:

2. The negative beliefs I have about myself that mirror those are:

3. The qualities I love about you are:

4. The qualities I love in myself that mirror those are:

5. The thing/s I have been afraid to tell you are:

6. The thing/s that I have been afraid to tell myself are:

7. The thing I am supposed to learn from this relationship is:

8. What I now know about myself and my healing process is:

When you are finished, thank each other. No doubt, during this exercise you have learned that what you've been projecting onto each other is exactly how you feel about yourself.

The good qualities you see in your partner are also reflections of you, so don't skip those. You may be calling into your life someone who is very spiritual because there is a part of you that is very spiritual and you need to honor or develop it more. You may call in someone who has a great sense of humor so yours can come out. The good qualities of your partner are reflections, just as are the qualities you don't like.

If you feel your partner isn't fully with you, there are undoubtedly ways in which you are not fully with yourself. If you feel your partner lies to you, undoubtedly in some way you are lying to yourself. If you feel your partner cheats on you, undoubtedly you cheat on him or yourself. You call each other in as reflections of what is going on inside yourself. Once you recognize this, you have a great opportunity to create deep healing. In the sessions, you can see clearly what your challenges are and begin to deal with them.

It really doesn't matter who you choose to participate with you in this exercise. The same mirror and reflection of what is going on inside of you will result. Everything in life is connected and related. In fact, you can create healing for yourself while sitting at your desk at work. Do this same exercise inside your head with the people you just can't stand. Sorry, they too are a reflection of some part of you, or they wouldn't be an issue. If they didn't trigger some injury inside you, you would not have any emotion attached to their behavior. Whenever there is intense emotion or an inability to let go of your intense discomfort, you are usually projecting some issue onto the other person, and that's why they bother you so much.

I had a client who hated the injustice in the world. Anytime anyone did anything to him that felt unjust, he was infuriated. We finally got down to his issue, which was how unjustly he had been treated as a child because he was gay.

You may have to get creative in understanding how your partner's reflection is a part of yourself, but if you keep looking, you will find the mirror. For instance, for a long time I could not tolerate men who had a macho attitude. I thought it was just my feminist ire raising its head. But I had an opportunity to find out differently with one of my teachers at school. He was a chauvinist with an authoritarian air who catered to the pretty women in the class while having no special interest for anyone else. He consistently used argumentative confrontation with students who expressed differing opinions. He was insistent that we believe exactly as he believed on nearly every issue. He came into class with stories about women who were as "wide as they were high," and had derogatory things to say about gays and lesbians, people with money, and anyone with whom he felt personally conflicted. Every time I went to class I did so with a knot in my stomach. My denial was awake and active. This guy really ticked me off. So I asked him to work personally with me, and I told him how I felt. Through our process together, I discovered he was the perfect representation of what I felt negative yang energy to be, and since that was how my father also was, I wanted no part of it. In fact, I had disowned my own yang or masculine energy because of the fear that it would be similar to my father's and this teacher's, and in doing so I had disowned my own power.

Our process together brought about an incredible healing for me that I will never forget. I still remember the chills that went down my back as I realized my fear was a result of fearing my own disowned male energy. I still didn't approve of the teacher's manner, but neither was I afraid of him or men like him any longer. The bad feelings I was having were more about me than about him, and he had given me a great gift in our process together. I had called him in, as annoying as he was, to do just that. He was perfect in that my response to him was so strong that I was forced to explore the reasons behind it. Someone less abrasive might not have been enough to get my attention.

Everyone in your life with whom you have a relationship is there to teach you something wonderful about yourself if you will become open to it. What part of yourself is your sister, who hates you, reflecting back to you? Which part of you is your boss, who hates gays, reflecting back to you? Which part of you is your lover, who adores you, reflecting back to you? **It's all about you!** Take a look at the ways in which everyone in your world reflects some part of yourself, and begin your work. When you understand life in this way, you can embrace it and those around you in order to learn and grow. You no longer have to recoil from it nor feel stagnated and alone. You can deepen and enrich your present relationships, begin to create new ones, and, one step at a time, empower yourself in the process.

## Understanding Inner Child Issues

You've seen a lot of books lately about the inner child. Obviously, we don't have a real live kid inside us. However, we still have pain and trauma from having been hurt as children. When we are able to focus on that pain, identifying the *child* part of our psyche that sustained the trauma, we can create deeper healing. Most of the kids *inside* who have been hurt or abandoned are full of pain. Because you carry this intense feeling inside, it continues to guide your unconscious decisions throughout your adult lives. You avoid deep bonding in order to avoid abandonment. Or you pick people who are similar to your parents, hoping to finally get what you did not have as a child. But most of the time the people you pick are no more able to provide you with that kind of healing than your parents were. So most of us repeat the same patterns again and again.

Your work with each other can offer your inner kids a safe, cradlelike, energetic space in which to address these issues. One client told me he felt that the months we had spent in this energetic connection were for him like being held safely in the womb, an experience of safety he never had with his own mother. Without that experience, he felt he could never have learned to individuate and emotionally grow. He was finally able to experience feeling deeply fused with another human being during our sessions. This enabled him to stop seeking the mothering he never had as a child in his adult relationships with women.

My client Belle described this energetic connection:

"The healing experience has caused me to think about the concept of 'holding.' I realize that you have 'held' me often without ever touching me. The 'holding' sustained me and made me feel safe. It also undermined my emotional defenses. Built to protect me from abandonment, anger, dishonesty, and shame, my defenses call attention to themselves and their inappropriateness when encountering the 'holding' of the loving listener. Much like a bridge that spans a dry riverbed, my defenses became irrelevant. They don't instantly crumble any more than the bridge does in the absence of its river. But the 'holding' calls attention to my behavior's structure, and that can be demolished if I have the courage to try."

It is important in personal relationships to have times when either partner can feel safe enough to experience the inner child's feelings. However, when a partner is in this childlike state more often than an adult state, too much dependency is created, and an adult-to-adult relationship becomes impossible. One partner is then required to take on the role of parent while the other remains disempowered. Your healing work allows you to set aside a specific amount of time in which to deal with the inner child's wounds. The result of this kind of healing work is that relationships become more equal in power, and therefore, more mutually supportive. This is because some of our inner child's unmet needs within each of us can be met in these exercises.

Whether male or female, we are all too ready to either become the child who needs mothering or become the parent who needs a child to care for. Some of this work is necessary and appropriate, so long as you are well-grounded in the reality that **every pregnancy ends** and **every child needs to become a healthy adult.** In other words, you can't stay a child forever. Healthy adults are able to individuate and separate from their parents in order to reunite again as spiritual equals. We can do deep healing together with the child in each of us, but we too must grow up and reconnect as adults. Your work should feel that it is heading in that direction.

## Preventing Unequal Relationships

Part of the problem with relationships is that women move from being little girls into suddenly becoming adults, without having had enough healing to be fully empowered women. Men move from being little boys seeking power to suddenly becoming men, without having healed enough to become fully loving men. Our relationships often contain the same parent-child dynamic.

With this kind of unequal parent-child bonding we are paralyzed in unhealthy relationships. Having a partner leave can actually feel like you are losing your parent figure or experiencing the death of some part of yourself. It is almost as if you feel you cannot survive in the world without that mother/father energy. Many people choose to stay disempowered in this type of relationship because it is too frightening to leave. If this is to change, we must have a place for this kind of healing.

It's important to be careful to make sure that this inner child work is not the only work done, because it leaves one person feeling less empowered than the other. In fact, you might decide to do some of this work with friends or people other than your partner to take some of the strain of this parent-child dynamic off your mate relationship.

If you are doing this work with your mate, it must be done within the framework of the healing exercises designated for this issue and with *limited* amounts of time specifically set aside. In other words, you may want to focus on the child aspect of yourselves every other week or as the need arises. If you put all your energy into this inner child healing, you have created a situation in which one or the other of you is being a parent in all your exercises. This work must be done with the specific goal of achieving adult partnerships as the end result. Otherwise it becomes too easy to set a pattern of one partner always playing the role of parent for the other.

*When you teach love, you become it.*

## And This Is My Beloved

As you create greater intimacy in your mate relationships—in all your relationships—take time now and then to greet each other in awe. Stop and literally tell each person in your life how deeply moved you are that he or she has committed to this process of growth with you. You are both playing leading roles in each other's drama, in each other's soul work. The task of staying present, being truthful, and acting out of love is the hardest on the planet.

*Being who I really am begins when I stop pretending to be*
*who I think I should be or who I think you want me to be.*

When you ask a partner to commit to be open, to be willing to feel deeply and to stay present to pain and joy, you ask for the finest, most meaningful gift one can give. I hope that from this moment on, you will have a sense of the sacredness each opportunity holds.

*When you choose not to try, out of fear or disappointment,*
*you also choose not to accept success,*
*and you abandon your dream and purpose.*

Schedule time with someone you love, and as you sit across from him or her, with each of you encircled in your individual boundaries, do the following exercise. One partner completes each of the following seven statements and then the other person completes the same series.

1. The lessons I most need to learn in life are:

2. The ways that I see you helping me with these lessons are:

3. The ways I am helping myself to learn are:

4. The lessons I'm aware you are working on are:

5. The things I am doing to help you are:

6. The things I see you doing to help yourself are:

7. The things I most celebrate or cherish in our relationship are:

This is an exercise you can do periodically with your partners as you find your challenges and priorities change. As you grow, so should your relationships. You are at the very beginning of the most exciting adventure of your life. This adventure will bring you more power, more joy. In fact, it will bring you ecstasy, the kind that only those on a real path of enlightenment and spirituality experience. As you grow, so does the world grow and change in positive ways.

*The end of this world is simply the destruction of fear
and the endless creation of love.*

■ ■ ■

Now let's take a moment to reflect on these issues in a meditation. Close your eyes and get comfortable. See yourself back in your safe place, quiet and at ease. Imagine that you are having a celebration with the people in your life who have taught you so much about yourself. Starting with friends and family, see them, one by one, coming into your awareness. As you greet each one, tell each person the gift of awareness about yourself he or she has given you. Tell them the ways in which they are reflecting a part of who you are. Take all the time you need. Let your partner be the last person you greet. Greet this special person, your beloved. Take this time to greet him or her as if you were seeing each other for the first time. Talk to your mate about what you appreciate in him. Tell him how he is a teacher for you. Feel yourself remove any barriers to seeing him with awe, respect, and deep appreciation. Renew your commitment to each other in your visualization. Once you have finished, make a decision to tell all the people in your life what they truly mean to you.

# CHAPTER ELEVEN
# Finding and Maintaining the Ecstasy

*When you give yourself permission*
*to live life fully*
*you become the light*
*of your experience.*
*The space between who you want to be*
*and who you really are*
*disappears*
*and*
*authenticity and ecstasy*
*take the place*
*of*
*pretense.*

At Disneyland there are many exciting, thrilling rides. The most daring and thrilling of these used to be called E ticket rides. A tickets were for the little kids. E tickets were for the big kids. There are not enough E ticket rides in life. E ticket rides are the life experiences that take our breath away. They create profound and lasting changes in our life that are positive, empowering. They act as the fire in our aliveness. These precious experiences should be common occurrences. Instead, they are rarely found—and even more rarely authentic. When we finally have such an experience, we may find that it too is like Disneyland, fleeting, fading, and very often false. Could we be looking for ecstasy in all the wrong places?

For instance, you wake up the morning after a torrid romantic encounter and find you can't even talk about real feelings to the person lying beside you. Sound familiar? You have a flash of state-bound enlightenment while on a drug, only to find that the next day, while no longer high, you can't remember a single profound truth to put to work in your life. The people you seek out as teachers, mentors, leaders, or gurus fall off their pedestals with some not-so-spiritual behavior that comes from their own red wagon of fear. The books you once thought to be divinely inspired produce less-than sacred sequels. The lows get lower, your disappointments become greater, and the highs seem more elusive than ever. And, although at first it may not feel perfect, all of it is!

We hunger for ecstatic experiences but often look in the wrong places and to the wrong activities and the wrong people to find them. In romantic relationships, you expect your beloved to be responsible for keeping the ecstasy alive. She should be sensuous, alluring, exciting, and mysterious. When you find either you or she can't sustain these feelings over time, you push on to the next potential opportunity, the next possible romantic encounter, the next high—through money, drugs, sex, relationships, power, food, or any other excess of choice. All the while, Spirit continues to call us back to ourselves.

*Your ego will move you from one goal to another endlessly,*
*because nothing will ever satisfy you but Spirit.*

Authentic ecstasy comes only from a sense of union. Spiritual union. Ecstasy is an alchemical state of union or healing harmony that is experienced on a cellular level. Almost everyone is bereft of ecstasy, in need of healing, because most of humanity lives in a state of separation. We are separated from ourselves and our real feelings. We are separated from each other. And most of us feel a sense of separation from what we perceive to be divine. There are opportunities for ecstasy everywhere, but to find them you must be willing to be profoundly present with yourself. Then and only then, will you find ecstasy waiting and available to you. You will find it in:

- emotional and spiritual courage
- excruciating truth
- unconditional love
- profound presence
- unbounded joy
- soul-deep growth

- total vulnerability
- spiritual insight
-  voyages out of denial
- impeccable integrity
- passages through fear
- uncommon and ordinary acts of kindness

All of which are in you! In very simple terms, ecstasy is found in personal spirituality—not necessarily in religion, but in a spirituality of oneness with ourselves, others, the planet, and Spirit.

When we perceive ourselves to be at a place in life where we will no longer be able to find or feel ecstasy, we begin the death process. Some of us may say we are dying of AIDS, cancer, old age, or toxins in the environment, but in reality we are dying because we no longer believe we can experience ecstasy in life, so we give up wanting to stay alive. How many people with a terminal illness have been given a short time to live and through sheer determination will stay alive long beyond that time for an event they perceive to be important? When the event and the ecstasy are over, only then do they let go and die.

*When we shatter the walls of ego and merge with*
*the ocean of humanity, we share in its dignity and joy.*

I remember sitting with a friend over lunch, discussing why I had not been able to give up smoking. I could always count on in-depth explorations with this particular friend, until some meaningful psycho-spiritual answer was forthcoming. That's why I kept my most perplexing issues for our lunches together. For some reason I could not yet identify, I could not give up cigarettes.

"What feelings are they holding down?" she asked.

"I don't know, a sadness, perhaps. My life has been so full—maybe I'm finished," I answered. "Maybe there's no more ecstasy for me," I said, thinking about the peak experiences from my past.

With that statement, a flood of energy left my body, and I started to cry.

"God, I think I believe I won't have any more of those precious moments when I felt so much aliveness and union with myself and the divine. It's been so long, and nothing seems to do that for me anymore. So here I sit, trying to take myself off the planet with cigarettes, for heaven's sake!"

She confirmed a similar sense in her own life that she was giving up in some way and thought it to be simply part of the aging process. "I don't think so! In fact, I think we're just a couple of old dogs who have given up on dancing on the edge. Maybe we just need to recommit ourselves to having more ecstasy and less stress." And that's exactly what I did.

*The universe consists of possibility made manifest by personal choice.*

In the wonderful book *Healers on Healing,* by Richard Carlson, Ph.D. and Benjamin Sheild, Richard Moss writes of the transformational process:

No sooner is it grasped than it dissolves. In the end, healing must be a ceaseless process of relationship and rediscovery, moment by moment…Here then is the golden thread: relationships. It is our capacity to merge, to become at one, however briefly, with ourselves, with each other, and with life in a larger sense. Healing, whenever and however it occurs, brings each person and humanity as a whole toward more inclusive, more unobstructed relatedness to all that is emerging in this adventure of life. This relatedness is endless: to oneself, to one's sensations, thoughts, feelings, images, dreams; to other people in how we transcend the sense of separation. And it is relatedness to something more, however we conceptualize it: Self or God.

This gift of being present, being honest and acting out of love is the ecstasy of life. Our ability to be attentive to ourselves and all of life in a profoundly present way allows us to discover ecstasy again. When we have disconnected from ourselves or life around us, we slowly die.

We have no choice about whether we will suffer. We will. We have no choice about whether we are met with challenge. We will. We have no choice about whether we will experience pain. We will. But we have choice about how we respond to life with all of its suffering, challenge, pain—and joy and love. You have the choice to meet life with spiritual impeccability and the ecstasy it offers, or you may close down, stay in denial, and spend your life dying. These are your only two choices.

Ecstasy is not reserved solely for heroes, heroines, God's chosen few, or mystics. It is waiting for each of us as soon as we are open to creating it in our lives. Ecstasy lies in the authentic space between you and me, in the space between you and your friend or you and your beloved. It is in the silent space between each of your deepest thoughts and feelings. Ecstasy is captured on the released breath of acknowledgment and understanding of your denial. It is discovered in the unfettered vulnerability of orgasm. The reward comes with each new conquest of fear. Ecstasy arrives with each step we take inward to ourselves, outward to each other, and to the center to Spirit. It increases with our refusal to tolerate separation. It abounds in authenticity, self-acceptance, and self-love. It manifests in equal degree to our commitment to truth and aliveness.

> *As we gradually grow from being love to more love,*
> *we also go from smallness to greatness.*

If you are not experiencing ecstasy, you have in some way left yourself or your commitment to fully experience life and all it has to offer. You are in denial. You need only return to yourself to find the ecstasy again. Use the following exercise to help you focus on where and how to find it and yourself again:

1. When was the last time you experienced ecstasy?

2. What were the conditions or beliefs that helped create those experiences?

3. What illusions or false beliefs have you allowed to come between you and the experience of ecstasy?

4. What ramifications have your belief in the lack of ecstasy created?

5. In what ways have you given up hope, abandoned your dream, decided to die, stopped seeking ecstasy?

6. What steps can you take toward bringing ecstasy back into your life?

7. What fears or illusions prevent you from taking these steps?

8. Which is greater, your fear of having ecstasy or not having it?

9. Which is more painful, not having ecstasy or facing your denial?

10. What steps are you willing to take toward facing your denial and creating ecstasy in your life now?

11. One month from today, write down the fears you have conquered and the steps you have taken toward creating more ecstasy in your life. (Enter date here and on personal calendar, and then check your progress.)

## It's Your Choice—Ecstasy or Denial

Most of us, with the help of the media, focus on gloom and doom. We are inundated with prejudice, murder, bedlam, and chaos in a world that seems to have gone crazy. All the more reason to become committed to the process of creating more ecstasy in our lives.

*There is a vast difference between acknowledging what is*
*and feeding negativity. Choose love.*

From a philosophical perspective, the world is changing. It must change. It no longer works properly. We are collectively standing in the middle of that transformation in that place called "nowhere." The old has not completely left, and the new has not yet fully arrived. However, this is a great time of power in the world, just as it is in your personal life. It is now that we each must set new direction and priorities for the quality of our lives. This is the only opportune time to create tomorrow. Tomorrow will we still be giving society the message that we are more about sex than spirit? Will be still be treating our elders in our community as if they are without value? Will we still be hiding our relationships and our love for each other as if they are something we should be ashamed of? Or will we create relationships that are honorable and long-term? Will we step into society and take our place as change-makers of character and courage? Will we deliver the message that it matters not who we love—it matters only *that* we love, deeply, honorably, with principle and spirit? These changes start in you, and in me, in our relationships.

If we explore the nature of healing, we understand that it begins even on a global level, within each of us individually. If I am fully connected to myself and aware of the ramifications of each of my choices, I will begin making more conscious choices, and so will you. Rather than expecting the authorities to create peace with us in the world, we can begin to understand that peace will be in the world only when it is firmly established within the heart of each of us.

*In every sea of faces, there is always one who is choosing to be Spirit.*
*Choose to be that one.*

And so it is with presence, truth, love, compassion, understanding, authenticity. and wisdom. Today we are manifesting and living the separation that was in our hearts about who we are yesterday. Tomorrow we will live the principles of oneness that we choose to have in our hearts today.

*The past becomes irrelevant when you begin again in the now.*

Oneness begins with you and me choosing to be in union with the best and highest parts of ourselves. It begins with each of us making a personal commitment to improving our ability to stay present and love deeply, honestly. Then, and only then, are we able to connect with and call forth the best and highest in each other. Your deliberate decision to choose the ecstasy that is birthed through awareness has a critical impact on the very nature of our existence. It is your contribution to a community that takes pride in itself. It is your contribution to a more sane and loving world. Your contribution is critical to this change.

*You are only one, but it takes only one to change the world forever.*

You don't have to participate in a march or political movement, although I applaud your willingness and courage to do so. You can simply be in your living room, alone or across from a friend or your beloved, with the intent to learn about yourself. That's all it takes. Once you begin your healing, which in turn creates a space that opens the doors and windows to your heart and mind, a profound connection results. You have changed the world and made it an infinitely better place in which to live. I know this with every fiber of my being. I have lived it. Do not feel as if you can do nothing because you are only one. Do whatever you, as someone fully present, can do truthfully and lovingly.

Perhaps you're thinking that not everyone can do this. That's not so. My clients and I are no different than you. Their stories are filled with hardship. I am a child who left home at 13, now a woman with a couple of Ph.D.'s, who has discovered her passion and purpose.

*You have only failed or been defeated at the point when you stop trying.*

No matter how difficult your life may have been, you owe it to yourself to grasp the balance of your time here voraciously and turn it into a joy-filled experience. You owe it to yourself to bring back the ecstasy. You deserve it. You have every right to it. And now you can begin to create it.

■ ■ ■

Let's meditate. Close your eyes and return to your safe place. I want you to see your life before you in a panoramic view one year at a time, starting from left, as a child, and moving to the right, as the adult you are today. Don't be concerned if you don't have memories for each year. Just allow what you do recall to appear before you. As you see yourself grow from one experience to the next, thank the part of yourself that survived each of those years and made it to the next. Notice the skills and abilities, the qualities and principles that make up who you are. Give yourself credit for your courage and wisdom. Take all the time you need. When you have finished, take a moment to see the *you* that you are becoming. See yourself a vital part of your relationship, your community, and society. Allow yourself to step into that image and become it.

# CHAPTER TWELVE
# The Hope and the Promise

*You and I
set our own limitations
by refusing to believe
there are
none.*

Imagine what might happen if world leaders today were taken to a room and told to stay there until they understood and appreciated each other's differences and similarities. What could result if they were told that before a single foot could be set on foreign soil, they would each have to examine their own individual distorted needs for power and violence and resolve those personal issues? Hundreds of thousands of lives could be saved every year. War has never resulted in anything but more war.

*Evil is love experiencing itself through fear and separation.*

Let's ask the soldier who drove his tank proudly down the confetti-strewn streets of New York to sit in a room with the woman who watched her child shot to pieces in Saudi Arabia. Have them speak about their confusion and betrayal. Put Donald Trump in a room with the black or Hispanic woman from the ghetto who can't feed her children. Let them talk together about their isolation and aloneness. Let's put the heads of the gay men's community in that room together with the leaders of the lesbian community and ask them not to leave until they have an created an abiding respect and love for each other. Imagine what could happen if all people were made to stay in that room until they moved beyond their denial and were able to create a deep connection and mutual under-standing. No, I am not blaming our soldiers, the wealthy, or our own men and women. I am blaming us. You and me. It is our *collective* unconscious and denial that has created these events. Together we have created the fertile, hostile, materialistic ground in which these inhumanities grow. Together we are all responsible for fixing it.

In the end, we are all the same in some profound ways. We want to be safe and loved. We deal with feelings of power and powerlessness. We are all hurting. You and I must understand that *everything* that goes on in our world is about us. It's all a reflection of the pain and helplessness we feel inside. The sense of separation the world feels from the man or woman who has AIDS, or the differently abled person eating breakfast in a restaurant, or a daughter or son who is in love with a same-sex partner is exactly the same separation that breeds war in our world. The sense of separation we feel about our own spiritual choice to be gay or lesbian, honorable in our relationships or not, out or not, is the same. It's cumulative—thought by thought, decision by decision, denial by denial. We *pretend* we are not connected to each other as a human family. We *pretend* that what happens to one of us does not happen to all of us. But we *know* better. If the pain in the world is to be healed, we must begin by healing the pain we each have inside that prevents us from being fully present, telling our truth, and acting out of love with each other.

> *When one's actions are less than one's truth,*
> *oneness has not yet arrived.*

You see, it really does start with your willingness to heal and get connected to yourself and others. Your individual healing really is a community event—no, a world event—within. Our ability to fully experience shared understanding and empathy is the only answer. And the only way we can get to the kind of understanding that produces harmony and peace on the outside is if you and I commit to it in our personal lives, on the inside. Global peace comes from inner peace.

## Separation From Our Source

There's yet another kind of separation that is perhaps the most significant of all. It's one that is handed down and re-created in our personal relationships and is the one we have not yet discussed. Jon Klimo says it beautifully in his book *Channeling*.

"We are currently undergoing what I will call a 'spiritual reformation.' All of us—atheist and devout alike—now have the possibility of giving ourselves permission to renegotiate our own most meaningful relationship with the living ground of Being: to variously knock upon it and have it open to us. And it appears that this is to be done with less guidance than ever before from either the churches of organized religion or from the church of organized science. We can intentionally seek to reestablish ties and to align and identify ourselves with our Parent Consciousness and ground our being."

There is a sense of divine at-One-ment when you are able to connect with the part of yourself or your partner that is the Spirit-connected self. It doesn't matter what you perceive Spirit to be or whether you even perceive Spirit at all. No matter what your perspective, we are all moved and deeply touched by intense union. That's what Spirit is. Divine union. Union is the divine state. Somehow through that connection your heart becomes open, and you instantaneously have a greater understanding and appreciation for the Source or All That Is, no matter what you choose to call it.

You cannot sit with the God-self or higher self of another human being and not feel moved toward greater acceptance and understanding. It's impossible. Neither can you hate yourself for being gay and still claim to love and be connected to Spirit, because you are Spirit. You are Spirit Itself choosing in this lifetime to have a gay or lesbian experience. Why not have that fully and with great joy? Isn't that the whole point? Until you are able to embrace yourself and your life as a gay person, fully and without hesitation, you are not finished with your spiritual assignment. Until you are able to embrace your beloved with that same respect and honor, you are not finished. Once you become that love, then and only then have you accomplished what you came here to do.

*Integrity is simply Self being true to Self.*

Each of us has a higher self, a part of us that is connected to a greater vision. A Spirit. For some, however, it may be buried under the pain and disillusionment of childhood trauma. The process of tapping into that part of ourselves in and of itself brings us closer to our personal spirituality and Spirit. A single instant in that oneness makes doing the work of releasing the pain of your past infinitely easier. And once we are able to see that everyone is a part of the greater consciousness, responding in some way to the pain in his or her life, we can more easily become forgiving.

> *When you understand that Spirit is all there is,*
> *it is impossible to judge anyone.*

Most importantly, it is no longer possible to believe we are separate. It is no longer possible to pretend that what we do *to* others or what we do *for* others doesn't matter.

There's no way we can all rush into the nearest therapist's office or self-help seminar. Nor should we want to do so. It is time for all of us to stop projecting our power *out there,* onto others, while continuing to act out of denial, as if we are helpless. We all need to stop lying to ourselves individually and as a community. We need to get out of the denial of our own divinity. We all have our own answers right inside. We can all, for the vast majority of our issues, be our own therapists, our own teachers, indeed, our own masters. Even when we sit with those who are able to impart new information to us, *you and I* must still take the final responsibility for creating internal and external change. In fact, I believe we each have a moral and spiritual obligation to do so. It is why we're on this planet in the first place. To become spiritual human beings.

Once your soul has been ignited with this process—and trust me, your soul *will* be ignited—a number of new doors will open to you. Every time you meet someone new, an opportunity for healing exists. Every time you become aware of some deeper level of feeling, healing is at hand. Every time you reach a new level of awareness, you'll want to go deeper. You might even consider starting a group, people with whom you can commit to the ongoing process of growth. Most of my friends, the people I teach in workshops, my students, and some members of my family admit, along with me, they do know how other people live without this level of awareness. It gives us all so much joy, and the greatest joy is knowing that we can never go back to *not knowing* what we all now know. It has completely changed our lives, provided meaning and purpose.

Right now that idea may seem preposterous. But each time you reach a healing state, the possibility of doing this work with others becomes increasingly appealing. It also becomes less unusual, more a part of your everyday thinking and array of possibilities. More a part of who you are. Committing to an ongoing process of healing and creating more love in your personal world becomes your way of life. To live each moment present and aware, consciously focused on your own healing is a precious, exquisite high. **It's called enlightenment.** This high may be the one you've been looking for in substances, food, 12-step programs, altered states, and each other. It's right here, available and waiting exactly where ever you already are, now.

*There is exquisite freedom in being left alone*
*to make the discovery of Self.*

We are living in a time of great change. We are at a crossroads, and the direction we will take from here is not yet determined. It's up to you and me to decide the direction we will go. There's no miracle cure coming. There's no new Savior on the way. The answer lies in the tiny space you and I inhabit, and in our gift of free will. How shall we choose? How shall we spend our time in our space together? Can we become committed to the work of our souls? It's up to you and me to become the most active in healing our planet—healing our communities, healing our relationships—by being the most active people involved in healing ourselves.

*If you are fully living what you know in the moment,*
*you are on the path to enlightenment.*

Imagine how different life might look if each of us expressed more love without prejudice. What could happen if we understood that we are all connected and participants in creating a planet alive with love—or dying in its sense of separation and isolation? Your individual work results in your healed life. Healed lives result in healed relationships. Healed relationships result in healed families, healed communities, and eventually—depending on how intent we become—healed countries and a healed planet. Love moves from the inside out.

*The realization of your oneness*
*creates instant healing everywhere, with everything.*

The more we can confront and diffuse the places within ourselves that are motivated by fear and distrust, the more we can contribute to the healing of this planet. We must stop hating ourselves for being gay. We must stop hating our gay brothers and sisters, our ex-lovers, and those gay role models who stand up for us in society. We must stop the effects of our internalized shame. There is great power in our red wagons. Each time we enter the places in our heart and mind that cling to fear and come out victorious, we are more empowered. We have brought light into another recess of our mind and, therefore, in the same instant, into another dark recess of the planet. Just like a ripple on the pond that was first created by the pain inside of you, a ripple of healing is created when you are willing to express more love. Becoming enlightened is a world event within.

We need more opportunities to courageously look at the beliefs inside ourselves that keep us from deeply connecting to each other. We must find a way to do exactly that, one that is not costly to our spirit, does not require someone greater or more knowledgeable than we are, and is readily available. That way is the journey into your own heart and mind. First do it alone. Then do it with your lover, friends, or family members. Then be courageous. Give this gift of healing to as many as you can. Small, intimate groups of gay men and women are meeting once a month, once a week, who want to make a difference in the world and who may be all we need to turn our dire situation around. Join them. Start a support group for conscious relationships in your own communities. Get clean and clear commitments from your friends to uphold the inherent rightness of your relationships and the preciousness of your bonds with respect. You are going to stumble and fall. You cannot do this work "right"—you can only do this work. Each of you get a copy of this book and, one chapter at a time, begin your journey together.

> *You may not always see the results of having done the right thing,*
> *but you will never see results from having done nothing.*

I ask you to trust and honor the Spirit within you. You are a master coming home. A true master never withholds knowledge based upon the pretense that only some are worthy. Therefore, share your courage and your insights with an open hand and heart. Once you get out of the gay closet, get out of the spiritual one as well. Imagine the joy of doing this work with those you love.

## Where Are the Breakups?

Perhaps you are wondering, since this is a book about relationships, when the issue of breakups is going to be covered. Are we not, after all, nearly at the end of this book?

Well, my personal prejudice is that if you are committed to creating healing with the people in your life, you will never have to leave your relationships. Nor will you continue breaking up inside with pain and isolation. You may still wish to leave some situations, but you will do so without the painful confusion and frustration embodied in the expression *break up*. You will leave because your path requires you to do so. You will leave without breaking the bond that once brought you together.

Breakups result from projections, shaming, and a lack of understanding. In your desire for continued growth, you may change the form of your relationships from a lover relationship to a friendship, or from a friendship to an acquaintanceship or from an acquaintanceship to an unconditional release with love and best wishes. But you will do it with honor and integrity, remaining fully present, fully truthful, and fully with love.

> *Judgment is senseless. We are all learning the same lesson*
> *in different ways, at different times.*

On some level, you will remain in unity or at one with each other. You will not have to break your commitments or negate the very reasons you were originally drawn to one another. You will simply make the appropriate changes in your relationship or in the dynamic between you. You will do that because it is natural, the correct decisions for your own path and your own growth. Even if you perceive your partner or friend to be engaging in self-destructive behavior, you will be able to see that too as part of a learning experience needed by that person, as a next step in his own evolvement. In other words, you release that person with love, with your best wishes for a safe journey, or with both. You will stay present to yourself, be honest, and act out of love for both of you.

Once you understand the value of the other people in your life and the important roles they play in helping you understand yourself, you will find you are able to be much more compassionate. You will also understand that those with whom you do this work are valued and lasting partners in your dance of consciousness. Out of our community will come permanent spiritual playmates who will leave indelible footprints on your soul and become your truest family.

Therefore, the finest gift you can give yourself right now, before you even put this book down, is a commitment to begin. Give yourself permission to make mistakes, get frustrated, fumble around, fall down, and keep going. Give yourself permission to understand and forgive the unconscious beliefs inside you that have long sabotaged your sense of oneness with yourself and others. Give permission for those you work with to do the same. But begin! Aliveness is addictive! And this healing process is the way to that aliveness. I believe we can teach the world even more about love than we already have. Beyond our insistence on our right to love whomever we desire, we can also demonstrate great character and integrity and the ability to create honorable, loving relationships that last in spite of society's oppression. Imagine what gifts that will bring to our own communities. Imagine the strength loving relationships will bring to our lives as the very foundation of who we truly are.

Once you begin the process, your natural instinct will take over and you will continue in the passion, the pleasure, and the pure ecstasy of finding yourself, much in the same way a plant reaches for the sunlight in order to survive. You will choose not to live without healing. You will know that it is impossible to do so. Consciousness and enlightenment have an inherent and beautiful quality; you can never *not know* a truth once you know it. And now that you have read this book, some part of you knows you have read the truth. Now *you* must begin.

I believe in us and our capacity to love. I do not want us to continue doing business as usual in the same destructive ways that straight society has conducted relationships. The fire in our souls suggest we can do more. Shall we?

# Seven Steps to Creating Conscious Relationships

Use the following consciousness contract, or create your own, and begin your journey now.

1. **I commit to staying present.**
I commit to recognizing and clearing away the obstacles *I* put in the way of my ability to be fully present. I will identify and name the defense mechanisms and denials I use to close my heart and abandon myself, my partner, friends, or family members in order to avoid connection, intimacy, and healing.

2. **I commit to respecting my own boundaries and spiritual path as well as the boundaries and spiritual paths of others.**
Conscious relationship means showing respect for my own and other people's boundaries and spiritual path. I will honor my right and my partner's right to reveal information only as it is safe to do so. I will honor my partner's truth as a sacred trust and will not reveal it to others without his or her permission.

3. **I commit to releasing my denial.**
I accept that I am ever-changing, and so are those I love. I will not hold onto pain or anger from the past. Neither will I hold onto negative behaviors that diminish my self-worth or are harmful or demeaning to myself or others. I promptly admit my mistakes. I do not take responsibility for or cover up for the mistakes of others. I commit to staying in the process until the issues are resolved or there is an agreement to disagree.

4. **I communicate and reveal my truths.**
Conscious relationship means microscopic truth-telling. I will not conceal parts of myself, even those of which I am not proud. Holding parts of me back in relationship is self-defeating. I can't be committed

unless I am fully present and willing to be transparent and truthful.

## 5. I take full responsibility for my life and my healing.

I have the power to take charge of my life and stop being a victim. I have the power to stop my dependence on any substance, obsessive activity, relationships, or people who I have made responsible for my happiness, self-esteem, and security. When I project blame and shame onto another, I have forgotten that I am in charge of my own reality and healing. I will not expect my partner to deal with the consequences of my refusal to do my own work.

## 6. I commit to ecstasy and laughter in my relationship.

I am aware that relationships take immense courage and commitment. Therefore, I also commit to creating equal joy and ecstasy. I accept the ups and downs in relationship as a normal part of the process and my personal opportunities for growth. I take the time to enjoy the strengths, creativity, and healing in my partner, in myself, and in our relationship.

## 7. I commit to Spirit and being love.

I invite Spirit into my life, my relationships, and all of my choices. As I grow in consciousness and become more aware of myself as a sacred human being, I can see how interrelated to all other sentient beings I am. I commit to actions that restore peace and balance to the planet. I commit to assisting others in the discovery and joy of conscious relationship and conscious living and resolution of their own issues.

Conscious relationships are a commitment and gift to soul. They teach you to:

- **be fully present and aware**
- **be honest, authentic, trustworthy, and truthful**
- **act out of love, not fear**

**And most of all, have great fun doing all of it!**

Take a minute, and in the silence between these words and your thought, feel the truth of this process. Imagine how much soul-deep work could be accomplished if you knew your partner would never cheat on you, lie to you, betray you, or leave you without an honorable end to your contract. These gifts of safety and integrity provide unlimited opportunities for growth, individually toward each other and in embracing Spirit. Remember...

*Every relationship you have is an opportunity to see how well you are doing both as a loving human being and a spiritual master.*
*It's all about you!*

# Conscious Connecting Exercises

These exercises are for couples who wish to connect safely and profoundly for the first time while creating deep intimacy slowly and with awareness and respect for each other. These exercises are also designed for couples who have been emotionally or sexually estranged from each other or those who are dealing with abuse issues in their relationships. It gives couples a progressive way to reconnect and move back into intimacy and lovemaking slowly and safely. Read this exercise together and make sure you both fully understand and agree on the process before you begin.

## Conscious Connecting Home Exercises

1. **Begin with energy exercises:** Feel free to use candles, soft music and background. **At any time during any process either partner can call "stop" and this must be respected.** Begin this exercise fully clothed, and once you have reached a place where both individuals are completely comfortable with the process, you can mutually opt to do the exercises clothed or unclothed if it feels safe to both parties. Make an agreement that sexual contact is not an expectation at the end of this process.

2. Sit across from each other and establish your boundaries. (Draw a circle around yourself to indicate where your boundaries are for your partner.) Begin to notice the rhythm of each other's breathing pattern and bring your own into sync. As your partner breathes out, you exhale and as he or she breathes in, you inhale. When you are breathing in the same rhythm, begin to connect with your eyes. If you feel a need to look away, notice what triggers this need and return to eye contact when you can. You may take a time out to talk about or process anything that has been triggered. Then attempt to return to the process or agree on another time to return to it. Make as many attempts and take as much

time as needed to do this process safely before moving on. It may take weeks or days to get to a place where you are both comfortable.

3. Once you have achieved a state of comfort with this breath exercise you can take the next step. Watch the pattern of each other's breath and as your partner breathes in, you breathe out. Establish an energetic circle going from you to your partner with the breath in the area of your heart. As he or she breathes in, you breathe out; as he or she breathes out, you breathe in until you have created a circle of breath/energy moving between you. Reestablish eye contact and begin to allow the energy or breath of your partner to move through you as it moves around the circle. Focus on receiving the energy. Continue this until you feel fully available to the process and safe.

4. Notice what makes you want to leave this intimate space and if or how you get back into it. You may take a time out to talk about or process anything that has been triggered. Then attempt to return to the process or agree on another time to return to it. Make as many attempts and take as much time as needed to do this process safely before moving on. It may take weeks or days to get to a place where you are both comfortable.

5. After you have finished each of these exercises, write down what you noticed and share it with each other or bring it into therapy.

At first, doing these exercises may take several weeks or even months. Do not rush to the next stage. The object is to become completely safe before progressing to the next step. There is no time constraint. Take as much time as you need to connect or reconnect safely.

Once you have the exercises down, practice them one or more times each week. This time, once you have become energetically connected imagine you are moving across the space to sit inside your partner's body and he or she is moving to your side of the space to do the same. Take some time while in this meditation to experience what it feels like to be inside your partner and try to experience his or her feelings. Talk about your awareness.

If you mutually choose to have sexual contact, do *not* have it immediately after this exercise. This space should be free of expectation and orgasm-oriented pressure. The object is simply to feel safe at deeply connected, energetic levels.

## Body-Touching Exercises

1. Set aside a time for mutual touching for at least 30 minutes per person. Each person should have plenty of time to experience the touching and being touched, so there should be no time constraints. The person doing the touching should use light fingertip stroking. **Stroking sessions progress very slowly from stroking hands only to arms and hands, to hands, arms and back, etc.**, until you have progressed to stroking all over your partner's body with the exception of genitals or breasts. This progression may take place over several sessions. The person being stroked has full control and gives directions as to the pressure, direction and location of touching. He or she is encouraged to put a hand on the touchers to guide the process. Dialogue might sound like, "A lighter touch at the crook of my arm feels better" or "Touching in long strokes behind my knees is very sensuous."

The exercise may begin with full clothing and may last for weeks or months before progressing to full body, without clothing touching. **Do not rush the process.** Begin with the energy-connecting, and then move into hands-only. The toucher's job is to explore the sensations that feel good to his partner. Give the partner full control and embrace a willingness to be told what feels best without taking anything personally. Do not interpret your partner's instructions as criticisms of your performance. Do not take an additional step of touching more parts of the body until both partners feel they have achieved a space of safety and an ability to receive and give without hesitation on each part being touched.

2. The full-body assignment is done without clothing, in a bed or other flat space and in a room that is kept a bit warmer than normal. Begin by doing the back or front of your partner's body with a desire to notice

which places on his or her body are sensuous, which places make your partner feel closer and loved as well as which places have no effect or have a negative effect. **The purpose of the exercise is to become fully acquainted with what your partner feels, likes, and dislikes during your touching.** Don't take any of the feedback personally. This is not about you, it is about becoming aware of your partner's needs and likes.

Stroking motions should blend into each other in a slow, continuous motion without losing contact with the body. Erection or excitement should not be given attention. Should masturbation become necessary, partners should do that alone and separately. The purpose of this assignment is to collect feedback, impressions, and signals from your partner to enhance your connecting process.

After you have finished each of these exercises, write down what you noticed and share it with each other or bring it into therapy.

Doing these exercises may take several weeks and in some cases several months. When touching has been associated with abuse or pain, it is necessary to set up a new reference point in the mind and body that can be associated with pleasure and safety. Take all the time you need to do this without rushing to the next stage. The object is to become completely safe before moving on to the next step. There is no time constraint. Take as many weeks or months as you need to reconnect safely.

Do this exercise one or more times over a period of a week. If you mutually choose to have sexual contact, do not have it immediately after this exercise. This space should be free from expectation or orgasm-oriented pressure. The object is simply to feel safe.

## Genital Touching Without Orgasm

Remember, you are encouraged to take as many weeks as necessary to get comfortable with each exercise before moving on to the next one. **The time these exercises take is not as important as getting to safely connected states.**

### First Session

Proceed as in the previous exercise, but limit the stroking to 10-15 minutes per side. After finishing the front, without switching roles, spend 10-15 minutes focusing on sensitive areas using the same light, stroking touch. Trace around ears, lips, breasts, genitals, and insides of upper thighs. The idea is to accept erections and/or lubrication as an indication or sign of pleasure, but to avoid compulsion to accelerate and instead continue stroking in an exploratory way. Wait a few days for the next session, or until you feel safe.

### Second Session

Again, do the 10-15 minutes of stroking, front and back, and as part of the front, cover sensitive areas working toward the genitals. The active partner should be sitting at the side of the passive partner, facing the feet. When touching the genitals, try to get information about your partner's preferences. Make sure you are checking in with your partner frequently, because conditions change at different stages of arousal. Avoid fast or heavy stroking. Men, if erection occurs, be sure it has subsided before returning to stroke the penis. In some cases this may require you to stop all stroking. When stroking female genitals, the natural fluids may reduce friction, but there should also be an opportunity for dry, very light, sensitive stroking as well. Attempt to sustain excitement without moving to orgasm. Wait a few days for the next session, or until you feel safe.

### Third Session

This assignment is the same as the previous one with the addition of unscented, nontoxic lubricants. Practice sustaining excitement and then allowing it to subside.

## Touching With Orgasm

This assignment extends the exercise to include orgasm. The exercise is to help you accomplish staying relaxed all the way to orgasm. This requires continuous monitoring by both partners. Frequent interruptions are usually necessary to avoid buildup of tension. This gives partners an opportunity to identify and describe their impressions. These frequent interruptions may be frustrating enough to rule out orgasm, and that is fine. The point is to notice the urge to push for orgasm rather than be giving and receiving.

Begin to notice the natural impulse to withdraw and break contact as you become aroused, to avoid looking away and being looked at and to not say anything. Make an effort to keep your eyes open and remain in contact. This will feel unnatural at first and may make you feel exposed or vulnerable. Simply notice the feeling that arises as you connect intimately.

You may also find that tension is created when we are put in one-sided roles as giver or receiver. It is important to keep the roles strictly separate. If you are not careful, when you are touched the compulsion takes over to regain control by stroking back physically or verbally. Try to restrain from giving back and instead notice any discomfort with receiving when you are the one being given to. Focus on being relaxed up to the point of orgasm.

Follow the same progression of stroking, however, where up until now your intent has been to create a good sensual experience, now the focus is to create relaxation in your partner. This may mean using deeper strokes—not a massage, however—on the neck, back, and shoulders. With the palm of your hand, move the muscles on either side of the spine by pressing and rubbing down toward each side, away from the spine. Continue down the back, over the pelvis and buttocks as your partner exhales.

On the front, smooth the forehead and cup the eyes using a mild, loving pressure. If your partner does not mind having his or her hair mussed, kneading the scalp can be relaxing. Use the same exhaling pressure on the chest area. Check for signs of body tension and focus on those areas. Lift legs and arms and let them drop freely. If there are signs of tension, work on those areas.

Once a fairly relaxed state is achieved, move into genital caressing.

Lubricants can be used. Since the object is to experience orgasm while being totally relaxed and passive, the active partner needs to monitor the levels of tension in the receiving partner. Many people automatically get tense during arousal, so take your time and slow things down when necessary. The passive partner may notice when tension occurs and take deep breaths, holding them for minute before exhaling. The active partner may also stroke an area of the body that is not arousing until the level of tension diminishes. Resting the left hand on the passive partner's forehead is helpful. If tension continues, go back to body stroking. Don't return to genital caressing in this session until partner is relaxed.

Try to avoid any temptation to accelerate touching as your partner comes closer to orgasm. Follow the receiving partner's instructions about how to do the genital touching, both before and after orgasm. Avoid orgasm altogether if it requires special effort to achieve it. Simply work up to whatever level of arousal is possible without strain for either partner and without an end result being anticipated.

### Second and Third Sessions:
Repeat this same assignment, paying attention to finer points and more subtle energy. Guys, notice pelvis tension and avoid tightening pelvic muscles or muscles at the base of the penis.

## Calling "Stop"
Calling "stop" is a formal way to interrupt the process that must be honored. Sometimes breaking contact is essential to getting in touch with what is going on. When partners emotionally leave or check out, "stop" should be called so that the partner that checked out can determine what the trigger was and process the feelings. This will help bring awareness to the surface about what each partner was feeling at the time. Once a partner says, " I want to call a stop here," physically separate. How far depends upon the issue. Sometimes you can call a stop and immediately identify the feeling and then resume. Other times you may need to call a stop to the entire session in order to sort out the feelings. Do not take it personally if your partner calls a stop. Move into

different rooms or another room if necessary to take the space to feel the feelings. Once you can identify the feeling, begin talking about what occurred and what you were experiencing. Take turns to hear each other fully. See how it feels to be back in contact and talk about that as well. Sometimes sensation can be heightened after your discussion, and at other times it will diminish. Neither is right or wrong. If the sensation is lessened, do not resume the exercise. Separating and then reconnecting gives partners the ability to say things they might otherwise hold back. Communication is obviously a critical part of this process. Because this is an important part of the process, just embrace it as an important part of your exercise and not a sign of failure.

Do not rush these exercises. Moving slowly from one level of intensity and safety to the next ensures your success. It also teaches you the joy of touching and being touched without performance or orgasm anxiety. Take all the time you need to enjoy the process and each other.

If you are interested in corporate or relationship workshops, seminars, or presentations in your area, call (602) 997-1200 or visit us on the Internet at http://www.In-Two-One.com.